Engaging Environmental Education:
Learning, Culture and Agency

Edited by

Robert B. Stevenson
James Cook University, Cairns, Australia

Justin Dillon
King's College London, UK

SENSE PUBLISHERS
ROTTERDAM/BOSTON/TAIPEI

A C.I.P. record for this book is available from the Library of Congress.

ISBN: 978-94-6091-159-0 (paperback)
ISBN: 978-94-6091-160-6 (hardback)
ISBN: 978-94-6091-161-3 (e-book)

Published by: Sense Publishers,
P.O. Box 21858,
3001 AW Rotterdam,
The Netherlands
http://www.sensepublishers.com

Printed on acid-free paper

TABLE OF CONTENTS

INTRODUCTION

ROBERT STEVENSON AND JUSTIN DILLON

1. INTRODUCTION TO ISSUES IN LEARNING, CULTURE AND AGENCY IN ENVIRONMENTAL EDUCATION

INTRODUCTION

The idea for this book emerged from a symposium at the Annual Meeting of the American Educational Research Association (AERA) in San Francisco in 2007. The title of the symposium was 'International Perspectives on Environmental Learning, Participation and Agency'. Not only were we, as discussants at that symposium, impressed by the quality of the papers presented, but we noted a common and important theme that was highly consistent with the perspectives on learning and learners embedded in the international goals and discourse of environmental education (EE) and education for sustainable development (ESD).

That theme, and the rationale for this book, emphasizes the importance of engaging learners as active agents in thinking about and constructing knowledge about the need for and the ways of developing a more sustainable and equitable quality of life on a global scale. Rather than treating students and adults as passive recipients of other people's knowledge, environmental learning and action are viewed as proceeding hand-in-hand and are viewed as holistic, collaborative, and democratically participative. The chapters in this book are intended to examine efforts - in formal, non-formal and informal educational settings in a wide range of international contexts - to create environmental learning that matches this rhetoric.

The title of this book is intended to reflect the dual challenge of the need for individuals, institutions and communities to engage with environmental education and for environmental education and learning itself to be engaging. The subtitle represents our recognition, as we read the first drafts of chapters that came in and with the benefit of hindsight, that an additional important theme was evident, namely the role of culture. Participation is still an important dimension of the book, as readers will discover for themselves, but the impact and effect of culture on learning and agency seems, to us at least, to be an even more fundamental theme.

We have tried to highlight the value and importance of culture by organising the chapters into pairs according to their context. So, for example, the first pair of chapters focuses on learning and agency in formal education contexts whereas the next are set in the contexts of communities. Within each pair, we hope that there will be sufficient contrast to enable readers to see the value of both perspectives and sufficient overlap to justify them being put in tandem.

R. Stevenson and J. Dillon (eds.), Engaging Environmental Education: Learning, Culture and Agency, 3–10.

In collections such as this one, the job of the editors is multi-faceted. The first task is to recognise the potential for a collection of contributions to add something to colleagues' work beyond cataloguing related studies. The idea to put together this book emerged within a very short time after the AERA symposium. However, on reflection, we decided that to tell a/the whole story, we should invite more contributors to add their perspectives and wisdom.

HOW THE BOOK IS ORGANISED

The book has five major sections with each section containing two chapters, as well as a concluding chapter.

Learning and Agency in Formal Education Contexts

In 'Exploring student learning and challenges in formal environmental education', Mark Rickinson and Cecilia Lundholm report on findings from two studies that focused specifically on learners' experiences of and responses to environmental curricula. The first study focused on students' learning within environmental geography lessons in three English secondary schools (Rickinson, 1999a; 1999b). The other looked at Swedish university students' learning about environmental issues within undergraduate engineering and biology (Lundholm, 2003; 2004a; 2004b). Through an integration of key aspects of these two studies' findings, this chapter seeks to highlight the complexity of the learning experience within formal environmental education and to draw attention to the need for improved research-based understandings of environmental learning processes. The authors present an integration of the studies' findings in terms of four kinds of learning challenges experienced by students in environmental education courses. The chapter ends by considering emerging issues for environmental education practice and research. Four emerging issues for research on environmental learners and learning are identified, but most importantly, the authors conclude that the major implication of their two empirical studies for environmental education theory and practice is the need to treat learners as active agents rather than passive recipients of environmental learning.

In 'Rainbow warriors: The unfolding of agency in early adolescents' environmental involvement' Natasha Blanchet-Cohen explores the nature of environmental agency of 10–13 year old children from many diverse cultures around the world who are involved in extra- or co-curricular environmental activities. Her study reveals that there are multiple ways in which these children engage with the environment and six forms through which they express their environmental agency are identified. Blanchet-Cohen observes that the way they position themselves in relation to environmental problems suggests they are "ready and open to engage in the complexity of environmental issues." Thus, she argues that teachers should embrace rather than avoid complexity. The data from her study offer an important counter to teachers' claims, reported in a number of studies, that they avoid discussing environmental issues in their classrooms because of their concern that it will create a sense of despair in children (Cross, 1998; Hicks, 2002, 1998).

Learning and Agency in Community Contexts

In 'Civic engagement in sustainability: The (trans)formation of an urban community', Arjen Wals and Leonore Noorduyn reconstruct the making of a 'sustainable' neighborhood as a social learning process of civic engagement in sustainability. This reconstruction is based on a study carried out five years after the initiators found a strong enough support base to start the creation of Eva-Lanxmeer in the Dutch town of Culemborg (Noorduyn and Wals, 2003). As the chapter progresses the authors increasingly mirror the outcomes of this study with recent thinking on social learning in the context of sustainability (Wals, 2007). First, the unique features of the neighborhood are presented, and then they focus in on the process of interaction that took place when the first people had moved in and collaboratively had to design the community garden that forms the heart of the neighborhood. Finally, some key principles or stepping-stones are drawn from the Culemborg experience that might be useful elsewhere. Perhaps the most notable of which is the precautionary recommendation that all those involved should be informed of the uncertainty and risks involved in participating in an interactive process of civic engagement in sustainability.

In 'Peer mediated environmental learning', Charlotte Clark draws on her doctoral work to look at the process by which voluntary collective actions form in communities. Clark's research described and characterized the formative process of learning and collective action in one U.S. community with a focus on issues with environmental implications. Clark followed the community's process of developing a policy on whether or not to allow domestic cats to roam freely outdoors (where they can prey on native wildlife). This narrative illustrates (a) the process by which a collective action agreement was formed, (b) the challenges faced during its formulation, (c) the potential changes to learning and behaviour that may have resulted within the community during its formulation, and (d) the corollary issues that proceed such a policy agreement, such as the need to orient newcomers, the need to document and reinforce information for all those to whom the policy applies, and the realization that consensus on a policy does not necessarily mean consensus on action.

Learning and Agency in Workplace and Informal Contexts

In 'If the public knew better, they would act better? The pervasive power of the myth of the ignorant public', Elin Kelsey and Justin Dillon argue that museums, aquariums, science centres, zoos and other informal science institutions (ISIs) are increasingly committed to engaging the public in issues connected to environmental conservation and sustainability. Although ISIs around the world may hold different views about what information the public should possess, they appear to share the belief that 'if the public knew better, they would act better'. They operate within a common discourse about the power of education to transmit information from those who are knowledgeable to those who are not (Kelsey, 2001). Kelsey and Dillon explore the implications of this particular discourse on environmental learning, participation and agency within informal science institutions.

5

More specifically, they examine a case study of conversational learning between guests (visitors) and volunteer guides in the galleries of a major US aquarium. This is a particularly timely topic, as the interaction between ISIs and the public has undergone significant change in the past decade. Throughout the 1980s and 1990s, environmental public participation programs operated in a type of 'decide-announce-defend' mode based on a 'one way' transfer of information from experts to the public (Duffield Hamilton & Wills-Toker, 2006). Such programs echoed the Public Understanding of Science (PUS) rhetoric, with its tacit assumption of public ignorance and its adherence to a deficit model (Lehr *et al.*, 2007).

In 'Participatory approaches to workplace learning for sustainable development in the hotel industry', Jeppe Laessoe and Monica Carlsson examine participatory learning projects on sustainable development at three conference centres in Denmark. The focal point of the chapter is the shaping of, and experiences with, employee involvement related to generating energy savings and addressing other environmental issues at these conference centres. The authors discuss examples of learning and participation in relation to sustainable development and subsequently identify potentials, constraints and dilemmas that influence the process of participatory learning. After a brief introduction to the topic and the concepts of participation and sustainable development, the authors present four thematic analyses: approaches to participation, power and participatory learning, key elements and concerns in sustainable development, and approaches to sustainable development. In particular, they describe a number of conflicts that illuminate the persistent role of power even in participatory processes. The chapter concludes with a discussion and an epilogue on educational research in the public interest.

Learning and Agency in a Media Culture

In 'The role and influence of mass media on learning about environmental issues', Martin Storksdieck and Cathlyn Stylinski examine the public's ability to respond to environmental challenges or contribute to current science debates. They note that the testing of "public knowledge" or "public understanding" by a set of multiple-choice questions has been likened to a "deficit model" of knowledge and understanding since it does not allow an individuals to express what that they do know, and it does not provide a learning context (for example, Falk, Storksdieck & Dierking, 2007). The alternative asset-based model of knowledge and understanding (for example, Falk *et al.*, 2007) suggests that much can be learned in adult life through informal, or free-choice, learning and that tests of what an individual knows or understands should be tied to the way we construct our knowledge and understanding outside of formal schooling. Free-choice learning is the basis for this knowledge construction; it is voluntary, non-assessed, self-directed and under the control of the learner. It is based on an individual's own interest and motivation and builds on his/her prior knowledge. It occurs wherever a person encounters information: in a conversation with others, during a museum visit, and while watching TV, reading the newspaper or surfing the Internet. We know little about what people learn from these sources or the degree to which this information is corrects or enforces misconceptions.

Various studies indicate that news media plays an important part in this type of learning, especially with regard to science and the environment (for example, National Science Board, 2008; Falk *et al.*, 2007; European Commission, 2001). However, few authors have attempted to determine the direct influence of the news media on learning about environmental topics and issues. Storksdieck and Stylinski try to indirectly assess environmental learning from the news media by examining the way in which environmental stories enter the news (including the forces that shape how they are reported) and then relating this reporting to national surveys and case studies of public understanding of environmental issues.

In "Popular media, intersubjective learning and cultural production," Marcia McKenzie, Connie Russell, Leesa Fawcett and Nora Timmerman explore a diverse range of media-based examples of pedagogical practices for engaging students in socio-ecological learning. They argue that engagement with media can involve pre-existing artifacts, products in creation, and/or interactive spaces. Examples or forms of media that they examine include "fiction and non-fiction, zines and comics, photography and visual art, film and documentaries, various web-based fora, and a range of other forms that cross-over or join these and other genres" (p. 147) These examples are presented within a framework which treats "engagements with media as intersubjective experiences that involve both the sensory and the cognitive, and suggest that a collective context can support or intensify this learning" (p. 147).

Learning Research and Research as Learning

In 'Understanding others, understanding ourselves: Engaging in constructive dialogue about process in doctoral study in environmental education', Jutta Nikel, Kelly Teamey, Seyoung Hwang, Benjamin Alberto Pozos-Hernandez with Alan Reid and Paul Hart attempt to stimulate debate about the processes and effects of undertaking a doctoral study, and being a doctoral student in this field. This chapter is based on a collaborative thinking and writing process, rooted in a common interest to promote critical and reflexive dialogues amongst doctoral students and their supervisors about understandings and experiences of carrying out doctoral work. Key to their exploration is the importance and opportunity of engaging in a constructive interpretive dialogue about process whilst focusing simultaneously on various personal and academic experiences at different stages during those selfsame processes.

Following an introduction to the academic context and research and debate in the area of doctoral studies in Higher Education, the authors propose three heuristics. These heuristics generate different reflections into the multitude and diversity of doctoral research experiences within and across personal, institutional, cultural, academic and discursive contexts and boundaries. The heuristics have been developed and revised in the course of reading literature and from abstracting shared and diverse elements and notions from their own stories and discussions. They then each share their own story to illustrate their points

7

surrounding the importance of interrogating and problematising the doctoral process, illuminating and fleshing out complexities of identity, agency, power relations and career progression associated with doctoral research. As members of the research community, their ongoing engagement with the current discourses and practices of the field of environmental education research and converging fields related to environmental education have been shaped and continue to be informed by mundane, transformative, and often painful learning experiences and encounters during the doctoral process. While the chapter title suggests 'understanding others' and 'understanding ourselves' as important constituents to supervisory discussions or conference interactions, both are understood as important processes servicing additionally wider goals: those of academic progression, professional growth, and progress in the field and balancing process and product within discussions of doctoral studies.

In 'Researchers as learners: Participatory approaches to researching environmental learning', Rob O'Donoghue and Heila Lotz-Sisitka propose attending to the ways in which environmental education research might engage with new forms of, for example, mediation structure and agency, culture and power, and experience and rationalization. They begin by exploring how a cultural turn in research is creating a stronger focus on literacies and agency within socio-historical contexts which has been accompanied by the emergence of educational research for the public good. They further note a new form or genre of educational research which they speculate may herald novel manifestations of reflexive mediation in the context of post-colonial Africa. This leads the authors to advocate, as a logical extension, the inclusion of local participants as researchers and to introduce the concept of research-as-pedagogy as embracing these new forms and genre.

Conclusion

In the concluding chapter, 'Environmental learning and agency in diverse educational and cultural contexts', Bob Stevenson begins with an overview of different conceptions and theories of learning before relating them to the particular context and challenges of environmental learning. A process of critical inquiry is identified and examined as a central learning process of EE/ESD/EfS, while real or authentic environmental issues are treated as the substantive content. A tripartite framework for critical inquiry of the dialogical, the dialectic and the deliberate (Sirotnik, 1991) is analysed, along with the need for deep reflection on one's own experiences, assumptions, beliefs and values, as well as on the contextual factors that shape ideas, values and practices, concerning human-environment relationships. Besides critical inquiry and reflection, imagination and action are discussed as necessary components of environmental learning: imagination to generate possibilities for creating more sustainable socio-ecological practices; and action to ameliorate current environmental concerns. The need for developing the capacity for appropriate and effective action raises the issue of learner agency which is framed as involving the three distinct forms of reflective, relational and transformative agency. Finally, in the last section of the chapter, Carolyn Stirling, examines the important role of research in learning and knowledge creation and how learning to research is a personal, professional and political project in complex and often culturally challenging contexts.

We hope that the following case studies offer significant insights into the challenges and complexity of engaging youth and adults in meaningful learning about and informed action on environmental issues, and most importantly, suggest ways in which these challenges might be addressed. Of course, we expect that they also will raise further questions for researchers, policymakers and practitioners. Beyond posing such questions, however, the success of this book might best be determined by the extent to which the contributing authors stimulate readers' ideas and actions for building the learning capacities of individuals and organizations for creating ecologically (and economically and culturally) sustainable communities and societies.

REFERENCES

Cross, R. (1998). Teachers' views about what to do about sustainable development. *Environmental Education Research, 4*(1), 41–53.

Duffield Hamilton, J., & Wills-Toker, C. (2006). Reconceptualizing dialogue in Environmental Public Participation (Mikhail Bakhtin). *Policy Studies Journal, 34*(4), 755–775.

European Commission. (2001). *Europeans, science and technology: Eurobarometer 55.2* (December 2001). Luxembourg: Office for Official Publications of the European Communities.

Falk, J. H., Storksdieck, M., & Dierking, L. D. (2007). Investigating public science interest and understanding: evidence for the importance of free-choice learning. *Public Understanding of Science, 16*(4), 455–469.

Hicks, D. (2002). *Lessons for the future: The missing dimension in education.* London: Routledge Falmer.

Hicks, D. (1998). Stories of hope: A response to the 'psychology of despair'. *Environmental Education Research, 4,* 165–176.

Kelsey, E. (2001). *Reconfiguring public involvement: Conceptions of 'education' and 'the public' in international environmental agreements.* Unpublished PhD Thesis, King's College London, UK.

Lehr, J. L., McCallie, E., Davies, S., Caron, B. R., Gammon, B., & Duensing, S. (2007). The role and value of dialogue events as sites of informal science learning. *International Journal of Science Education* (Special Issue on Informal Science Education). *29*(12): 1467–1487

Lundholm, C. (2003) *Learning about environmental issues. Undergraduate and postgraduate students' interpretations of environmental content.* Unpublished PhD Thesis, Stockholm University. (In Swedish).

Lundholm, C. (2004a). Case studies–exploring students' meaning and elaborating learning theories. *Environmental Education Research, 10*(1), 115–124.

Lundholm, C. (2004b). Learning about environmental issues in engineering programmes: A case study of first-year civil engineering students' contextualisations of an ecology course. *International Journal of Sustainability in Higher Education, 5*(3), 295–307.

National Science Board. (2008). *Science and Engineering Indicators.* Arlington, VA: National Science Foundation.

Noorduyn, L., En Wals, A. E. J. (2003). *Een tuin van de hele buurt* [Creating a Neighborhood Garden]. Wageningen: Wetenschapswinkel Wageningen UR, 72 p.

Rickinson, M. (1999a). *The teaching and learning of environmental issues through geography: A classroom-based study.* Unpublished DPhil Thesis, University of Oxford.

Rickinson, M. (1999b). People-environment issues in the geography classroom: Towards an understanding of students' experiences. *International Research in Geographical and Environmental Education, 8*(2), 120–139.

Sirotnik, K. (1991). Critical inquiry: A paradigm for praxis. In E. Short (Ed.), *Forms of curriculum inquiry* (pp. 243–258). Albany, NY: SUNY Press.

Wals, A. E. J. (Ed.). (2007). *Social learning towards a sustainable world.* Wageningen: Wageningen Academic Publishers.

Robert B. Stevenson
The Cairns Institute and School of Education
James Cook University, Australia

Justin Dillon
Science and Technology Education Group,
King's College London, UK

LEARNING AND AGENCY IN FORMAL EDUCATION CONTEXTS

MARK RICKINSON AND CECILIA LUNDHOLM

2. EXPLORING STUDENT LEARNING AND CHALLENGES IN FORMAL ENVIRONMENTAL EDUCATION

INTRODUCTION

There is growing recognition for the significance of learning within debates about sustainable development. The United Nations has proclaimed 2005–2014 as the Decade of Education for Sustainable Development with the overall goal of 'integrating the principles, values and practices of sustainable development into all aspects of education and learning' (UNSECO, 2005). In their book entitled *Sustainable Development and Learning*, Scott & Gough (2003, p. xiv) argue that 'there will be no sustainable development where learning is not happening'. Their view is that 'it is not enough to say that sustainable development and learning need to go hand in hand'; rather sustainable development itself needs to be understood as a learning process (p. xiv). Along similar lines, Sterling's ideas about *Sustainable Education* work from the basis that 'the difference between a sustainable or a chaotic future is learning' (2001, p. 10).

Recent reviews of research in environmental education, however, make clear that insufficient attention has been given to questions of learners and learning (Hart & Nolan, 1999; Rickinson, 2001; 2006). For much of the last decade, there have been few investigations into what Scott and Gough (2003) describe as 'learning which accrues from an engagement with the environment or environmental ideas' (p. 14). During the period 1993–1999, for example, there were many studies investigating characteristics of school students (e.g., what kinds of environmental attitudes or knowledge they have) but few exploring the process or outcomes of their environmental learning. In particular, there has been a tendency to overlook the process aspects of environmental education so that there is 'a marked predominance of evidence on learning *outcomes*, but very little about learning *processes*' (Rickinson, 2001, p. 216).

In the light of this situation, this chapter reports findings from two studies that focused specifically on learners' experiences of and responses to environmental curricula. The first focused on students' learning within environmental geography lessons in three English secondary schools (Rickinson, 1999a; 1999b). The other looked at Swedish university students' learning about environmental issues within undergraduate engineering and biology (Lundholm, 2003; 2004a; 2004b). Through an integration of key aspects of these two studies' findings, this chapter seeks to

R. Stevenson and J. Dillon (eds.), Engaging Environmental Education: Learning, Culture and Agency, 13–29.

highlight the complexity of the learning experience within formal environmental education and to draw attention to the need for improved research-based under-standings of environmental learning processes.

The chapter begins with an outline of the focus and methods of the two studies. We then present an integration of the studies' findings in terms of four kinds of learning challenges experienced by students in environmental education courses. The chapter ends by considering emerging issues for environmental education practice and research.

THE TWO EMPIRICAL STUDIES

The studies that inform this chapter were undertaken independently but drew on similar theoretical perspectives and methodological approaches.

Study 1: Environmental Issues in Secondary School Geography in England

This study focused on the teaching and learning of environmental issues within secondary school geography lessons in three English secondary schools (Rickinson, 1999a; 1999b). It was a qualitative investigation into the ways in which three teachers and twelve of their students (aged 13–15 years) dealt with controversial environmental issues within the geography classroom. This focus was motivated by the lack of exploratory classroom-based research in the field of geographical/environmental education at that time.

More specifically, the research investigated:
– the ways in which environmental curriculum topics were being taught by the teachers, and the thinking that lay behind these practices
– the ways in which such teaching was experienced by their students
– the similarities and/or differences between the perspectives of the teachers and the students.

These foci were explored in the context of lessons on environmental topics that were perceived by the teachers to be issues-based (as opposed to purely factual). Examples included lessons on rainforest development, nuclear power and indigenous peoples.

The research involved three sequential case studies of geography lessons, each of which lasted two months. Data were generated through lesson observation and audio recording, pupil lesson impression sheets and post-lesson interviews with teachers and students. Analysis of the data involved detailed examination of the actions and interactions of each individual teacher and student within the controversial issues lessons. This analysis was based on lesson transcripts and observational field notes (pictures of classroom practice), as well as post-lesson interview transcripts (commentaries on classroom practice) (see Rickinson, 1999b). Central to these methods was a desire to understand the teachers' and students' actions from their perspectives.

There were strong methodological links with several previous studies of teachers' and students' perspectives on classroom teaching and learning (for example, Connelly & Clandinin, 1986; Ghaye, 1986; Edwards & Mercer, 1987;

Cooper & McIntyre, 1996). This work also drew upon a conceptual approach that sees the curriculum as becoming manifest within classrooms, through teachers constructing and enacting particular combinations of subject matter and learning tasks (that is, subject matter-tasks) that are interacted with, and experienced, by students (cf. Nespor, 1987; Doyle, 1992; Erickson & Schultz, 1992).

Study 2: Swedish University Students' Learning about Environmental Issues

This study investigated Swedish university students' learning about environmental issues as part of undergraduate programmes in civil engineering, biology and doctoral environmental research (Lundholm, 2003; 2004a; 2004b; 2005). It consisted of three cases studies based on different kinds of environmental content:
– first-year engineering students' interpretations and learning during a compulsory ecology course
– biology students' learning during an environmental auditing task, which encompassed issues relating to economics, business and administration
– doctoral students' interpretations of the task of writing a thesis in the environmental field, focusing on natural science, social science or both.

The purpose of using these different kinds of environmental content was to explore possible differences in students' learning in relation to the content being natural or social scientific. Furthermore, the research sought to explore the students' learning processes and the way in which they interpreted and experienced tasks and courses in the environmental field.

In the first case study, interviews were carried out with six first year civil engineering students following a compulsory course in ecology. In the second case study, the dialogue between a group of four biology students was tape-recorded while they were working on a task about environmental audit reports. The third case study was based on interviews with six postgraduate students regarding their interpretations of environmental research and the task of writing a thesis. The empirical examples presented in this article are taken from the first two case studies with the engineering and biology students.

The transcripts of interviews and group discussions were analysed from an intentional perspective, that is, a perspective which takes into account the students' aims defined as 'projects' (Halldén, 1988, 2001; Halldén *et al.*, 2007). When analysing a student's interpretation of a task, it can be described as a 'problem' that s/he is solving. The 'problem' that the student is working on can be interpreted as part of a future goal or 'project', such as to pass a particular exam, to successfully complete a whole course, or to gain knowledge for personal or professional reasons. Analysing data from such a project-oriented viewpoint means asking questions concerning the kind of 'problems' that the students are working on and the kinds of 'projects' in which these activities are made meaningful. Such questions give the researcher a chance to understand what the students are saying and doing, and may reveal possible explanations as to why they interpreted the content or task in a particular way.

Similarities and Differences between the Studies

As stated earlier, these two studies were undertaken separately at a time when the authors had no knowledge of each other's work. It is therefore important to contextualise the subsequent discussion of their findings with a brief consideration of the similarities and differences between the two pieces of work.

There are some important commonalities in terms of the two studies' approaches to researching environmental learning. For example, there were similarities in their:
− focus on the student perspective − both studies had a clear focus on accessing experiential accounts of the students' environmental learning experiences
− methodological approaches − both sought to access student accounts through classroom observation and audio recording, and post-lesson interviews
− conceptualisation of curriculum processes − both drew on concepts from research on students' interpretations of learning activities, in particular the distinction between the task as presented by the teacher (the enacted curriculum) and the problem (or 'project') as understood by an individual student (the experienced curriculum) (e.g., Halldén, 1988; Erickson & Schultz, 1992; Entwistle & Smith, 2002).

Alongside these commonalities, though, were differences in educational context. There is a clear distinction in the age groups of the learners, in that the English study focused on school students aged 13–15 years, whereas the students in the Swedish study were 20–45 years old. Connected with this difference, the learning contexts were distinct in the sense that the English study was concerned with compulsory schooling while the Swedish one looked at post-compulsory university studies. The foci of the environmental courses also differed: controversial issues in geography as compared with ecology for civil engineers and environmental auditing for biologists.

The motivation for writing this chapter was the degree of common ground that was evident between the two studies' findings *despite* the clear differences in educational context and age of learners. What became clear to us was that there were a number of challenges that the students in both studies were experiencing (albeit in different ways or to different degrees) that seemed to be related to the environmental subject matter and learning tasks that were being studied. It is to the nature of these learning challenges that we now turn.

FINDINGS RELATING TO STUDENTS' ENVIRONMENTAL
LEARNING CHALLENGES

Based on an integration of the two studies' findings, it is possible to identify four kinds of learning challenges that were experienced by students in their environmental education courses (Figure 1).

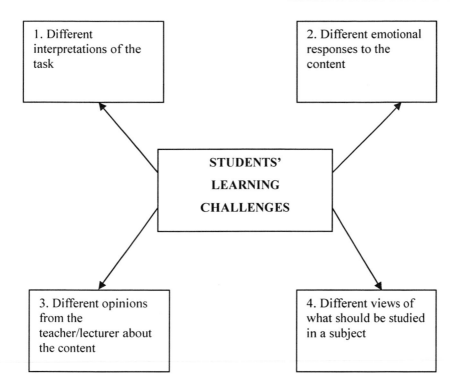

Figure 1. Learning Challenges Experienced by Students in Environmental Education Courses.

The challenges outlined in Figure 1 focus on incidents of students holding and expressing:
– different interpretations of the task – where individual students understand and enact learning tasks in varying ways
– different emotional responses to the content – where students' learning experiences are shaped by an emotional reaction to an aspect of the topic being studied
– different opinions about the content as compared with the teacher/lecturer – where there is some kind of conflict between the beliefs or views of a student and the beliefs or views of the teacher/lecturer
– different views of what should be studied in a subject – where students feel that a certain type of task or content is not appropriate for them to be studying within a particular subject.

Each of these differences is now discussed in more detail using examples from the data of the two original studies.

Different Interpretations of the Task

The first type of challenge that was evident amongst the English school students and the Swedish undergraduates stemmed from the way in which learning tasks were interpreted in different ways by individual students. In the English study, this was seen very clearly with two students during a lesson about the indigenous peoples of the Amazonian rainforest. After watching a film on this topic, the students were asked to 'write a poem of a day in the life of a Kayapo Indian'. The teacher envisaged this as an empathetic writing task, based on the view that it was important for students to develop the ability to empathise with different perspectives on issues such as deforestation. Through talking with students after the lesson, though, it became clear that this task was understood quite differently by two students. Box 1 shows the poems that Joanne and Aiden, both aged 13, wrote in this lesson and what their thoughts were about this task.

For Joanne, it would seem that this task was understood as an exercise in creative writing, as reflected by her concerns with the rhyming of words and the rhythm of her poem. Aiden, meanwhile, was more concerned with putting 'some sort of content in it' and trying to include information about what 'they might think'. In contrast to Joanne, then, Aiden undertook this task as an exercise in empathetic (rather than creative) writing. What is interesting here is the way in which the task acted as a barrier rather than a facilitator to Joanne's engagement with the subject matter. In other words, she was caught with writing a poem that rhymed, rather than thinking about the lives of the Kayapo Indians. This is an example of the way in which students' differing task interpretations can present challenges for environmental learning.

In the Swedish study, the issue of task interpretations was seen in the case study of the biology students undertaking a task entitled 'Environmental Reports: Superficial or Meaningful?'. This was one of five tasks all related to the social scientific environmental domain. The class was divided into groups of four and one of the groups chose the topic of environmental reports. The task was rather open-ended but the overall aim was to learn about environmental reports and understand how they were used in companies at the time. Audio recordings of the ongoing conversations of one of the small groups revealed a number of different possible interpretations of what had to be done. One idea was that the task would require the group to investigate and reflect on the environmental practices of the companies. Another view was that the task should involve comparing the companies' environmental practices with what is stated in their environmental reports. A third option was that the work should focus solely on the environmental reports themselves regardless of what might or might not be known about the companies' actual practices. In contrast to the poetry writing task discussed above, this was a group activity that took place over more than one session. What was interesting here was that these different interpretations of the task became an ongoing issue for the group and one that they kept coming back to and struggling with. Underlying these struggles was the question of the students' own values and beliefs about the companies and the extent to which these should be allowed to influence the ways in which they carried out this task. This brings us onto the next source of challenge, namely, students' different emotional responses to the content.

Box 1: Joanne and Aiden's Poems about the Kayapo Indians

Joanne

I'm a Kayapo
you know what I mean
I live by the grass along the stream
In my village, where I live
with my dad and my uncle Viv
I go fishing with my dad all
my mates think I'm sad.
The tribe was started long ago
by a couple of people all named Joe

'It was a bit harder because I thought it would be easy and I started off really well and then I started, like no words left, no like words and I started making up a few [...and...] when I got things like [reading from her poem] 'I live in the grass along by the stream, My face is painted yellow and green', and then I couldn't think of anything else 'cos that line, when you put it with that it didn't go because you'd be like this [acts out a gasp] gasping for air.'

Aiden

In the undergrowth of the forest floor
Wild boar roam free again
As our tribe is environmentally-friendly
the Western people corrupt and pollute.
As we fish for food
the women prepare vegetable stew.
While the children practice their hunting
skills, the men do the real thing.
The Western people want to change us
But we will not change our ways.
We are the Kayapo strong and true.

'Well I wanted some sort of content in it, so I put that in ... I just put that in there to sort of put it in as a view, you know they might think. Well, they're not using CS gasses or anything like that, are they? They're just using what they have in the forest but whereas we just, well we buy it in gases, we use chemicals and so on [...] I just thought it would be good since I was writing a poem from their view and what they would probably think.'

Different Emotional Responses to the Content

A second area of challenge was where students were having to grapple with their own emotional responses to the subject matter they were studying. This issue was seen very clearly with Melanie, a 13-year-old student in the English study. Shortly after a lesson that involved watching two short pieces of film about rainforest destruction in Amazonia, Melanie described how one of these films had provoked a strong emotional response for her:

> The second video [...] didn't seem very interesting - cutting down trees, I don't think that's very my sort of thing, I don't like things like that. I don't like cutting down trees, I don't like animals being hurt or moved or anything. I don't like anything like that. Yeah I'm very against it, I think it's awful.

What's important is that her emotional response to the images within the film had a very real effect on her engagement (or, more accurately, disengagement) with the lesson. For, as she described:

> I was hardly watching it, I was just paying a little bit of attention 'cos I don't watch things that are boring. If I think they're boring I don't watch them. [...] I just judge things before I see them and I didn't think it was really very exciting ... If I've got my own opinion on them, yeah I like hearing other people's opinions because it's their opinion, but no matter what you can't change my opinion. You can try till you're blue in the face but I will not change.

This can be seen as an example of a student pursuing a strategy of minimal engagement ('I was just paying a little bit of attention') as a result of emotions about the content of the lesson ('I don't like cutting down trees, I don't like animals being hurt or moved').

For the Swedish undergraduate biologists, the difficulty was the extent to which they should allow their personal values and emotions to shape the way they carried out the task about the companies' environmental reports mentioned earlier. This is well illustrated by the following interchange within a small group shortly after they had set the task of examining the series of company environmental reports:

> Karin: We can't get too emotionally involved, that's the problem!
> Hans: No
> Karin: We can't actually include what we **think**
> Nina: But yes, we can include what we **think**
> Karin: No, not what we think about these companies and their-
> Lena: We can't say 'I think they're crap!'
> Nina: No, exactly 'MoDo is a hell of a company, cutting down the forest' – no!
> Hans: We share a common view of the companies –
> [All the students are talking at the same time. Difficult to hear the different voices.]
> Nina: Yes, yes, but I think the same way – companies suck! [She laughs].
> **That** judgement we should not include
> Karin and Lena: No

In a similar way to Melanie, one can see the way in which students' feelings and emotions about the topic (namely, the environmental practices of large corporations) influenced their engagement with the learning activity. In the extract above, the group seems to reach some kind of consensus that getting 'too emotionally involved' would not be helpful and what is really needed is an impartial engagement with the task. What is interesting, though, is that this issue of impartiality remained an ongoing tension throughout the process of the group carrying out this piece of work. Even in their last group meeting, they were still debating what was and what was not 'relevant to the focus of our work'.

While there are differences between the minimal engagement of Melanie and the impartial engagement of the engineering students, what they all have in common is students having to deal with their own individual emotional responses to environmental subject matter.

Different Opinions from the Teacher/Lecturer about the Content

This third category of challenge brings the teacher or lecturer into the picture alongside the students. Research on teachers' thinking in environmental education has made clear that teachers can hold strong views on the issues that they are teaching (see, for example, Fien, 1992; Kyburz-Graber, 1999; Corney, 2000; Cotton, 2006). We have seen in the last section that the content of environmental courses can evoke strong feelings amongst the students. It is therefore possible for students and teachers/lecturers to hold strong and diverging views about the topics with which they are dealing. Negotiating such differences in viewpoint can present real difficulties for students, especially when they are only too aware that it is the teacher/lecturer who will be grading their work.

This type of situation was clearly seen amongst the engineering students in the Swedish study. In the interviews about their ecology course, several students brought up the issue of the lecturer's perspective. Tobias, for example, talked about how he felt the course had been 'angled from an ecological perspective [i.e.] everything that humans do has an impact on nature and if you affect nature, it is bad'. He went on to explain how this conflicted with his own views on this topic:

> But, actually, humans are a part of the whole ecosystem too and therefore one has to live in harmony with nature. Humans did not used to do that, people in the Stone Age killed all the animals they saw. It wasn't all that environmentally friendly as one might think. [Compared to me, the lecturer] values environmental problems in **one** way and 'This is the right way'.

Tobias' views were echoed by one of his classmates called Ola:

> Our dear ecology lecturer has the viewpoint that man was God's biggest mistake. Humans have only destroyed and so on. Many of us [students] have got this impression and then it feels kind of meaningless to discuss how we can solve these problems if the best solution is if everybody kills themselves. This was crudely put, but it is a bit of this kind of atmosphere that has

evolved. When somebody has asked a question about solutions to a certain problem you've got an answer that has been angled in that way [...] He has these values that see man as an evil creature.

What is interesting in Ola's comments is what he has to say about the ways in which his engagement with the course is affected by his perception of the lecturer's perspective.

I think you quickly kill all interest in discussing, nobody wants to, what the hell I don't want to pick a fight. It is also this exam, I think that's a big part of this. If he has that opinion then you let him have it, then you don't go into discussion because you know that, even though it shouldn't be that way, the lecturer will be affected by discussions. I think, if you discuss the wrong things and have very different views and you don't want to become an enemy to someone who is going to **correct** your exam. There are a lot of values in a subject like this. I mean, just think about environmental issues!

Here we see a student deciding not to express his real opinions on the topic for fear of 'picking a fight' with the lecturer and 'becoming an enemy to someone who is going to correct your exam'.

A similar sort of situation was evident amongst some of the English students in their geography lessons. There was an important difference, though: for the university students, the difficulty was with having an opinion that conflicted with that of the lecturer; for the school students, the challenge was not having a strong view either way on an issue about which the teacher felt they ought to have an opinion. One example comes from a lesson about nuclear power, where the pupils had been asked to answer the question 'Do you think nuclear power is a good thing?' after watching a video about the Chernobyl disaster. Lisa, a 14-year-old student, explained her difficulty with this task as follows:

I could put 'No nuclear power is not a good idea', but I'd rather just write 'No' full stop. [...] It's not exactly hard to write what you think, but sometimes you're thinking, you don't write what you think, but you're thinking of something, but it's not what you think if you sat down and thought about it for ages. It's just a spur of the moment thinking for what would be right to put down. [I wouldn't want more time though..] because I don't find it interesting. I wouldn't sit around for an hour thinking full-on about whether nuclear power is a good idea, I wouldn't find it interesting, it would just be a waste of my time. Maybe not for miss [i.e., the teacher] or for other people, but that's generally what people think in our class.

In talking further about the nuclear power lesson, Lisa explained how she had developed a strategy for dealing with this problem of having to express opinions about topics which she was not personally concerned about.

I just usually write what I think, just the truth ... but sometimes I find it difficult, it depends. There's been some things on what you think and [looking back through her book] I remember what it was, about when there was that acid rain thing with the trees and miss said write what you think of what you see when you see those trees. I didn't really think anything so I just put that [pointing to what she wrote which said: 'When I see the effects of acid rain, I think it's just deserted with nothing much exciting, but I feel sorry for the trees'] ... I didn't really feel sorry for the trees, it was just something to write because that was what Miss was trying to make us look at the effects the trees had from the acid rain. So I thought it was the thing to write down, it would make sense feeling sorry for the tree. Cos you wouldn't want, like if these trees [pointing to trees outside window] were cut down, you wouldn't want them cut down so I just wrote that, but I wouldn't really care to be honest

[Researcher: Right, but you wouldn't write that down - that you don't really care?]

No. Cos miss wouldn't tell me off and she wouldn't say 'Well done', she'd just make me write it out again, she'd just have a conversation with me to see what I **really** think, so I just write that down and it saves me.

What we see here is an example of a student adopting a particular approach to the learning task that involves going through the motions or appearing to do what was expected without really doing it. The parallels between Ola in Stockholm and Lisa in Oxfordshire are striking in the sense that both are choosing a particular strategy in order to deal with the fact that they hold different views to their teacher/lecturer about the subject matter. This, we would argue, represents another important challenge for learning and teaching about environmental issues within formal education settings.

Different Views of What Should be Studied in a Subject

This final category of learning challenges stems from students holding strong views about the type of content that should be included within a particular school subject or university course. One example of this came from a 13-year-old school student in England who felt that learning about the peoples of the rainforest was 'not really geography'. When interviewed shortly after a lesson in which he had watched a video and written a poem about the Kayapo Indians, he said: 'In geography today I did not learn anything to my benefit'. When asked to elaborate on this, it became clear that this was related to his view of what was legitimate content for a geography lesson. As he explained,

Today we were mainly focusing on the people, and not the rainforest, and their habits in the rainforest. But that's not really learning about the rainforest, it's about learning things that people do in the rainforest. It's like you're learning architecture and learning what people can do in the house in many ways. You're learning how to build a house, and they're telling you what people can do in this house. It's not really talking about the architecture of the house.

23

Far from being geography, Aiden felt that 'You probably would have learnt about the Kayapo in history as history is about things that happened and people in many ways'.

In Lundholm's study, there was also evidence of students experiencing difficulties with the nature and structure of their environmental curricula. An issue for the engineering students for example, was whether the course content was helpful to them in terms of working as an engineer in the future. Their complaints were that the content of their ecology course was:

(i) too focused on problems as opposed to solutions – One student, for example, argued that 'I think ecology, it should relate to cases and actual examples instead of just saying how very bad everything is. For example, if you are building a road in the jungle you have to cut down the trees. Okay, that's easy to understand, but what should you do?... The course ought to give solutions to problems and not only the problems. So that it is more adapted to construction. I think that would make the course more interesting for the students as well. And I think that more students would feel more involved and concerned. Some students did not prioritise the course because they felt it was just so much mumbo jumbo.'

(ii) overly concerned with the big picture - 'Ecology, I don't know, let's say the water cycle ... You don't really need the big picture. It's enough to know that in this place, water runs from here and on. It is rather extensive, it's not absolute, sort of. And then the fact that it doesn't relate to what you want or to what you are here for. It is kind of on the side or how to say. So it becomes - it feels, I don't think you have to take the ecology course to become a good engineer. It is only a thing you have to do to get through'.

The common theme here is of students expressing personal evaluations of the content and the way it is organised within an environmental course or series of lessons. This observation suggests that another challenge associated with environmental curricula is that students can attach low priority to environmental content if they see it as inappropriate to the subject and/or unhelpful to a future professional training.

DISCUSSION AND CONCLUSIONS

The challenge of sustainability is one that necessitates learning at all levels within society:

> the learning that will need to be done transcends schools, colleges and universities; it will be learning in, by and between institutions, organisations and communities. (Scott & Gough, 2003, p. xiv)

What this chapter provides is the early beginnings of empirically-based insights into the complexity of such learning within the formal education context (for further empirical analysis in this area, see Hopwood, 2007; Lundholm, 2008; Lundholm et al., 2008; and Rickinson et al., 2009). The studies reported in this chapter suggest that learning about environmental issues within settings such as

schools and universities is far from straightforward. We have identified four areas of difficulty that can present challenges for students involved in environmental education. These occur where:
- individual students understand and enact learning tasks in varying ways
- students' learning experiences are shaped by an emotional reaction to an aspect of the topic being studied
- there is some kind of conflict between the beliefs or views of a student and the beliefs or views of the teacher/lecturer
- students feel that a certain type of task or content is not appropriate for them to be studying within a particular subject.

We would argue that the first of these challenges is not particularly new or unique to learning in environmental education. That students can enact learning tasks in differing ways that have more or less correspondence with the teacher's original intentions has been well evidenced in previous classroom-based studies (e.g., Nespor, 1987; Halldén, 1988; 1999; Wistedt, 1994; Cooper & McIntyre, 1996; Pollard et al., 1997). The challenge of students getting caught up in the procedural (rather than the substantive) aspects of a task, as we saw with Joanne's focus on making her Kayapo poem rhyme, has also been noted in other contexts. For example, Edwards and Mercer's (1987) study of creative learning activities in the primary school classroom highlighted the danger that children's 'understanding of things will remain at the level of specific experiences and practical procedures, while the hoped-for principled understandings are never grasped or articulated' (p. 85). In this respect, then, the use of open-ended creative activities such as role plays and empathetic writing in environmental education comes with similar challenges as when they are used in other curriculum subjects.

However, the other three challenges – emotional responses, student-teacher conflicts and appropriateness of content – seem to be more closely related to the values-rich nature of environmental subject matter. These challenges all have a strong affective (and in some cases, normative) dimension, and in this sense, seem more particular to learning within environmental education. In the words of Ola, one of the Swedish engineering students, 'There are a lot of values in a subject like this. I mean, just think about environmental issues!' The findings reported in this chapter suggest that the ways in which such values play out in school or university classrooms are an important issue for practitioners and researchers involved with environmental learning.

Implications for Practice

We see important messages stemming from this work for teachers and lecturers seeking to facilitate environmental learning amongst their students. Perhaps the most important message is that environmental education can present a number of quite particular kinds of learning challenges for students.

Environmental subject matter can evoke strong emotional responses amongst learners, which can influence the nature and depth of their engagement with any learning activities set up by the teacher/lecturer. As we saw earlier, Melanie's dislike of 'cutting down trees and animals being hurt' resulted in her 'just paying a little bit of attention' to a video about deforestation. This idea of students choosing how and when to engage with emotive issues is supported by Watts and Alsop's (1997) work on undergraduate students' learning about radiation and radioactivity. One of their key findings was that 'where issues are unpalatable or unsavoury there is a tendency for people to ignore them, to undergo "conceptual avoidance" '(ibid., p. 361). The key point here is that teachers/lecturers need to recognise that students' difficulties with environmental learning activities can be as much due to issues of emotions and values as to challenges of knowledge and understanding.

Connected with this point, teachers/lecturers need to be aware that the similarities or differences between their own views and those of their students can be problematic for student learning and engagement. This issue was seen with the Swedish engineer Ola, who struggled with his 'dear ecology lecturer's viewpoint that man was God's biggest mistake', and as a consequence avoided 'going into discussion [for fear of] becoming an enemy of someone who is going to correct your exam'. It was also evident with the school student Lisa who explained how she had developed a strategy for dealing with her teacher's requests for her to express an opinion about issues that she did not see as particularly interesting or controversial. In her words, 'I didn't really feel sorry for the trees, it was just something to write because that was what Miss was trying to make us look at the effects the trees had from the acid rain'.

Finally, there is the important point that it cannot be assumed that students will share teachers'/lecturers' belief in the importance of dealing with environmental/ sustainability issues within particular curriculum subjects. The engineering under-graduates in Lundholm's study were far from convinced that their ecology course was helpful to them in terms of working as an engineer in the future, while one of the school students in Rickinson's work felt strongly that learning about the indigenous peoples of the rainforest was 'not really geography'. These examples suggest that curriculum developers and practitioners need to think much more carefully about the ideas that students bring to the learning situation about what is and is not appropriate and helpful to study in different curriculum contexts.

A further point relating to all of the above challenges is that their occurrence in school and university classrooms may well be *largely hidden*. Students may well have very good reasons for wishing to keep their differences of opinion or views about the subject matter hidden from their teacher or lecturer. This point highlights the importance of renewed efforts to improve our understanding of environmental learning from the perspective of the learners which brings us to the implications for research.

Implications for Research

In our view, there has been all too little in-depth investigation into the dynamics of environmental learning, particularly in terms of the experiences of learners. As Payne noted in the late 1990s, there has been 'a lack of consideration in environmental education theory and research practices about the children who are the subjects of environmental education' (1998, p. 20). In comparison with fields such as science and mathematics education, environmental learning has been both under-researched and under-theorised (Dillon, 2003; Rickinson, 2006). Furthermore, as pointed out by Falk (2005), 'It is becoming more widely appreciated that narrowly focused and limited views of environmental learning limit both its understanding and a meaningful assessment of its impact' (p. 273).

In view of this situation, we see a need for more serious research attention to be given to issues of learners and learning within environmental education. The case studies discussed in this chapter suggest a need for more sophisticated understandings of several aspects of the learning situation. In particular:

- the role of values and emotions in the learning process and the relationship between the affective and the cognitive aspects of students' experiences
- how the relationships between the beliefs and values of teachers and students can influence students' learning
- the factors that can facilitate and hinder learners' willingness to engage with and benefit from environmental learning opportunities
- the extent to which the kinds of learning challenges reported in this chapter may be relevant within different educational contexts.

Developing and improving understandings on these matters will require research that is empirical as well as theoretical, concerned with learning as well as teaching, and grounded in ideas from beyond as well as within environmental education. Most significantly it will need serious recognition for learners as active agents rather than passive recipients of environmental learning.

REFERENCES

Connelly, F. M., & Clandinin, D. J. (1986). On narrative method, personal philosophy and narrative unities in the story of teaching. *Journal of Research in Science Teaching, 23*(4), 293–310.

Cooper, P., & McIntyre, D. (1996). *Effective teaching and learning: Teachers' and students' perspectives.* Buckingham: Open University Press.

Corney, G. (2000). Student geography teachers' pre-conceptions about teaching environmental topics. *Environmental Education Research, 6*(4), 313–329.

Cotton, D. R. E. (2006). Teaching controversial environmental issues: Neutrality and balance in the reality of the classroom. *Educational Research, 48*(2), 223–241.

Dillon, J. (2003). On learners and learning in environmental education: Missing theories, ignored communities. *Environmental Education Research, 9*(2), 215–226.

Doyle, W. (1992). Curriculum and pedagogy. In P. W. Jackson (Ed.), *Handbook of research on curriculum.* New York: MacMillan.

Edwards, D., & Mercer, N. (1987). *Common knowledge: The development of understanding in the classroom.* London: Routeledge.

Entwistle, N., & Smith, C. (2002). Personal understanding and target understanding: Mapping influences on the outcomes of learning. *British Journal of Educational Psychology, 72*, 321–342.

Erickson, F., & Shultz, J. (1992). Students' experience of the curriculum. In P. W. Jackson (Ed.), *Handbook of research on curriculum.* New York: Macmillan.

Falk, J. H. (2005). Free-choice environmental learning: Framing the discussion. *Environmental Education Research, 11*(3), 265–280.

Fien, J. (1992). *Education for the environment: A critical ethnography.* Unpublished PhD thesis, University of Queensland.

Ghaye, A. (1986). Outer appearances with inner experiences: Towards a more holistic view of group work. *Educational Review, 38*(1), 45–56.

Halldén, O. (1988). Alternative frameworks and the concept of task: Cognitive constraints in pupils' interpretations of teachers' assignments. *Scandinavian Journal of Educational Research, 32*, 123–140.

Halldén, O. (1999). Conceptual change and contextualization. In W. Schnotz, S. Vosniadou, & M. Carretero (Eds.), *New perspectives on conceptual change.* Amsterdam: Pergamon.

Halldén, O. (2001). Social constructionism, constructivism and intentional analysis as an heuristic tool. In O. Halldén, M. Scheja, & H. Jacobsson Öhrn (Eds.), *Intentional analysis.* Research Bulletins from the Department of Education, no. 65, Stockholm University. (In Swedish)

Halldén, O., Haglund, L., & Strömdahl. (2007). Conceptions and contexts: On the interpretation of interview and observational data. *Educational Psychologist, 42*(1), 25–40.

Hart, P., & Nolan, K. (1999). A critical analysis of research in environmental education. *Studies in Science Education, 34*, 1–69.

Hopwood, N. (2007). Environmental education: Pupils' perspectives on classroom experience. *Environmental Education Research, 13*(4), 453–465.

Kyburz-Graber, R. (1999). Environmental education as critical education: How teachers and students handle the challenge. *Cambridge Journal of Education, 29*(3), 415–432.

Lundholm, C. (2003). *Learning about environmental issues. Undergraduate and postgraduate students' interpretations of environmental content.* Unpublished PhD thesis, Stockholm University. (In Swedish)

Lundholm, C. (2004a). Case studies–exploring students' meaning and elaborating learning theories. *Environmental Education Research, 10*(1), 115–124.

Lundholm, C. (2004b). Learning about environmental issues in engineering programmes: A case study of first-year civil engineering students' contextualisations of an ecology course. *International Journal of Sustainability in Higher Education, 5*(3), 295–307.

Lundholm, C. (2005). Learning about environmental issues. Undergraduate and postgraduate students' interpretations of environmental content. *International Journal of Sustainability in Higher Education, 6*(3), 242–253.

Lundholm, C. (2008). Discourse, cause and change: A study on economics students' conceptions of child labour. In J. Öhman (Ed.), *Ethics and democracy in education for sustainable development. Contributions from Swedish Research.* Stockholm: Liber.

Lundholm, C., Hopwood, N., & Rickinson, M. (2008, April 24–28). *Developing lenses for understanding environmental learning.* Paper presented at the annual meeting of the American Educational Research Association, New York.

Nespor, J. (1987). Academic tasks in a high school English class. *Curriculum Inquiry, 17*(2), 202–228.

Payne, P. (1998). Children's conceptions of nature. *Australian Journal of Environmental Education, 14*, 19–26.

Pollard, A., Thiessen, D., & Filer, A. (Eds.). (1997). *Children and their curriculum.* London: Falmer.

Rickinson, M. (1999a). *The teaching and learning of environmental issues through geography: A classroom-based study.* Unpublished DPhil. Thesis, University of Oxford.

Rickinson, M. (1999b). People-environment issues in the geography classroom: Towards an understanding of students' experiences. *International Research in Geographical and Environmental Education, 8*(2), 120–139.

Rickinson, M. (2001). Learners and learning in environmental education: A critical review of evidence. *Environmental Education Research, 7*(3), 207–317.

Rickinson, M. (2006). Researching and understanding environmental learning: Hopes for the next ten years. *Environmental Education Research, 12*(3/4), 445–457.

Rickinson, M., Lundholm, C., & Hopwood, N. (2009). *Environmental learning: Insights from research into the student experience.* Dortrecht: Springer.

Scott, W., & Gough, S. (2003). *Sustainable development and learning: Framing the issues.* London: RoutledgeFalmer.

Sterling, S. (2001). *Sustainable education: Revisioning learning and change.* Dartington: Green Books.

UNESCO. (2005). *United Nations decade of education for sustainable development (2005–2014): International implementation scheme.* Retrieved September 9, 2008, from http://www.unescobkk. org/fileadmin/user_upload/esd/documents/ESD_IIS.pdf

Watts, M., & Alsop, S. (1997). A feeling for learning: Modelling affective learning in school science. *The Curriculum Journal, 8*(3), 351–365.

Wistedt, I. (1994). Everyday common sense and school mathematics. *European Journal of Psychology of Education, 9*(1), 139–147.

Mark Rickinson
Independent Research Consultant and Research Fellow,
University of Oxford, UK

Cecilia Lundholm
Research Fellow,
Department of Education and Stockholm Resilience Centre,
Stockholm University, Sweden

NATASHA BLANCHET-COHEN

3. RAINBOW WARRIORS: THE UNFOLDING OF AGENCY IN EARLY ADOLESCENTS' ENVIRONMENTAL INVOLVEMENT[1]

Stop stop I shouted
And made my presence noted
Leaving behind my fear
I made a tear
Land is our mother
And trees are her lungs
Stood the men sorry
With concern and worry
Ashamed of their terrible deed

Nandhini, 11, Kenya

When Nandhini recited the poem, I was struck by her bold yet subtle approach to environmental action. While there is increased recognition of the unique perspectives, intellectual contributions, and abilities of children, what is the nature of their contributions? How are children *"Warriors of the Rainbow,"* referred to in the Cree prophecy as people who will restore health and values on earth?

To understand the nature of early adolescents' environmental action, I undertook research with 10–12 year-old participants in the International Children's Environment Conference (Blanchet-Cohen, 2008). Rather than action, I found agency as the cross-cutting element. Agency more than action captures how children are constantly interacting with their social and physical environments: they are manoeuvring, and being strategic. I identified six dimensions of children's environmental involvement which are presented under the following headings: connectedness, engagement with the environment, questioning, belief in capacity, taking a stance, and strategic action. These dimensions form the basis of a framework that highlights the multi-layered nature of children's environmental involvement. To illustrate how the framework helps in understanding a child's story, an annotated vignette is provided for each of the four profiles of environmental involvement: initiator, creative, member, and grounded. The concluding section discusses implications for education of valuing children's abilities in engaging with their environment.

R. Stevenson and J. Dillon (eds.), Engaging Environmental Education: Learning, Culture and Agency, 31–55.

LOCATING THE RESEARCH INQUIRY

The study builds on the contributions and critiques of research on significant life experiences (SLE) (see *Environmental Education Research* special issue 1999). Just as in SLE research, I saw value in learning from environmentally involved individuals; therefore, participation in an environmental conference was one basis for selecting the participants. I wanted however to go beyond singling out sources of environmental concern and motivation, and to explore the emerging activism of children (Chawla, 1998; 1999).

A focus on early adolescents raised questions on methods, because SLE research has largely been with adults on their memories of childhood. As articulated by Gough (1999), environmental concerns and behaviours are very different for those aged below 30: "Rather than treating students as 'innocent pets' and forcing them to replicate our experiences we should be helping them to find their own significant life experiences within the context of the SLE of their near peers" (p. 390). The interest in children's perspectives also comes from a growing recognition of the need to involve children in decisions that affect them, given the UN Convention on the Rights of the Child (John, 2003).

Moreover, there are several indications that early adolescence is pivotal in children's awakening to environmental issues (Cobb, 1977; Hutchinson, 1998). While classic theorists of child development, such as Freud and Erikson, devalue the significance of early adolescence, buried in the literature is evidence that this is a unique period, as also identified by several authors studying children's spiritual experience. Scott (2004), for instance, explains: "Children have the capacity to transcend themselves and enter into a moment or series of experiences without distraction, caught up in the event that may lead to a sense of oneness beyond the self " (p. 182). Parallels between spiritual awakening and feelings of concern and care for the environment are worth emphasizing (Hart, 2003). For several reasons, therefore, early adolescence could represent a window of opportunity for environmental awareness and action.

Initially, the literature review pointed to action as the focal concept for the study. Largely, this was in response to the extensive literature that distinguishes between behaviour and action. Emmons (1997) explains: "Action has an intentional quality that may or may not characterize behaviour" (p. 35). Action is deliberate, taken with an intended result, whereas behaviour may be automatic or involuntary, and the outcome may or may not be a conscious intention. Jensen and Schnack (1997; Jensen, 2002) consider that to be an action, distinct from an activity or behaviour, requires being both (a) directed at solving a problem, and (b) decided upon by those preparing to carry out the action.

I also was interested in broader conceptualizations of action, that include less tangible and subtle elements such as making a decision, posing a problem or question, or expressing a feeling (Clover, 2002). The broad perspective is critical to recognizing, for instance, that adults listening to children's perceptions may be as important as physically changing the environment (Hart, 1997). Noddings (1984) describes how action is an integral, though often covert, aspect of caring. Smith and Williams (1999) discuss environmental education as being about transforming relationships, establishing personal affinity, sense of place, and experience of community. Community action research identifies action as involving change in the areas of relationships, of ideas on issues, and of institutional policies and practices (Reitsma-Street, 2002).

To capture the richness and complexity of children's environmental involvement, I turned instead to children's agency as a focal point for the study. The appropriateness of agency flows from recognizing children's perspectives. As articulated within the new sociology of childhood, it is part of recognizing that "children are and must be seen as active in the construction and determination of their own social lives, the lives of those around them and of the societies in which they live. Children are not just the passive subjects of social structures and processes" (James & Prout, 1997, p. 2).

Agency shines the light on how children act relationally with themselves, the natural environment, and society. As Mayall (2001) identifies, there is an important distinction between children as social actors and agents:

> They are not merely "actors" – people who do things, who enact, who have perspectives on their lives. They are also to be understood as agents whose powers, or lack of powers, to influence and organize events – to engage with the structures which shape their lives – are to be studied. (p. 3)

Studying children as agents is fascinating given that more than most adults they live in situations of dependence, yet seek to influence their own experiences and their world. So the question becomes how do children interact with the structures that affect their lives? What shape and form does children's leverage take?

The agency concept is also appropriate in understanding how children's perspectives can contribute to social change. At one level, agency is about the continuous and reflective internal dialogue which we practice; as Archer (2000) articulates, our power lies in our inner conversations which are what defines our humanity. Agency reflects Giddens' (1979) theory of structuration, which views change as the outcome of agency and structure interrelating in the same moment. Emirbayer and Mische (1998) consider human agency as: "a temporally constructed engagement by actors of different structural environments … which, through the interplay of habit, imagination and judgement, both reproduces and transforms those structures in interactive response to the problems posed by changing historical situations" (p. 970). Combined, the expressions of children's agency, while subtle and seemingly mundane, are incrementally significant, leading to social change and potentially a redefining of the nature of environmental awareness and action (James & James, 2004).

Few studies have focused on early adolescents' interface with the environment, or the active and complex nature of children's agency interactions with structure. King's (1995) study amongst children 5 to 15 years old in the United States examines how children's views on the environmental crisis are manipulated by mass media. Children receive conflicting messages on their role, their power, and their future responsibilities. King considers environmental action to be confined to personal, private decisions about changing behaviour, such as turning off the tap or recycling. King calls for a radically new set of social relations between human and nature, where children have the opportunity to be "prototypical frame breakers" (p. 121). Wals (1994) carried out action research with children aged 12 to 13, living in the poorest neighbourhoods of Detroit, on their perceptions and ideas of nature and environmental issues. Similarly to King, Wals places little emphasis on the role of the individual child, seeing few children who challenge the distribution of wealth and natural resources or who question the precepts of capitalism.

Punch (2001), on the other hand, studied children's strategies in Bolivia to renegotiate adult-imposed boundaries. She shows how children assert their autonomy by gaining control over their use of time and space. She considers this process to be a critical aspect of children transitioning to adulthood and an expression of children's participation in their community. It is a focus on the seemingly small yet significant processes that I turn to in my study to capture the significance of children's stories, as illustred in Nandhini's poem.

METHODOLOGY

The 2002 International Children's Environment Conference (ICEC) in Victoria, British Columbia, Canada provided a site for the research. ICEC was of interest in that it brought together 400 children, aged 10-12, representing 66 countries, who were interested in the environment or already involved in environmental activities. As articulated in research on significant life experiences (Chawla, 1998; Palmer, 1996; Tanner, 1980), an analysis of environmentally active children is thought to give insight about experiences and understandings that can be replicated more widely. Significantly, the conference was more than a 4-day event. There was a 9-month planning period with a 12-member junior board which included one face-to-face meeting of the entire board three months before the event (Blanchet-Cohen & Rainbow, 2006). Following the conference, there was also a one-year book legacy project.

One limitation of this study is that these children were privileged. Some subsidies were offered, but travel costs to Victoria as well as conference fees prevented children from attending. In addition, there were the hurdles of hearing about the conference and receiving adult support to complete the application. Thus, while coming from different parts of the world, the children are mostly from the middle class (as suggested by the parents' professions) and actively part of a global community and culture (as evidenced by a familiarity with Harry Potter books).

Three methods for gaining an understanding of children's perspectives were used (Christensen & James, 2000; Lewis & Lindsay, 2000). Forty-two open-ended one-on-one interviews, using both literal and metaphorical questions, allowed children to share their stories and explore their perceptions and beliefs about the environment. Ten to twelve years is an age at which children have the language skills to express themselves articulately; semi-structured interviews provide for a level of interaction between the researcher and participants (Kvale, 1996). The 19 questions in the interview questionnaire covered three areas: (a) reasons for coming to the conference, (b) stories of environmental activism, and (c) metaphorical questions. Four questions using metaphors were placed at the end to capture the covert expression of children's environmental involvement (Lakoff & Johnson, 1980; Snively, 1986). Children responded well to all the metaphorical questions, despite language concerns. It was interesting to note changes in facial expression when answering the metaphorical questions, as though the children were reaching to another side of their brain.

Mind-mapping activities involved respondents relating one of the conference themes (either water, climate change, resource conservation, or healthy communities) to themselves (i.e., how the issue impacts them, actions), and what they want world leaders to do to address the issue. The mapping activity itself was a metaphor, with the outline of the child representing the boundary between themselves and the world leaders. Maps were either done collectively or individually. They left space for children's creativity, allowing them to express themselves visually or in words within loose guidelines.

A visual survey appropriately engaged children while providing quantitative data to substantiate the findings. The visual survey was selected to achieve greater congruence between the study's theoretical framework and methods. Several researchers (Alerby 2000; King, 1995) have used drawing to explore children's relationships to the environment. The survey was handed out to 116 conference participants representing over 25% of children attending. The 98% rate of return suggests that the survey was successful in engaging children.

The researcher's field notes supplemented the data. These were largely enriched by my involvement in the conference planning committee and a subsequent legacy project. Being part of planning the conference was critical to making the research possible – a reality increasingly recognized in qualitative research as contributing to the research itself and a basis for validity rather than an impediment (Denzin & Lincoln, 1994; Hart & Nolan, 1999).

Data from all tools were categorized to identify patterns and relationships, somewhat like in grounded theory. The environmental agency model emerged from the search to answer "What is the story line?" (Strauss, 1987). The following section presents the six dimensions of the framework, followed by annotated vignettes for the profiles of environmental involvement.

THE ENVIRONMENTAL AGENCY RAINBOW FRAMEWORK

The environmental agency rainbow framework (see Figure 1) visually represents the study's findings. I selected the rainbow as the unifying metaphor for a number of reasons, but above all because it figured prominently in the data. Though it was not mentioned an inordinate number of times, when it was identified the references were powerful (Rubin & Rubin, 1995). The bands of the rainbow represent the six dimensions of children's environmental agency: connectedness, engagement with the environment, questioning, belief in capacity, taking a stance, and strategic action. Agency expresses itself differently in each of the dimensions. The shape of the rainbow arc and blending of the bands is a reminder that children's involvement is interlinked. It is a process that has not (and may never) come to a full circle.

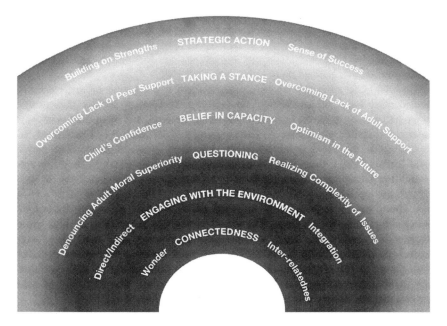

Figure 1. Environmental agency rainbow framework.

The sense of mystery that surrounds the image of the rainbow parallels the nature of children's environmental involvement. Just as the rainbow is widely believed to be a sign of good luck, the success of children's environmental initiatives is unknown but somewhat magical. Thus the connection with the Cree prophecy that speaks about a time when the *Warriors of the Rainbow* will come to end the destruction of the Earth and instil new values and sustainable livelihoods. Is there reason to believe that today's children are Warriors of the Rainbow, as reflected in the wisdom of their words, and their commitment to bringing about change?

While the six bands are presented as distinct and in a specific order, just as in a rainbow where each colour merges into the next, in this framework elements of each dimension remain as one proceeds from one dimension to the next. In other words, there is a flow between the dimensions, as environmental involvement cannot be explained by a linear framework.

Band 1: Connectedness

Connectedness opens the rainbow, setting the foundation. Connectedness is about children immersing themselves in their environment, exploring and relating to their surroundings on an emotional, intuitive level. In the context of the data, I identify children's expression of connectedness under two subheadings: (a) wonder and (b) interrelatedness.

Wonder refers to the sense of fulfilment and contentment in being in nature. Children often experience wonder in their special places. Florence from Québec, for instance, describes a specific rock beside the water covered with moss where she *"feels more at home than anywhere else."* The rock gives her a sense of security, of unity, where, in her words, *"you are entirely alone with nature."* Many accounts of connecting with nature have a spiritual component. Oren refers to the *"energy"* of his special tree.

Children demonstrate creativity in giving meaning to special places even in the midst of a city's concrete. Karanfil from Turkey expresses the joy provided by a particular tree in her grandmother's apartment building garden: *"There was a tree it smelled so good.... I always got under its leaves, sometimes I read a book. Sometimes I fell asleep. I felt really comfortable there, it was wonderful to be there."* Children express agency in connectedness by singling out compelling features, and finding meaning in them.

Interrelatedness, on the other hand, refers to children's relationship with the physical environment. Children comment on the impact of the environment on their well-being: *"When I'm inside I feel kind of locked up, so I'd prefer to be outside. I just really love it, so I just usually sit on the beach, and just watch the sunrise and sunsets."* Often, there is a personification of the environment. Maria, Guatemala, says, *"If we are happy, also nature will be happy with us."* Yvonne, Kenya, views herself as a twin to the environment *"because we both need each other. We need to work together."*

In answer to the metaphor questions, where children spoke of their beliefs and responsibility towards the environment, children's responses conveyed a respect for the environment. When asked, if the environment is like a hotel would they see themselves as the owner, the guest, or the employee, the majority answered either employee or guest. Carissa, Canada, says, *"We're the guests. It's really Mother Nature's, we are just visiting."* Florence, Québec, stated that *"those who care for the environment also care for others,"* thereby identifying a parallel between relating to people and relating to the physical environment. In the maps, there were many drawings of hearts. Connectedness with the environment has an affective, almost magical element to it. There is agency as children intentionally give meaning to places, in being absorbed by the mystery of nature, and often engaging in imaginative interactions with their special place.

Band 2: Engaging with the Environment

Engagement with the environment involves learning about the environment, moving from an intuitive connection to a deeper discovery, either through direct or indirect contact with nature. Engagement with the environment concretizes the connection with the environment, moving from wonder to curiosity to knowledge of how the environment works. For instance, at the base of Vivek's campaigning for the protection of an endangered species of bats is fascination with its unique tail: *"It has a tail like a mouse and wags it like this* [gesture].... *I thought this cool and I got interested.*" This initial connection led Vivek to learn more about bats through books and observation, particularly of bat excrement. "*Some bats have long things and some bats are short. Some are fat and round things.*"

Interestingly, children spoke about their limited access to the outdoors, often appearing unaware of the significance of spending time outdoors close to home. Children give increased meaning to one-off events, television, the Internet, and books (see Table 1). According to the survey, 63% identify the Internet and books as either often or always useful. In the interviews, books are identified as the preferred medium for learning about the environment. While recognizing that these children are of a particular socio-economic stratum and that 75% are urban, the study raises questions about the impact of the loss of direct contact with nature. Research on significant life experience amongst adults consistently identified childhood memories of spending time outdoors as key. What does this mean in an increasingly urban world? The study shows that children are creative in compensating for the lack or absence of direct experiences with nature, another expression of children's agency. But does the resulting personal affinity parallel that provided through direct experience?

Beyond accessing information on the environment, there is integration. Adults play a key role in nurturing children's interest in the environment. Small-scale behaviours and opportunities often have, from the children's perspective, the greatest impact. For Adrian, USA, his grandfather watering the plants with used bath water stands out in his recollections. For Carissa, Canada, the grade-five teacher allowing them to "*walk in our socks to see what would grow on them*" created a strong impression. Processing of knowledge comes from interaction and engagement. The active element can simply involve sorting through multiple sources of information and translating them into a child's own language. Children deepening their understanding reflects agency, which allows children to become more invested and hence more responsible.

Table 1. Sources of learning about the environment

	Never %	*Sometimes %*	*Often %*	*Always %*
Books	9	28	31	32
Internet	10	27	28	35
TV	28	40	16	16
Mother	2	27.5	37.3	33.3
Father	4.9	38.8	27.2	29.1
Teacher	8.8	25.5	31.4	34.3
Other Adult	18.4	49	21.4	11.2

Band 3: Questioning

After connection and engagement, environmental involvement is about children critically interfacing with society's behaviours and attitudes towards the environment. Questioning deals with the awakening of children's critical consciousness and sense of justice; in considering the bigger picture children become aware of the contradictions and complexities in the world. There is agency when children react to what they observe or feel by raising concerns, denouncing contradictions, or making claims on moral and practical grounds.

Questioning is expressed primarily in denouncing adults, and in realizing the complexity of environmental issues. Children seek and receive support from specific adults, but blame adults as a whole for destructive behaviours. In children's criticism, adults are often bluntly portrayed as the destroyers and the children as those who repair. Questioning permeates statements in the collective maps: "*World leaders should start a way to dump trash somewhere else than the ocean,*" "*People should have an equal amount of water,*" or "*World leaders can stop wasting so much money on the military and instead help the environment.*" An underlying judging tone made me initially ask whether children's accusations were not made at the expense of taking on responsibility (Blanchet-Cohen, Ragan, & Amsden, 2003). Viewed within the context of the other dimensions, questioning is part of children tackling systemic issues and seeking their place and voice.

Questioning includes children realizing the complexities of solving environmental problems, and how they hinge as much on resolving economic, social, and political questions. Children raise questions, pointing to contradictions such as unequal distribution of resources and over-consumption. Children discover that adults

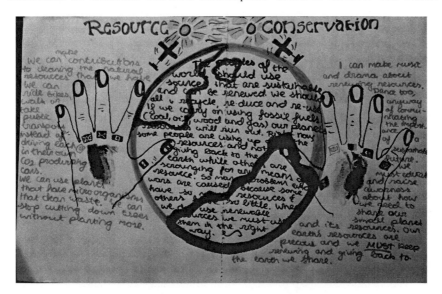

Illustration 1. 'Resource conservation'

are subject to larger forces and do not have all the answers. Maybe unlike adults, children easily raise questions. *"The people of the earth should use resources that are sustainable and can be renewed.... So many problems and wars are caused because some have so many resources and others so little,"* states Alicia, Scotland, in her drawing (see Illustration 1). Children often discover adults covering up for loopholes in the system. This is the case for Brian and Nicole, who discovered that despite city bylaws requiring pet owners to clean up after their pets, the city has no disposal method for dog feces. The adults interviewed by the children often defended the system, or sent them to other departments.

> We asked a lady at the Delta Municipal Hall in the bylaws department if you are allowed to put doggy doo in the landfill. She said 'Yes'. We said: 'No, the landfill says you are not allowed to put it in your garbage because it is considered offensive material.' The lady checked this out and returned saying: 'Oh! You are right. We are not allowed to put it in the garbage, but they will accept small quantities.' She also explained to us that the SPCA was in charge of enforcing the doggy doo bylaws.... After visiting the Delta SPCA we were told there were 9,000–15,000 dogs in Delta. We also learned that the Delta SPCA have never fined anybody for not picking up after their dogs! (excerpt from story essay, n.d.)

Nicole and Brian continued their quest for effective alternatives for disposing of the dog feces. Questioning initiated their interest and continued to motivate them to search for solutions and concrete action.

Raising concerns, denouncing contradictions, and making claims on practical and moral grounds are in many ways part of growing up. It is in responding and reacting that children develop their identity. Questioning reflects agency as children take a critical look at real-life happenings, and make judgements. While the two previous dimensions take place at the individual level, often internally, questioning involves outward thinking.

Band 4: Belief in Capacity

Belief in capacity constitutes the fourth band of the rainbow. It involves children framing the issue positively, and viewing themselves as capable of making a difference. It refers to children's confidence in their own capacity and optimism for the planet's future. It has to do with an attitude or a conviction. Belief in capacity relates to the notion of hope, identified by environmental educators as a necessary component for children to care for the environment (Hicks, 1998). Belief in capacity places increased emphasis on the active role of the child, better reflecting the children's own phrase "We can do it."

Belief in capacity is the crystallization that brings a child to express care for the environment beyond his or her own self. I identify two components of the belief in capacity dimension: confidence and optimism. Confidence awakens consciousness, and gives an individual the power to follow through on his or her beliefs and feelings. Children need to be intentional to *"put their minds to it"* says Rebekah from

Canada. It is confidence, not knowledge that allows children to overcome the challenges of environmental involvement, such as confronting peer pressure. Peer pressure was repeatedly mentioned. Sarah, from the UK, comments:

> I'm like, the only one that really cares a lot about the environment. And, most of them really, they're all – how I look – and like that. But I think it doesn't really matter just as long as you know that you can do something special. ...When I talk about it they call me a hippy and a tree hugger, and I think that's really cruel. Because they actually, I [think that] they do care deep down, but they're just not showing it because it's not fashionable.

At issue is not so much the lack of interest, but having the strength to act on one's convictions despite perceived lack of peer support. Children portray confidence as a characteristic that can be acquired and nurtured, and express that undertaking environmental initiatives does not require having all the answers. Samantha, Jamaica, explains: "*I don't think that they [children] have to have an idea of what they are going to do and why they are going to do it.*" In other words, confidence rather than merely knowledge carries one through the challenges of environmental action. This may be seen as a wise commentary in the area of the environment, where we do not have all the answers.

Besides confidence, children need to feel optimistic about the planet's future. According to the survey, 85% of children said they disagreed or strongly disagreed with the statement "It is too late to care about saving the environment." In the metaphor questions, children selected images that spoke to their active role in restoring the planet's health. To the question, "If the environment is like a car, do you see yourself as the passenger, mechanic, or driver?" an overwhelming number of participants (26 out of 39) identified themselves as mechanics. They are optimistic, in other words, about being able to fix and repair the health of the planet. "*I see myself as a mechanic. Because I try and fix the environment where it's been spoiled, yeah.*" The data suggest that children's optimism comes from being realistic about their environmental roles, and viewing environmental problems as everyone's concern. "*I feel it is my responsibility, but not just mine . . . as long as you are using something from the planet it is your responsibility to take care of it,*" says Yvonne, from Kenya. This is agency because children are making the choice to make environmental problems manageable, rather than being overwhelmed.

Band 5: Taking a Stance

The fifth band, taking a stance, is about going beyond a simple refusal or the status quo; it is about actually committing to a position. It is about the 78% of respondents who answered agree or strongly agree to the statement "I would speak out if someone treats the environment poorly." As Jonas expressed in a drawing, he goes ahead distributing his brochure on the use of pesticides despite the fierce community looking over his shoulder (see Illustration 2). In fancy handwriting, he writes on the side "hot stuff," indicating that it can be popular to be environmentally active.

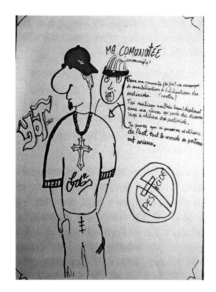

In my community, I did an awareness campaign against the use of pesticides. I created a (very good) brochure with my class that describes the harms of pesticide use. I think that if no one uses pesticides everyone will be well.

Translation from French

Illustration 2. 'Hot Stuff'

Peers and adults represent the biggest obstacles to children's environmental involvement. Children who express their environmental concerns have to deal with adult or peer opposition, or both, in varying degrees depending on the situation. Children spoke about the hardships of being lonely, and the competition between environmental concerns and other preoccupations, such as looks, sports, and social activities. Bereniz, from El Salvador, comments, *"They are more into their own things at home . . . watching television. They get into fights, play football, they don't care if the plants get broken."* Chris, from Kenya, was emotional when he talked about being bullied by his classmates, *"being seen as a servant"* because he was picking up the garbage. There is often a high price to pay for being environmentally involved.

Several participants spoke about their peers' preoccupation with looks, sports, or other social activities taking precedence over concern for the environment. Adults, on the other hand, assign children to specific roles and activities, and the environment is often not one of them. The adults are portrayed as "pulling us along." Taking a stance is about deciding to no longer be the passenger, and take an active part in caring for the environment. It involves children overcoming adults' demeaning attitudes by proving themselves, and negotiating with adults: *"So in order to get people to listen to you, you have to do important things within your community and school, and people will see how you're not just some kid"* (Mathew, British Columbia). Rangi Marie, from New Zealand, makes a similar point: *"But I don't think they would listen to kids, but only if a kid really made it stand up and showed them, and like, really put it in their face about what's happening."* There is agency in taking a stance as children refuse the status quo by positioning themselves in front of adults and peers. Taking a stance is particularly significant at this age when children are emotionally, socially, and physically dependent and place such importance on adults and peers.

Band 6: Strategic Action

Strategic action represents the sixth and final band of the framework. The word strategic reflects children's purposeful and conscious approach; the environmental action undertaken results from children positioning themselves within a given social and physical context. There is agency in children defining and selecting their approach. Children are not mere receptors; they are empowered actors. Strategic action stems from the previous five dimensions of environmental agency. Its significance, however, does in no way overshadow the importance of the five previous dimensions. Each dimension continues to unfold as strategic actions are carried out.

The concrete environmental activities undertaken may be classified in six categories: recycling, restoration, fundraising, awareness, study of nature, and other. According to the survey, children are generally involved in more than one environmental activity; recycling (75 responses) is the activity that they most often carry out to help the environment. This is closely followed by learning about the environment (64 responses), tree-planting (63 responses), and protecting animals (60 responses). The environmental activities are most often carried out in the school (73 responses), followed by in the home (58 responses), and in the community (55 responses). An examination of the reasoning behind the activities undertaken suggests that building on strengths, and having a perceived sense of success are determining factors. As explains Bereniz, *"The most we can do is to plant trees, pick up bottles, do small things."*

Agency is reflected in children's explanation of and actual approach to resolving environmental problems. Children are purposefully selecting a focus that builds on their strength, recognizing the context within which they find themselves. Kalareit, from Turkey, describes how small things do not require the help of adults: *"We don't need adults for doing these things. So, we can just find some people that we can work with, and do everything we want. We can start small things, and then, I think it will grow."* Children see small actions as being part of the process. Justin, from Canada, comments, *"If you start in one little area, then you can work your way bigger and bigger."*

Within the constraining context in which children manoeuvre, raising awareness is identified as the way they can make the biggest difference. Children recognize the appeal of their freshness and innocence. Rangi Marie, from New Zealand, speaks to this skill: *"They can also make a difference now by telling other people, because children are really good at that. ... And they can make a difference ... not only when they grow up, but now, as they most of them are doing."* She identifies this strength as a resource that can be drawn upon now and in the future. Some respondents explained children's vantage point:

> We can like, we can go around doing, like, we can spread news, because, parents love their children, and children, can like, when they learn stuff about the environment, they can tell their parents, and children can set examples. Because parents love them, they want to listen to them, and like when you tell them something they can say "oh yeah, that's true." (Sarah, UK)

43

It is similar for Nandhini in her poem; she uses a moral argument to stop the men from cutting down the trees.

Children are surprisingly aware of the unclear and indirect impact of their environmental involvement. They exercise agency in seeing themselves as contributing to resolving problems, while being realistic, and speaking in terms of "*doing the most I can.*" This is where their power lies.

PROFILES OF ENVIRONMENTAL INVOLVEMENT

To verify how the six dimensions, or rainbow bands, of environmental agency play out in the life of an individual child, I chose vignettes. I did so recognizing that narratives effectively serve to capture and investigate experiences of human beings in time, in space, in person, and in relationship (Clandinin & Connelly, 2000). Or as Hart (2002) points out, "Narrative inquiry helps understand reasons for actions which are motivated by the beliefs, desires, theories and values" (p. 141).

The vignettes are based on the interviews, follow-up communications, and illustrations produced. Early on in this study, I realized that children's involvement varies. Based on my study, four profiles of environmental involvement were identified: the initiators, creatives, members, and grounded. In each, the dimensions of the environmental agency model are reflected, but to varying degrees. The framework helps give meaning to children's involvement. To present the profiles an abbreviated vignette is provided.

Initiator Profile

The initiators are children who took a leading role in designing and implementing environmental initiatives. While receiving support from a significant adult, the child played a key role in the inception of the initiative. The child's own interest and undertaking was critical. The novelty for initiators is often not the idea. Many draw on already proven approaches (i.e., Internet, video, team work). Rather, the context and method of using the approach are unique. The type of activity undertaken includes sending out weekly environmental messages to a list-serve by email, fund-raising for wells in Africa, hosting a radio program, founding clubs, producing and disseminating a pesticide brochure, or researching and creating a video on disposal of dog feces. The wide range of approaches and environmental areas demonstrates children's capacity to concretely channel their environmental concern.

Included in the 11 initiators identified is Yvonne, age 13, who lives in the Athi region of Kenya. Her environmental activism began 4 years ago with questioning when she noticed the pollution in the river close to her home and formed an environmental club. This led to her attending international conferences, and meeting a Kenyan minister who followed up with a visit to the local factory and subsequently ordered the factory to close down. As she says, "*My life as a child activist had begun*" (personal communication, October 7, 2002).

Repeatedly, Yvonne's agency is reflected in the type of action carried out, her responding and manoeuvring as the actions unfold, and her own reflection on the events. For instance, Yvonne has been involved in working with her peers to convince supermarkets to eliminate plastic bags. For the campaign, children strategically emphasized the ugliness created by disposed-of plastic bags, an aspect of the problem that would be of great concern to supermarket managers and officials concerned about their public image. Yvonne's parents did not initiate her interest in the environment, rather teachers played an important role in fostering her engagement and supporting action.

A number of times, Yvonne spoke about the difficulty of being an environmental activist and gaining the support of her peers. In taking a stance, she has had to believe in her capacity, and select appropriate partnerships. In the interview, I asked Yvonne whether she considered herself successful in her environmental involvement. She qualified her response and said it depended on how success was defined, reflecting back on the factory that was reopened after there was a change in government. Despite "failures," Yvonne believes in her capacity to make a difference in her country. She explains her biggest success as having been in creating awareness. Thus her interest in hosting a television program on the environment and work in promoting children's rights with UNICEF.

Throughout the interviews, Yvonne alluded to her spiritual connection to the environment even though from her interview, it was not clear whether Yvonne spends lots of time outside. She speaks about the need to revisit our relationship with the environment, abandoning humanity's conception of ownership. *"You know, that we're not the only people—it doesn't belong to only us."* Further on, Yvonne explains how she considers herself a twin of the environment: *"I see myself as a twin and the environment as another twin, because we both need each other. We need to work together. And when we are together, so much can happen, so much good comes out of it."* The framework highlights the multiple levels of Yvonne's involvement as an initiator instead of only highlighting the strategic action.

Creative Profile

The creative profile brings together individuals who are outspoken about their concern for the environment. They have reflected on an environmental question, but they have not initiated environmental activities that involve a group, nor does membership in an environmental group define their environmental involvement. There is a focus on processing and reflecting, caring for the environment taking place through a range of activities including creative expression, whether drawing, writing or poetry, or speech.

Included in the 13 participants in the creative category is Andrea, age 12, from Winnipeg, Canada. Drawing and poetry have been key in expressing her concern for the environment. It is on the basis of a poem that she was selected for the conference's junior board. Andrea also likes drawing. The drawing which she gave

Illustration 3. 'Clean Mother Earth, and father wind'

me at the follow-up interview (see Illustration 3) expresses spiritual connections to the environment. The big blue drop teardrops that flow from Mother Earth depict the hope and belief in capacity as conveyed by the overlooking figure, a rainbow-headed, open-armed, and wise-looking woman cloaked in black.

Books also play an important role in Andrea's engagement with the environment, nourishing her imagination and creativity. In the metaphorical question "If the environment is like a tree," she identifies herself with branches like those of the weeping willow in the Harry Potter series of books. Andrea upon learning about other children's environmental involvement re-examined her own involvement. It seems that dimensions of environmental agency – such as taking a stance and strategic action – were not fully expressed. In her first interview about what she has done for the environment, she responded: "*I'm not sure. I recycle at home. I'm not sure.*" Interestingly, while she attended an Eco-labelled school she does not feel it made a difference because she was not given the opportunity to take on initiatives herself. She wrote to me:

> My writing is my gift and I thought it was my way of helping the environment. When I met the other kids, they showed me that what I was doing was not enough.... Since I've gotten back, I've done more. I've recycled more. I have downloaded the SEEDS Green School program

information from the Internet, have met with the vice-principal about starting the program in my school, and have met with the President of the student council. (personal communication, March 3, 2002)

In reflecting on the issues, Andrea is taking ownership and expressing her agency across the dimensions. She feels that concrete actions are more significant than words. This raises a question about the nature of an environmentally healthy planet. The Cree prophecy refers to the Rainbow Warriors as people who will give *"principles or rules to follow to make their path right with the world."* Does not Andrea's creativity play as important a role as the tangible actions of the initiators in guiding people on a new path?

Member Profile

For members, it is the group context that defines environmental activism. Being part of an environmental group is in the members' profile the tangible expression of their care for the environment. Children speak of the importance of group work, and the support provided by group facilitators. As in the creative profile, the children have reflected on the environmental question and have lots to say about it, but they have not undertaken a range of environmental activities on their own. Unlike the initiators, members do not see themselves taking on a leading role in establishing a project at this point.

Included in the 14 members is Nonjabulo, age 10, from Swaziland, who is part of a group called Siswati Bhukwana – Swazi Stars Towards a Brighter Future. It is a school group that focuses on air pollution awareness.

Nonjabulo is connected and engages with the environment. She enjoys going outside and playing sports, particularly in the forest behind her house. Its mystery attracts her: *"You know it's kind of bushy, so I'm not really allowed to go there. But it's kind of fun, it's really fun to go."* She portrays the environment as having a functional purpose for human beings, seeing the environment as being a "good quilt." Nonjabulo questions incessantly, grappling with environmental issues and their solutions, although her knowledge of environmental problems is sometimes restricted. She sees, for instance, pollution in the rivers to be the biggest problem in her community because *"People go and wash their clothes in there, you know, people who live in poverty."*

Nonjabulo realizes that solutions to environmental problems are difficult. While she identifies ignorance as the biggest problem in her community, she acknowledges that providing information is not sufficient to solve environmental problems. *"I can tell you now to go and pick up litter at your house and you could just go home and cook."* Nonetheless, Nonjabulo believes in her capacity and is optimistic about the planet's future. She speaks about seeing herself as the one who walks the extra 15 miles to get clean water. To the metaphorical question "If the environment was a tree, would she be the branches, fruits, or the roots?" she responded fruits, and gave the following explanation: *"We're environmentally born children. So, when the environment produces the good fruits, somebody eats it, and it like, goes into their heads."*

Membership remains a dominant attribute of Nonjabulo, as part of being the good fruit. To the metaphorical question "If the environment is like a hotel, do you see yourself as the owner, a guest, or an employee?" she responded, *"Employee. Because I kind of work for the environment.... So, an employee would like, you know, um, contribute to how the hotel works."* Through her membership in the Swazi Stars Towards a Brighter Future and the activities carried out, Nonjabulo is taking a stance. She is engaged in her surrounding community, and also connects to nature in her free time. In carrying out her activities, she has also been dwelling on the complexity of solving environmental issues. She is perceptive, recognizing that there is no quick-fix solution to environmental problems.

Unlike Andrea, there is no indication that Nonjabulo is dissatisfied with her involvement as a member. Of significance, however, is how within her group there is a space for participation and for her to express agency, as the group members are involved in planning and carrying out the group activities. The environmental agency framework serves to highlight these critical components that are considered necessary for children to be Warriors of the Rainbow.

Grounded Profile

The grounded profile includes people who view their environmental involvement as a way of life, rather than a project. They are closely connected to nature as demonstrated through their daily activities. It is inappropriate to ask about their first memory of having done something for the environment. They speak in terms of living in harmony with nature, of the inter-relationship between humans and the environment, and the need to honour that as a way of being. They are grounded in that they take a holistic approach to the environment, one that is rooted in their way of life.

Included in the 4 participants who fit the grounded profile is Oren, age 11, who stood out at the conference because of his attire, which included a Dr. Seuss-like hat. He lives on a mile-long island off Vancouver Island, hard to access in difficult weather, and is home-schooled. His engagement with nature comes from direct experience. He talks in detail about loving to explore the outdoors. *"I love like walking in it, I love exploring in it and I love going on adventures and climbing and just all sort of fun things."*

Repeatedly, he refers to his spiritual connections to nature. He speaks about a huge tree with eight trees growing out of it as his special place on the Island. He likes going to that tree *"because it's umm it's like unique, it's big, it's umm got lots of energy in it."* Oren sees the environment as alive because *"everything has a spirit cause it all came out of the earth."* In describing his inter-relationship with the environment, he chose a value: trust. *"I trust the environment and I hope the environment trusts me."* The environment takes on human-like characteristics, and becomes capable of judgement.

Oren doesn't see caring for the environment as separate from his life: *"I feel like it's also like part of my life to help protect it."* His environmental involvement takes place in activities as well as in his behaviours. He mentions a number of specific activities he has been involved in with his parents, such as being part of the Clayoquot protests, cleaning the beach after an oil spill, campaigning against fish farms, and collecting bottles from the beaches. He questions the extent to which people relate to the environment intimately: "*If more people lived around the environment and in it, I think they would realize what is going on and what they would lose if they don't try and make a difference.*"

Oren speaks to belief in capacity but is careful not to overemphasize his role, nor his capacity. He is realistic, and sees himself not as fixing the planet but helping it. "*I do what I can do. There is only so much one person can do.*" As with other children, Oren does not take on all the world's environmental problems, nor is he overwhelmed by them. In his assertion, he shows how personally he feels empowered and responsible to protect the environment. Oren's articulation of and expression of his relationship to the environment reflects his taking a stance and his strategic action. In his drawing, he beautifully encapsulates the critical place of environmental agency (see Illustration 4).

Through this powerful image, the necessity of water, green trees, and food to sustain all life forms stands out. In placing around the body an alternative for a healthy environment on one side, and the harm done to the environment on the other side, Oren suggests we have a choice; there is hope and we are not mere receptors of the situation. The glasses and earrings, as Oren describes, represent our own perception and take on the world, and the need to have the courage to express ourselves, given our uniqueness. This articulately encapsulates the concept of environmental agency.

The green inside the body symbolizes a green planet. The water is for unpolluted water. Water is one of the most important things in the world. Without the green trees we will die without food we will die. The trees on the left signify how the government should create the sewer tank. On the right symbolizes pollution and air and water pollution.

The glasses and earrings symbolize your own personality and to be who you want to be and not to be influenced.

(transcription of Oren's verbal explanation)

Illustration 4. 'Your own personality'

DISCUSSION

The current study shows that concrete environmental action is the tip of the iceberg; there are several underlying components. I identify these as the dimensions of environmental agency. In each of the six dimensions, there is an active element. In connectedness, children intentionally give meaning to places, and relate to the environment as well as to other people. In engaging with the environment, children learn about it through first-hand discovery and/or processing of the knowledge gained. In questioning, children respond to the world, awakening to the contradictions and complexities of our world. In belief in capacity, children take on a positive perspective of the planet's future and their own capacity to effect change. In taking a stance, children express themselves by articulating their concern for the environment, often despite external disapproval. Finally, in strategic action children define and select their approach to addressing environmental issues.

Further research could lead to identifying other dimensions or a re-labeling; most significantly however the research points to the multiple forms and significance of children's environmental involvement. On its own, for instance, Brian's beach cleanup may not have an immediate significant environmental impact, but it is part of his journey. In becoming more aware of his capacity in making a difference, and in connecting with the beach and the people with whom he carries out this activity, Brian is establishing relationships with the physical and social environment and learning both about himself and his responsibility to care for the environment.

Agency defines children's participation. In each dimension, children explore and define themselves in relation to the rest of the world, and to specific issues. Children's participation becomes meaningful as they engage in critical thinking, imagination, and action. This study shows how children's participation is critical to human development and learning (see Rogoff, 2003) with environmental involvement facilitating children's growing up and their search for a voice and a place.

Responding to the world's environmental problems is not easy. Often a child is involved in a paradoxical process of both seeking out and distancing himself/herself from the sources available. A child, for instance, engages with the environment and nurtures relationships with significant adults on the one hand, but on the other takes a stance to differentiate himself/herself from peers and adults. Children ambivalently go back and forth between expressing feelings of strong connection to the environment, and positioning themselves in front of environmental problems. While Florence speaks about feeling most at home on a rock in the woods, she is also involved in organizing a home-based environmental club. In this case, her connection to the environment translates into action. In other cases, an initiator may be connected to a special place at home, yet focus on a single distant environmental issue. In going back and forth in this way, events, places, and relationships become meaningful for children. The constant defining and refining of children's environmental activism mirrors in some way the awkwardness of growing up, as they find their place in the world (Cobb, 1977; Hart & Nolan, 1999; Hutchinson, 1998).

The current study suggests that the influences that shape environmentally involved children are varied and complex. Adults, peers, formative experiences, discovery of special places, T.V., Internet, and books all play a role. While these sources were identified in SLE research (Chawla, 1999), my study places the emphasis on how a child seeks his/her voice and place through critical thinking, imagination, and action. Of as much interest as the specific sources of environmental concern, is how a child interacts and engages in the situations or resources at hand. Of significance are both a person's context and opportunities, and the individual's role in giving significance to these. Therefore, one understands how children whether living in highly dense urban areas or in rural areas identify a particular place in nature to relate to, or give importance to one-off experiences far from home.

Children's awareness of their skills and limitations explains the predominant focus on awareness-raising, recycling, and restoration as environmental activities. Part of children's maneuvering aims at making environmental problems manageable; thus, for example, children may value small-scale actions. In other cases, children focus on a single issue. In awareness-raising, children can afford to denounce contradictions and call for profound environmental changes; age in this case can be an advantage as children can reach adults in unique ways. Hence, what might appear to be barriers to involvement can also become strengths to bring about positive environmental change.

Throughout the stories and words of the children who participated in the study, there are indications that children are Warriors of the Rainbow. The study speaks to social change as emerging from the interaction between the context and the individual child's strategic maneuvering, whether it be through critical thinking, imagination, or concrete action. While these children were unique and privileged, there are several implications for education.

Implications for Education

This study re-enforces the importance of participative learning to sustainable development, and of the need to nurture the capacity of people to modify and shape the future of our society to guide its social, economic, technological, and ecological changes along the lines of sustainable development (de Haan, 2006). Early adolescence may indeed represent a unique window of opportunity as involvement in environmental activities facilitates growing up, meeting the young person's need to discover both oneself and one's place in the world (Snively, 2001; Sobel, 1995). Like Scott (2004), who is concerned about the later impact of ignoring young people's spiritual development, one must wonder about the implications of devaluing the expression of children's environmental agency.

While educators are indeed placing emphasis on the critical role of action, this focus needs to be accompanied by an understanding of the significance of small and non-tangible actions. I conclude with two specific recommendations for educators.

Educators need to embrace the complexity and inter-connectedness of children's environmental involvement. This study shows that environmental awareness and activism is not about providing a single type of experience, nor only

51

giving environmental knowledge. Rather, it originates from multiple sources. The rainbow model speaks to how a child's environmental awakening arises from all of his or her life experiences; the school is significant among these experiences but does not stand on its own. The arc-shape of the model is an affirmation that children's environmental involvement is an evolving process – whether the journey involves critical thinking, imagination, or tangible action, it is significant. The dimensions interact, feeding on one another. It is not merely about achieving a final once-and-for-all bonding with nature, and moving on to the next level.

The absence of a common or conclusive trajectory amongst young environmental activists in this study points to the need for implementing environmental education broadly in the curriculum, repeatedly, and in ways that honour interrelationships. As articulated in the new paradigm for ecological literacy, educators need to think in terms of "relationships, connectedness and context" mirroring the web of life (Capra, 1996).

Children's involvement is critical to learning. In each of the dimensions, children are learning about the environment, themselves, or finding their place in the world. An oversimplification of environmental knowledge disconnected from the reality does not help students; rather, it stifles their learning. Both children and teachers need to intellectually engage in the complexity of environmental issues, to discuss values, to critically examine their society, and to reflect on their own behaviour (Ballantyne, Connell & Fien, 2006).

Agency describes the complexity of children's environmental involvement; it is an outcome of the interplay in and amongst the dimensions as children intentionally engage, position themselves, and respond to experiences. Each dimension builds children's identity, providing children with a sense of accomplishment, allowing them to go deeper or move on to something else. The result of this process is an increase in children's self-efficacy, in believing in their capabilities.

Teachers and parents are often wary of involving children, as though adult authority will be overridden. This research demonstrates the importance of involvement and how it provides for learning. Teachers often stay away from environmental issues because of their complexity and the fear of leaving students with a sense of powerlessness should difficulties in effecting positive environmental action occur (Hammond, 1997; McClaren, 1989). A child is empowered by being involved in designing and carrying out activities, by being able to imagine himself/herself as a creature of nature, or by connecting with nature. Should educators fear a focus on empowerment? In children's questioning of adults' behaviours, they seek out partnerships with adults – as social beings, but also because children realize the need to work together for addressing environmental problems. As Oren says, *"One strand of rope can be broken, but many cannot."*

Opportunities for empowerment in the curriculum are many and varied. They depend mostly on how subjects are taught, and on educators valuing the process and paying attention to the opportunities for involvement. As teachers, parents, and citizens, we need to nurture early adolescents' environmental awakening and concern in as many children as possible. In this way, it is more likely that the ephemeral nature of rainbows will have long-lasting impacts on the future of our planet. Like the calm that follows a rainbow after a storm, this could mean greater balance, equity, and peace in the world.

NOTES

[1] The research was carried out as part of doctoral research in the Faculty of Education, University of Victoria (Supervisors: Dr. Gloria Snively, Dr. Ted Riecken, Dr. Daniel Scott, Dr. Nancy Turner). The study is also reported on in the June 2008 *Environmental Education Research* issue.

REFERENCES

Alerby, E. (2000). A way of visualising children's and young people's thoughts about the environment: A study of drawings. *Environmental Education Research, 6*, 205–222.

Archer, M. (2000). *Being human: The problem of agency*. Cambridge: Cambridge University Press.

Ballantyne, R., Connell, S., & Fien, J. (2006). Students as catalysts for environmental change: A framework for researching intergenerational influence through environmental education. *Environmental Education Research, 12*(3–4), 413–427.

Blanchet-Cohen, N. (2008). Taking a stance: Child agency across the dimensions of early adolescents' environmental involvement. *Environmental Education Research, 14*(3), 257–272.

Blanchet-Cohen, N. (with Rainbow, B). (2006). Partnerships between children and adults? The experience of the international children and environment conference. *Childhood, 13*(1), 113–126.

Capra, F. (1996). *The web of life. A new understanding of living systems*. New York: Anchor Books.

Chawla, L. (1998). Significant life experiences revisited: A review of research on sources of environmental sensitivity. *Journal of environmental education, 29*, 11–21.

Chawla, L. (1999). Life paths into effective environmental action. *Journal of environmental education, 31*, 15–26.

Chawla, L. (2001). Putting young old ideas into action. The relevance of growing up in cities to LA21. *Local Environment, 6*, 13 25.

Christensten, P., & James, A. (2000). *Research with children. Perspectives and practices*. London: Routledge Falmer.

Clandinin, J., & Connelly, M. (2000). *Narrative inquiry: Experience and story in qualitative research*. San Fransisco: Jossey-Bass.

Clover, D. (2002). Traversing the gap: Concientizacion, educative-activism in environmental education. *Environmental Education Research, 8*, 315–323.

Cobb, E. (1977). *The ecology of imagination in childhood*. Dallas, TX: Spring Publications (Original work published 1969).

De Haan, G. (2006). The BLK '21' programme in Germany: A "Gestaltungskomptenz'-based model for education for sustainable development. *Environmental Education Research, 12*, 19–32.

Denzin, N. K., & Lincoln, Y. S. (1994). Introduction. Entering the field of qualitative research. In N. Denzin & Y. Lincoln (Eds.), *Handbook of qualitative research* (pp. 1–17). Thousand Oaks, CA: Sage Publications.

Emirbayer, M., & Mische, A. (1998). What is agency? *American Journal of Sociology, 103*, 962–1023.

Emmons, K. M. (1997). Perspectives on environmental action: Reflection and revision through practical experience. *The Journal of Environmental Education, 29*, 34–44.

Giddens, A. (1979). *Central problems in social theory: Action, structure and contradiction in social analysis*. London: Macmillan Press.

Gough, A. (1999). Kids don't like wearing the same jeans as their mums and dad: So whose 'life' should be in significant life experiences research? *Environmental Education Research, 5*, 383–394.

Gough, N. (2002). Ignorance in environmental education research. *Australian Journal of environmental education, 18*, 1–10.

Hart, P. (2002). Narrative, knowing, and emerging methodologies in environmental education research. *Canadian Journal of Environmental Education, 7*(2), 140–165.

Hart, P., & Nolan, K. (1999). A critical analysis of research in environmental education. *Studies in Science Education, 34*, 1–69.

Hart, R. (1997). *Children's participation. The theory and practice of involving young citizens in community development and environmental care.* London: Earthscan.

Hart, T. (2003). *The secret spiritual world of children.* Maui, HI: Inner Ocean Publishing.

Hicks, D. (1998). Stories of hope: A response to the 'psychology of despair'. *Environmental Education Research, 4*, 165–176.

Hungerford, H. R., & Volk, T. L. (1990). Changing learner behaviour through environmental education. *Journal of environmental education, 21*, 8–22.

Hutchison, D. (1998). *Growing up green: Education for ecological renewal.* New York: Teachers College Press.

James, A., & Prout, A. (1997). *Constructing and reconstructing childhood: Contemporary issues in the sociological study of childhood* (Rev. ed.). London/Washington: Falmer Press.

James, A., & James, A. (2004). *Constructing childhood. Theory, policy and social practice.* New York: Palgrave Macmillan.

Jensen, B. B., & Schnack, K. (1997). The action competence approach in environmental education. *Environmental Education Research, 3*, 163–178.

Jensen, B. B. (2002). Knowledge, action and pro-environmental behaviour. *Environmental Education Research, 8*, 325–334.

John, M. (2003). *Children's rights and power. Charging up for a new century.* London: Jessica Kingsley Publishers.

King, D. L. (1995). *Doing their share to save the planet: Children and environmental crisis.* New Brunswick, NJ: Rutgers University Press.

Kollmuss, A., & Agyeman, J. (2002). Mind the gap: Why do people act environmentally and what are the barriers to pro-environmental behavior? *Environmental Education Research, 8*, 239–260.

Lakoff, G., & Johnson, M. (1980). *Metaphors we live by.* Chicago: University of Chicago Press.

Lewis, A., & Lindsay, G. (2000). *Researching children's perspectives.* Buckingham: Open University Press.

Lincoln, Y. S., & Denzin, N. K. (1994). The fifth moment. In N. K. Denzin & Y. S. Lincoln (Eds.), *Handbook of qualitative research* (pp. 575–586). Thousand Oaks, CA: Sage Publications.

Mayall, B. (2001). Introduction. In L. Alanen & B. Mayall (Eds.), *Conceptualizing child-adult relations* (pp. 1–10). London: Routledge Falmer.

Noddings, N. (1984). *Caring. A feminine approach to ethics and moral education.* Bekeley, CA: Regents of the University of California.

Palmer, J. A., & Suggate, J. (1996). Influences and experiences affecting the pro-environmental behavior of educators. *Environmental Education Research, 2*, 109–121.

Palmer, J. A., Suggate, J., Bajd, B., Hart, P., Ho, R. K. P., Ofwano-Orecho, J. K. W., *et al.* (1998). An overview of significant influences and formative experiences on the development of adults' environmental awareness in nine countries. *Environmental Education Research, 4*, 445–459.

Punch, S. (2001). Negotiating autonomy: Childhoods in rural Bolivia. In L. Alanen & B. Mayall (Eds.), *Conceptualizing child-adult relations* (pp. 23–35). London: Routledge Falmer.

Reitsma-Street, M. (2002). Processes of community action research: Putting poverty on the policy agenda of a rich region. *Canadian Review of Social Policy, 49/50*, 69–92.

Rogoff, B. (2003). *The cultural nature of human development.* Oxford: Oxford University Press.

Rubin, H. J., & Rubin, I. S. (1995). *Qualitative interviewing. The art of hearing data.* Thousand Oaks, CA: Sage Publications.

Scott, D. (2004). Spirituality and children: Paying attention to experience. In H. Goelman, M. Sheila, & S. Ross (Eds.), *Multiple lenses. Multiple images. Perspectives on the child across time, space and discipline* (pp. 168–196). Toronto: Toronto University Press.

Smith, G., & William, D. (1999). *Ecological education in action. On weaving education, culture and the environment.* New York: State University of New York Press.

Snively, G. (1986). *Sea of images: A study of the relationships amongst students' orientations and beliefs, and science instruction.* Unpublished Doctoral Dissertation, University of British Columbia, Canada.

Sobel, D. (1996). *Beyond ecophobia. Reclaiming the heart in nature education.* Orion Society.

Strauss, A. (1987). *Qualitative analysis for social scientists.* New York: Cambridge University Press.

Tanner, T. (1980). Significant life experiences: A new research area in environmental education. *Journal of environmental education, 11,* 20–24.

Tanner, T. (1998). Choosing the right subjects in significant life experiences research. *Environmental Education Research, 4,* 399–417.

Wals, A. E. J. (1994). *Pollution stinks! Young adolescents' perceptions of nature and environmental issues with implications for education in urban settings.* De Lier: Academic Book Centre.

Natasha Blanchet-Cohen
Department of Applied Human Sciences,
Concordia University, Canada

LEARNING AND AGENCY IN COMMUNITY CONTEXTS

ARJEN E. J. WALS AND LEONORE NOORDUYN

4. SOCIAL LEARNING IN ACTION:
A RECONSTRUCTION OF AN URBAN COMMUNITY MOVING TOWARDS SUSTAINABILITY

INTRODUCTION

"By now I should have gotten used to it, but the thrill is still there every time I pass Lunetten station and get off the train in Culemborg to take that short walk home and to enter this ocean of flowers. And even though I had all kinds of dreams of this neighborhood before moving here, I never imagined that it would be such a paradise to live in for Keri and Job." (Jan Willem, father of Keri and Job, inhabitant of Eva-Lanxmeer)

In the evolution from nature conservation education and environmental education to learning towards sustainability, one can see a shift from a focus on individuals (and their attitudes, behaviors, and so on) to a focus on communities (and the lifestyles and systems they support). With this shift towards the collaborative and the communal, there is increased attention for things such as capacity-building, agency, participation and forms of collaborative learning. This shift is partly fed by a realization that the creation of a more sustainable world is complex, contested, contextual, and marinated in uncertainty. We do not and cannot know what the most sustainable way of living is. What we *do* know is that current systems and lifestyles are fundamentally unsustainable and that we need to engage people, organizations and communities in a creative search for more sustainable ones. How do we engage people at the community level in such an existential quest? What kinds of learning processes seem promising in utilizing the diversity different members of society bring to this quest? These are the main questions this chapter addresses using an authentic case of community development from The Netherlands. The chapter culminates with a social learning perspective on community engagement. This perspective holds that social cohesion and social capital are essential for developing agency, utilizing diversity, safeguarding inclusivity and sustaining commitment to jointly agreed change.

In the late 1990s, the Dutch Ministry of Environment, Housing and Spatial Planning developed legislation that encouraged municipalities and individual citizens to promote sustainable housing. Citizens could get all kinds of subsidies, for instance, to move towards energy efficiency, while municipalities could get national grants when they allocate municipal land to housing development that meets certain sustainability criteria. In 1999 a number of sustainability-minded citizens were interested in developing an entire neighborhood (over 200 households)

R. Stevenson and J. Dillon (eds.), Engaging Environmental Education: Learning, Culture and Agency, 59–76.

founded on principles of sustainable living as outlined by themselves (i.e., a community garden owned, designed and maintained by all members) and by the government (i.e., with regards to the building materials used, double water system, solar energy, triple-pane glass, etc.).

The group was given seed money by the town of Culemborg to organize themselves and to hire a process facilitator. The process of reaching agreement about what a sustainable neighborhood actually means and the design and implementation of the generated plans required a great deal of interaction and mutual learning among the various stakeholders. In this chapter, we will reconstruct the making of a 'sustainable' neighborhood as a social learning process of civic engagement in sustainability. This reconstruction is in part based on a study[1] carried out five years after the initiators found a strong enough support base to start the creation of the new neighborhood in Culemborg (Noorduyn and Wals, 2003) and on mirroring the outcomes of this study with recent thinking on social learning in the context of sustainability (Wals, 2007). First, we present some of the unique features of the neighborhood and then we focus in on the process of interaction that took place when the first people who moved in collaboratively designed the community garden that forms the heart of the neighborhood. Finally, we distil some key learning principles or stepping-stones from the Culemborg experience that might have some transfer value (i.e., might be useful elsewhere).

THE ORIGINS OF A 'SUSTAINABLE' NEIGHBORHOOD

In 1994, people with different backgrounds but with similar concerns and interests met in a series of workshops focusing on creating a sustainable urban neighborhood from scratch. During the workshops the idea emerged of an exemplary development project which combined ecological construction, organic design and architecture with active citizen participation. In the fall they created the EVA Foundation (Ecological Center for Education, Extension and Advice) to develop this idea further. EVA identifies the principles of permaculture as key guiding principles in the design process (Mollison, 1991). One consideration was the scale of the community they wanted to create. Founder Marleen Kaptein: "If you really want to show what sustainable building and living means then we need to move up in scale. Not just create a few unique buildings but an entire neighborhood with hundreds of houses. Only then can citizens come to know what a sustainable community looks like."

The town of Culemborg (27,000 inhabitants), just south of the city of Utrecht, was sympathetic to the idea of experimenting with sustainable design at the neighborhood level. Culemborg was already actively supporting energy efficient housing and ecological management of green spaces within the city boundaries, but never at the neighborhood level in an integrated way. The local government was also keen on experimenting with creating (more) space for citizen participation. They wanted to see citizens have more influence on the design of their houses and the layout of their neighborhood. With the newly envisioned neighborhood – by now called Eva-Lanxmeer (www.eva-lanxmeer.nl), the town realized both ambitions at once. The experiment would also provide experiences that would be valuable for improving the quality and sustainability of existing neighborhoods but also that of future ones. In the words of one of the local officials: "We came aboard because we wanted to go one step further. We already had neighborhoods with ecological park and green border maintenance and did promote energy efficiency, but now Eva-Lanxmeer gave us an opportunity to realize everything in one neighborhood."

In 1995, the EVA Foundation presented its plans to the Municipal Board of Culemborg to develop a sustainable neighborhood in the older 'Lanxmeer'. They developed and fine-tuned their plans interactively with high involvement (e.g., through consultation meetings and workshops) of a project group consisting of potential future inhabitants. Their plans called for development of an area consisting of 24 hectares, 200 houses and apartment buildings along with a number of businesses, offices and ateliers. Furthermore, a green conference center and an ecological city farm was envisioned. The housing was to consist of a mix of social or public housing (30%), middle-income level rental and private property (20%) and upper middle/higher income level private homes (50%), in line with one of the guiding principles that call for a socio-economically integrated neighborhood. The entire neighborhood was to be created between the year 2000 and 2002 with the conference center and city farms following shortly thereafter.

OVERALL DESIGN

The final design of EVA-Lanxmeer called for a spatial zoning (Box 1) of the buildings that would encourage social interaction, while the location and design of the green zones or corridors called for near-natural transitions and connections between the different functional zones[2]. The agricultural zone, which surrounds part of the neighborhood, for instance, transitions from intensive agricultural use to extensive agricultural use. The design and management of these different zones corresponded with these different uses [i.e., management of the extensively managed zones focused on promotion of (agro)biodiversity, natural dynamics, compatibility and connectivity between the various (landscape) elements, places and processes (i.e., natural cycles)]. All the zones are connected in different ways:
– physically: by the design of the waterways, green corridors and the cycles of nutrients, organic materials and products;
– spatially: by an enhanced perception of unity or 'wholeness';
– ecologically: by an increased biodiversity and vitality of the entire area;
– socially: by collaborative use and management by those living in the area.

The principles underlying the design are not only translated spatially into different zones but also physically into the construction of the homes and the functional systems supporting the neighborhood. Below we list a few examples of how this was done.

Energy: energy use is to be as low as possible. The aim is to have an 'energy neutral' and 'CO_2-poor' neighborhood by using cutting-edge insulation techniques and materials, re-capturing heat-loss, and using solar panels. The design of the houses enhances energy efficiency. For instance, the roofs are high, sloped, and oriented in such a way to allow for optimal use of solar power. Some houses,

Box 1. The zoning of EVA-Lanxmeer

Zone 1: The immediate area bordering the physical structures (houses, offices, etc.) includes, for example, the private gardens and terraces. Inhabitants may place a border between their own garden and their neighbours' to create some privacy and quietness. However, the border may not be too high and will need to be made of 'sustainable' and 'natural' materials (for instance a fence constructed out of willow shoots or made out of non-tropical, local hardwood).

Zone 2: The semi-public space in between the private gardens and the public green area that forms the core of the neighborhood. This area is considerer semi-public, since the owner of this land (the town of Culemborg) has given the inhabitants the right of passage and the responsibility of maintance for a nominal fee. This space is considered highly suitable for fruit trees, play areas and common hang-out places.

Zone 3: The public area, accessible to anybody. This public area will contain a *jeu-de-boules* field, a vegetable garden and a 'natural' water playground. This public green space is characterized by ecological connectedness, biodiversity and edible gardens that follow the permaculture principles.

Zone 4: A peripheral functional area containing water retention basins (also of naturally, helophyte-filtered waste water from the houses), the ecological city farm which produces fruit and vegetables and holds small livestock, but also provides educational and recreational functions.

facing north, have an extra double glass wall as a buffer to minimise thermal transfer. Wind energy and a local biogas energy plant that uses sewage water and other organic 'waste' (food waste, garden waste) further help the neighborhood become energy neutral.

Water: water conservation is a key principle. The residents agree to reduce the use of tap water, to minimize wastewater and to slow down the drainage of rainwater. They even want to go further by closing the water cycle. In order to do so, the houses have separate water systems in their houses each having their own taps. Clear drinking water can be accessed in the kitchen and bathrooms. The second system contains so-called household water that is used for flushing toilets and for cleaning and washing purposes. The used household water or 'grey' water has a separate drainage systems, which takes the water to a field with helophytes where it is filtered and turned into, again, household water. Then there is the so-called 'black' water or sewage water which enters yet a third system. The black water is piped to a local biogas plant where is generates energy that again is made available to the people living in Eva-Lanxmeer. In order to make this all possible it was important that the neighbourhood's infrastructure included the piping for these three systems.

Green 'waste': the so-called city farmer who also collects the green waste created in other neighbourhoods of Culemborg collects the green waste created by the households and the maintenance of the gardens. The city-farmer brings this organic waste to local biogas plan (also referred to as the Sustainable Implant).

Mobility: the initiators felt it was important to minimize the number of cars entering the neighborhood. On the outskirts there are special parking areas: it is not possible to park your car on or near your own property. Only in special circumstances (i.e., accidents or when moving in or out) can cars get close to the homes. There is no traffic going through the neighbourhood. Short and high quality bike and walking paths to the town's railway station and city centre stimulate the use of bikes and public transportation. The parking lots are made of so-called 'wadis': a layer of water draining stones that prevent rapid run-off and allow for gradual infiltration.

Chain management: the use of natural resources is minimized. The use of durable materials is mandatory in the building and construction of both the homes and the public spaces. At the same time, the re-using of materials is promoted.

In order to have all these elements become a living part of the entire community, the neighborhood association, BEL, has translated these guiding principles into an agreement that all future residents will have to support and sign before being allowed to buy or rent a house.

This chapter focuses on the creation of the so-called green commons that form the publicly accessible heart of the community (zone 3 in Box 1). The green commons were designed while the first houses were built and created once the first residents moved in.

DESIGNING THE GREEN HEART

Most of the neighborhood's design principles and distinguishing features had already been decided upon when the neighborhood's infrastructure was created, and the houses were actually built: before people actually moved in. Up until that point, the community participation consisted mostly of those who were a part of the foundation of EVA and already knew for a long time that they wanted to help create and live in a sustainable neighborhood. As the houses were being built, however, new people came in who were attracted to the concept of EVA-Lanxmeer but who had not been a part of its creation and did not yet know one another. EVA therefore created a support group for guiding the design process of the public space that forms the green heart of the community. This support group also helped the new inhabitants become more familiar with the principles of permaculture. The town of Culemborg makes money available for this design process (money the town otherwise would have spent on designing and developing this public space). This money is mostly intended for assuring that the design process is done in a participatory and professional way.

The people moving into Eva-Lanxmeer share, at least for Dutch standards, quite a bit of public land that forms the core of the neighborhood that they jointly can design and manage. This was the next challenge in the creation of this sustainable neighborhood. Since not all new residents were known at that stage and not all residents were able to participate in the design process for various reasons, a project group consisting of roughly 10 residents was formed (the number fluctuated over time as people moved in and out over time). One community member put the challenge ahead as follows: "How can a group of different people create a joint concept everybody is happy with or that at least everybody is comfortable with and considers a solid base for future collaboration?" The municipality, as a key supporter and stakeholder of Eva-Lanxmeer, wanted to know what the inhabitants will make of the green commons. The town officials were not so concerned about the emerging design but much more about the quality of the *process*, after all one of the town's conditions is that the creation of the commons is done in a participatory and professional way. In the words of one of them: "Whether they decide to create one big lawn or fill the commons with playgrounds or fruit trees, it's all fine with us, as long as it is done in a professional way." To assure some level of professionalism, four experts were asked to help guide the design process:

-   A landscape architect, responsible for the quality of the design and the blending of the green commons with the entire neighborhood which he co-designed;
-   a professional landscaper and gardener responsible for overseeing the actual implementation of the design, establishing smooth transitions between the commons and the private gardens and participating in the maintenance of the public green spaces in the neighborhood;
-   a technical facilitator with expertise in permaculture and ecological gardening and landscaping but who also knows how to involve citizens in co-designing public spaces;
-   a process facilitator who orchestrated and managed the participatory design process and coordinated the work of the other experts involved.

The external experts (many of the future residents were also experts in a range of aspects relevant to the neighborhood's development but they were considered internal experts) play an important role in the whole process. They organized many of the meetings and helped set the agenda. They also outlined various options and choices and showed the potential consequences of each of them, for instance in terms of the evolution of a landscape over time, the type of management required, the financial implications of each design choice, etc. In the words of the technical facilitator:

> "Right from the beginning I help them imagining the possible 'end picture' even though that picture is not yet fixed. When someone wants a traditional beech hedge then you need to explain what the costs are, what kind of management is required, the way the hedge will look in the various seasons and how it will transform over time in the years to come, but I also show how the maintenance of such a hedge can be shared."

The project group divided all activities and meetings into different phases or categories such as the starting-up, visioning, designing, execution (i.e., the actual landscaping and planting activities), evaluating and documenting (i.e., keeping records, logs, picture and a video database) for both a sense of history and accomplishment but also for future learning. After this train of activities, the project group got a clear mandate from all inhabitants to implement the plan. This flow of phases much resembles the phases of social learning as distinguished in Figure 1 by Wals *et al.* (2009). The figure distinguishes a macro learning cycle,

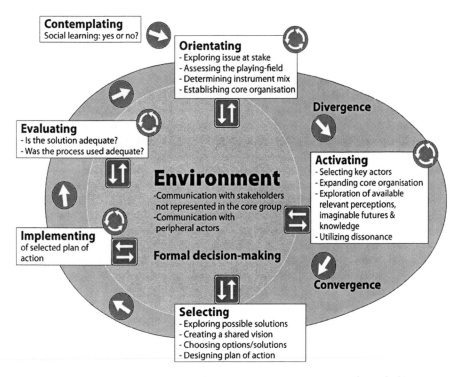

Figure 1. Possible phases in social learning processes (source: Wals et al., 2009)

spanning the whole change process, and a number of micro learning cycles, depicted by the roundabouts, which illustrate that action and reflection take place continuously during all phases.

Guided Self-determination

During the first phase of the design of the green commons, the team of experts did take the lead but provided enough space for the project group of new residents to move forward independently. In the words of the technical facilitator: "The idea was that we would help get them on their way but that we would emphasize that the green commons were their green commons, not ours. They are the ones who will have to manage and maintain the area."

Finding a balance between giving spaces for citizens' self-determination and providing professional input is not so easy. Again the technical facilitator: "How do you create a situation in which you provide ample support, yet allow sufficient room for people's own ideas? There is a tension there. To what extent do you take over responsibility when there seems to be a vacuum or a stalemate? And how do you know whether the inhabitants are able to take on that responsibility themselves again?"

Divergence

The project group organized an 'inspiration day' to generate ideas for private garden designs and the execution of suggested elements of the green commons, but also to help people to get to know one another. The children participated as well (Box 2). To get in the right mood, everybody picked an image from an enormous pile of pictures depicting a range of, sometimes extreme, situations. One picture, for instance, showed a dry bare dessert, another was filled with birds. Everybody picked a picture that was appealing to him or her and explained why to all present. The people who have already moved in the neighborhood gave a tour of their part of the neighborhood and shared their experiences so far. In the afternoon, everybody, children included, sketched or drew their desired image of the green commons (or the elements thereof they found most important. Later on, during a so-called 'design session' led by the external facilitators, the participants wrote key words indicating their expectations of the green commons. Some emphasized *gezelligheid* – a Dutch catchall word referring to coziness, intimacy and pleasure – others wrote about the presence of birds, safe play areas for children, etc. They also told each other stories about gardens and natural areas they had been to that were special to them. Then there was a homework assignment: to make a rough sketch of their preferred designs and design elements using pictures, drawings, models, photographs from magazines - whatever works best. The children too got to make their own rough sketches.

A few weeks later, the rough sketches were exhibited in the local school. In groups, the residents walked past every exhibit where its creator clarified and explained. One of the facilitators: "All these images do quickly give a sense of what

Box 2. Children's participation

For the children the project group and the external facilitators also organize a separate meeting. Every child age four and up gets a personal invitation. "You will not only move into a beautiful new home but there will also be a big garden for the whole neighborhood. With all the adults we have been collecting good ideas for this garden. We believe that you can think of some good ideas as well" (quoted from the original invitation). First the 4, 5 and 6 year olds get to work, followed shortly thereafter by the 7, 8 and 9 year olds. The younger group focuses on the inner-part of the green commons that borders with private gardens. The idea is that the parents will want to be able to keep an eye on them when they play. The older kids primarily focus on the outside periphery of the commons as it is assumed their physical play boundaries will be wider. The younger kids tell each other in a circle what they like to do at home, at school, inside and outside. The older group watches slides, makes drawings and discusses. They conclude that flowers are important, as is a swing, a climbing wall, a tree hut and hiding places for playing hide-and-seek and for pranks. They also agree on their favorite color: pink! The children all think it is wonderful to contribute and feel very important. One proudly reports to his parents that he attended a 'real meeting.'

people want and do not want... One thing that became clear was that everybody wanted it to be possible to walk the green commons bare-footed! ... But there were differences as well: some people wanted a low-maintenance wild-flower garden, with natural lawns, fruit trees and hay. Others wanted small paths meandering through fields of herbs that allowed for intensive gardening. Those are fundamentally different views!"

After over one year of meetings, design ateliers, town hall meetings, workshops, excursions and feedback sessions, a design of the green commons was ready that all were happy about. This was not the only result with which the people were happy. The preparation year had strengthened the social cohesion between the new inhabitants. One of them stated "We not only now have designed a wonderful green heart for our community, we have also strengthened our social ties because you do meet each other a lot." In the words of one of the facilitators: "Half of what we want to realize is the product itself, the other half is the process which allows the people to contribute and get to know each other."

Convergence

During all the sessions, the landscape architect observed what is going on and took note of the key outcomes. He took home all comments, ideas, desires, concerns, expressions of consent but also of disapproval, and sketches. Using all the input from the inhabitants, adults and children alike, the previous rough plans made by the project group which he helped shape, and taking the overall principles and foundation of Eva-Lanxmeer at heart, he created an integrated and coherent design. This much anticipated design was then presented to all involved. "This was a suspenseful moment," one of the inhabitants stated. "You do wonder what he will have done with all our input." The general response to the composite plan is one of approval. "In the design, the fundamental differences that indeed were there have been camouflaged more-or-less. There is something in this design for each of us. To divide the commons in eight distinct squares and a half circle is ingenious," in the words of another inhabitant.

There were a few dissonant voices, however, that raised some objections to parts of the design but since time has become a factor, these objections were not discussed any further which resulted in some participants going home disappointed. Later, a few further changes were made to the design, which led to general acceptance of the master plan. In retrospect, some of the unhappiness was a result of different interpretations of the status of the design. Some thought it was a binding and prescriptive plan which would leave little room for people's own initiative and inter-pretation, whereas it was meant as a guiding framework that still would require the creative input of the people living there to make it work.

The disagreement did lead to a discussion about the decision-making process. How can decisions formally be made? A few of the participants decided to focus on this question as they suspected that this question would surface again in the future. They came up with the following proposal: a decision is only made when there are no longer any well-founded arguments presented that go against the proposed decision.

This directive does not mean that everybody has to agree or that full consensus is required for decisions to be made. The strong point of this way of making decisions is that the underlying reasoning for being against a proposal will need to be made explicit, whereas full consensus, which may never be reached, is not necessary for things to move on. One inhabitant noted that in most cases, formal decision-making was not necessary and things happened in a more or less fluid and natural way: "Things happened by themselves, without problems. So that there is no reason to be formal." It also became clear that the social cohesion formed during all the common activities allowed for this informal decision-making to blossom. This occurred partly because the established 'chemistry' between the people involved made them more open to others and made them more willing to engage with ideas different from their own. This chemistry proved to be crucial, as people were more willing to share, open-up and, indeed, make themselves vulnerable: all ingredients for creativity and a genuine participation process. The people working together to create Eva-Lanxmeer shared a common vision, even though they had different ideas about the operationalization of this vision and certain elements of the design. This common vision and the social connections proved stronger than the emerging differences. The safe and open environment in which the process took place made it possible to confront and discuss them. In the end, not everybody agreed with one another but the people involved became more understanding and accepting of the differences that remained.

IMPLEMENTATION

Once the first houses were completed and people moved in, the social ties strengthened even more and the informal contacts increased. There were social-get-togethers, housewarming parties, 'get-your-hands-out-of-your-sleeve' days with coffee and sandwiches. The people of the adjourning neighborhood, completed a few years earlier, threw a neighborhood party to which the people moving in were invited too. The making of the green commons always surfaces in the conversations at one point or another. Now that the design is actually implemented people could see the impact of their actions immediately, whereas the impact of the hours, days and, indeed, months of meetings was oftentimes hardly noticeable. People seemed to forget the long road that preceded.

The seemingly endless meetings within the project group and later with the other inhabitants proved to be necessary to lay the social groundwork before the first spade penetrated the soil. In the words of one of the participants: "Having meetings really is essential. You need to explore the extremes in order to grow closer to another. It is much easier to accept a dissenting voice from someone you actually know a little. By getting to know each other, you become more tolerant and flexible. As a result, it is easier to find common ground. Should some tensions remain under water, then they need to be made explicit and openly discussed." The latter is important otherwise tensions might come back to haunt the whole process later on. Having meetings also provided a space for, literally, meeting but also for expression of ideas and the ventilating of feelings and concerns. The facilitators were very aware of creating this space and the safe atmosphere required to stimulate openness, honesty and transparency. Altogether, the entire process of creating the green commons in Eva-Lanxmeer took two years of preparation. By scheduling regular meetings and by frequently reporting outcomes, sharing ideas, distributing an electronic newsletter, and so on, the project group was able to keep the fire burning.

Continued involvement turned out to be essential, not only during the design and implementation of the commons, but also when all appeared to be done. Daily, weekly and annual management activities were required to allow the design to become what was envisioned. Some earlier working groups ceased to exist, as they were mostly concerned with design aspects (i.e., the group pre-occupied with equipment for the children's playgrounds or the group focusing on transitions between private and public green space). New working groups were formed: a tree-trimming group, a garden group, a pruning group, a playground maintenance group and so on. Also new structures were needed for communication and decision-making.

Looking to the future,who will take the lead? How do we bring in new people who have just moved in or will move in the future? Will they be equally committed and enthusiastic, even when they were not a part of the process that led to the green commons as they are today? New inhabitants likely bring in new ideas and help determine future directions of the neighborhood's development. In all likelihood, they will share the basic ideas underlying the neighborhood as they will have consciously chosen to live in it and will have signed the memorandum of understanding. At the same time the 'pioneers' will also continue to help shape the neighborhood if only because they are aging, as are their children. A new phase in their walk of life will likely lead to new ideas about the way the commons should develop. Playgrounds for children may come and go over time as the demographics of the neighborhood change over time. Perhaps the neighborhood will become more multi-cultural over time given the 'multi-culturalization' nature of Dutch society. This, too, will likely affect the development of the commons.

LESSONS LEARNT

There are no recipes for successful citizen involvement in moving towards a sustainable neighborhood. The circumstances, participants and challenges are just too varied to allow for a kind of blueprint or roadmap. In fact, it can be argued that this is precisely why a participatory approach is required in the first place. Nonetheless, there are some lessons to be learnt both from theory and practice that may help increase the odds of realizing a fruitful learning process with worthy outcomes and meaningful impacts.

Not Everything Needs to be Done Interactively

Interactivity may be the preferred *modus operandi* when seeking a sustainable world, but this does not mean that every decision needs to be made interactively and that there is no place for, for instance, instruction and more authoritative decision-making. Interactivity needs to be applied selectively depending on a number of variables such as scale, history/baggage, sense of urgency, complexity of the issue at stake, make-up of the group, perceived interdependency among stakeholders, and the various 'stakes' people or groups of people bring to the table. What often happens is that the easier issues (i.e., issues that are not threatening and non-controversial) are tackled in a participatory way, while a small group of insiders makes key decisions about more important issues that are then presented to the larger group as a *fait accompli*. Indeed, sometimes it is better (i.e., more efficient) to make key decisions in a small group. The key is that this small group has been given a mandate by the larger group, but also that there is transparency in what issues the smaller group tackles and in the way they go about tackling them.

Harmonize Expectations

Another lesson learnt here is that different people have different expectations about what the process will result in and to what extent they themselves can influence the process. These expectations vary from very low (the cautious, the pessimistic, the realistic, etc.) to very high (the empowered, the optimistic, the dreamers, etc.). Some have modest expectations (i.e., everybody will compost in the neighborhood and the compost will be used in the community vegetable garden) while others have very high ambitions (i.e., a model sustainable neighborhood based on permaculture principles, closed cycles, social well being and ecological integrity). It is crucial to have participants express these expectations at the beginning to begin harmonizing them a bit early on, in order to avoid disappointment later on when people find out the process is not at all going where they thought is was supposed to be going.

Make Progress Visible

At the onset of a process such as the one described in this chapter, people are enthusiastic, energized and ready to get going and spring into action right away. However, creating a more sustainable neighborhood does not occur overnight: it is time consuming and requires a lot of patience. However tempting it may be to 'get moving,' it proves to be wise to reflect thoroughly on what is desirable and feasible and to take ample time to build social capital and cohesion in the group of core participants and the other stakeholders involved (municipality, building and construction company, landscape architect, water board, etc.). This time for reflection and social capital building can easily be seen as 'stalling'. The initial energy can easily evaporate when the participants do not see any progress and feel there is a lot of talk but no action. Yet, things *are* changing continuously: people get to know each other better (create social capital), develop a joint vision and a sense of ownership, are better at articulating what they want and do not want, and are involving new people and new stakeholders who were out of the picture in the beginning.Therefore, even though no spade has penetrated the ground and no soil has been moved, a lot is happening. The point is that when these changes in views, positions, involvement, ownership, relationships, etc, are not made visible, it will seem as though nothing has happened. People often define progress in terms of 'hard' results such as a playground, compost bins, benches made of non-tropical, FSC-certified hardwood, a sound barrier to block highway noise, a community vegetable garden, but overlook the 'soft' results that are created in the process leading up to these hard results: increased respect, understanding, sense of community, and so on.

Dare to Share

Oftentimes a small group of very committed people comes up with a number of creative ideas and solutions that then do not resonate with those who are to approve and/or work with them (i.e., the other people who are to live in the community or even one's own spouse or children). It is quite easy to form small elites of very motivated, dedicated and inspired people who get along great and communicate very well with one another but forget to share with others and fail to take them along in their thinking. The result might be a kind of innovation elite who have, without realizing it, lost touch with the larger group. This is why high quality communication with all involved is so crucial. All steps, choices and results need to be shared in formal (newsletters, minutes, website, community paper) and informal (at the kitchen table, in the local bakery, at the schoolyard where parents wait to pick up their children, etc.) ways. Only then is the process transparent enough so that those who are more at the periphery out of choice or out of necessity can follow what is going on and can jump in when they feel their own ideas are being compromised or marginalized in unacceptable ways.

Upgrading Facilitation

Usually people do not enter a process like this because of the process itself but because of its focus on what they see as a high quality of life without compromising the future of the Earth too much. As they participate they value being able to contribute on an equal basis. They do not always appreciate it when one member dominates the process or positions him or herself above the group and takes charge, no matter how knowledgeable or experienced that person may be. This is one of the reasons for hiring a process facilitator who is a relative outsider yet accepted by everyone: someone who speaks the language of the participants and has a genuine interest in both the process and in what it seeks to achieve. In order to establish good relationships, the facilitator will also need to get to know the life-world of those involved in the change process and come to understand the local context in which the process is to take place.

The facilitator is also someone who monitors and stimulates openness and safety (i.e., no intimidation, equal opportunity), access (people should be able to move in and out freely) and transparency (no hidden agendas). At the same time, he or she deals with conflict, asks questions, maintains focus when needed, shows progress, maintains a sense of urgency, and helps create a positive and stimulating atmosphere. As if that is not enough, he or she is also able to introduce innovative methods that are appropriate in certain stages of the process (i.e., brainstorm techniques, creative thinking techniques, role-playing, excursions, etc.). Finally, the facilitator has to be socially and emotionally competent as well: a good listener, empathetic, an animator, humorous, a navigator of force fields, diplomatic, etc. All these qualities are hard to find in one single person which is why for processes like these, it might be best to have two or even more facilitators. At the same time it should be acknowledged that many of these qualities are, sometimes latently, present among the participants and will, under the right conditions, emerge and make the facilitator's job a little easier.

Living with Uncertainty

In a process like the one described here, the specific outcomes are unclear and only slowly emerge over time. For some this leads to a feeling of unease and causes stress, others accept this as a given and are comfortable or even excited by it. The latter group flexibly adapts to changing circumstances and prospects whereas the former group can easily become frustrated by the lack of clarity and the seemingly never-ending uncertainty. Much like the harmonizing of expectations, it is important to inform all involved about the uncertainty and, indeed, the risks involved in participating in an interactive process of civic engagement in sustainability. Making this clear at the on-set will make the process more attractive to uncertainty-minded people, and may make those who are not more understanding of what it is going on later on in the process (or may lead to the more certainty-minded people to opt out). Nonetheless, there will always remain a mix of personalities who jointly will have to create the 'chemistry' needed for a collaborative learning process that hinges on things such as commitment, involvement, ownership and creativity.

Keep it Alive!

The interactively created and managed green commons of Eva-Lanxmeer are, to a large degree, the result of a good deal of positive energy and very committed people. Especially in the start-up and implementation phases, the energy level is very high. However, over time these levels are likely to decline. Two factors often cause this decline. First, the new people who have not taken part in the start-up and implementation, move into the neighborhood, do not feel the same kind of ownership, and do not relate to the commons in the same way. Second, some of the original pioneers who have spent hundreds, if not more, hours creating the neighborhood are moving on to other challenges, some elsewhere, while those remaining are beginning to think: 'I have done my bit. It's time for others to pitch in now!' How can the process remain alive? How can we stop the green commons being neglected? In the words of one of the pioneers: "It is important that the green commons are seen as a living place that is not finished but is continuously changing, also in directions that may not be desirable and undermine some of our original ideas." This is why continued communication about what needs to be maintained and how this is done is crucial, as well as continuous reflection on the functions and functioning of the commons and its various components (as suggested earlier, new people, new phases in life, etc. may lead to a rethinking of some of the original ideas and designs). In fact the process has a cyclical nature and needs to repeat itself repeatedly over time, although perhaps at a smaller scale and with a mix of new and old participants.

Nonetheless, there will be moments of "being stuck" which will threaten the process. One strategy that might work to get out of this situation might be to look elsewhere. How did others deal with this? How were they able to overcome adverse conditions? What kind of process did they use at this stage? Careful investigation of such cases could reveal an amalgamation of a variety of smaller actions and a number of critical decisions might be needed (Monroe, 1990). Social psychologist, Karl Weick noted that since smaller problems are more easily solved that big ones, framing an issue in smaller pieces provides enormous psychological benefit (Weick, 1984).

CONCLUSION: A CASE FOR AND A CASE OF SOCIAL LEARNING

The Eva-Lanxmeer case has been presented as a form of active civic engagement in creating a neighborhood that is considered more sustainable than any of the neighborhoods the participants ever lived in before. In this final section, we will interpret the process that helped create this neighborhood from a social learning perspective. We referred to social learning already, without really clarifying the term, which is here understood as a collaborative reflexive process involving multiple interest groups or stakeholders. This process is grounded in the multitude of actions, experiences, interactions and social situations of everyday life (Vandenabeele and Wildemeersch, 1998). Through discursive dialogue and cooperation between people who often share common interests but act within different configurations or frames (i.e., values, worldviews and contexts) such learning can be intensified and can lead to change. Social learning, here, is an intentionally created purposeful learning process that hinges on the presence of the 'other,' others, and 'otherness' or difference. We should recognize that social learning also takes place in everyday life where intention and purpose may be less clear.

In social learning, the interactions between people are viewed as possibilities or opportunities for meaningful learning. The motivation to participate in a social learning process is not always naturally present, but does play a critical role. Much depends on the collective goals and common visions shared by those engaged in the process. Whether such collective goals and visions can actually be achieved depends on the amount of space available for possible conflicts, oppositions and contradictions to enter the learning process. A main point this contribution is trying to make, based on the Culemborg experience, is that any process that seeks to address sustainable living will inevitably involve diverging norms, values and constructions of reality even when all appears smooth sailing in the beginning. Hence, these differences need to be brought above the water table. By explicating and deconstructing them, it becomes possible to analyze their nature and persistence. This is an important step in the process since it helps both to improve the dialogue between the actors and helps identify strategies for utilizing conflict in the learning process.

Learning here can be viewed as a change process resulting from a critical analysis of one's own norms, values and constructions of reality (deconstruction), exposure to alternative ones and the construction of new ones (reconstruction). Such a change process is greatly enhanced when the learner is mindful and respectful of other perspectives. In addition, there needs to be room for new views that broaden the realm of possibilities. In other words, when there is space for dialogue rather than the mere transmission or exchange of points of view. Sustainable living seems to require a kind of dialogue that continuously shapes and re-shapes ever-changing situations and conditions. A dialogue here requires that stakeholders involved can and want to negotiate as equals in an open communication process. Such dialogue rarely emerges spontaneously but requires careful designing and facilitation.

One critical aspect of social learning is working on the edge of people's comfort zones (Wals, 2007). Both in helping people confront the normative underpinnings and limitations of their own positions, views, ideas, and values and in helping them reconstruct alternative ones, facilitators need to be mindful of these zones. "Confronting people with ideas that are radically different ideas from their own – no matter how good they might be - can be threatening in which case it might be more fruitful to introduce mildly dissonant voices that are strong enough to lead to the questioning of people's own thinking and acting" (Wals and Heymann, 2004, p. 239). Some people are very comfortable with dissonance and are challenged and energized by radically different views, while others have a much lower tolerance with regards to ideas conflicting with their own. The trick is to navigate the learning process towards the edges of people's individual comfort zones with regards to dissonance. If the process takes place too far outside of this zone, dissonance will not be constructive and will block learning. However, if the process takes place well within people's comfort zones, as is the case when homogenous groups of like-minded people come together, learning is also likely to be blocked. Put simply: there is no learning without dissonance, and there is no learning with too much dissonance. Ideally, facilitators of processes like these become skilful in reading people's comfort zones, and when needed, expanding them little by little. An important task of facilitators and, ideally, of the participants themselves, is to create space for alternative views that lead to the various levels of dissonance needed to trigger learning both at the individual and at the collective level.

Perhaps the essence and success of social learning towards sustainability lies in people's ability and willingness to let go of and transcend their own individual views of what is sustainable and what is not, so that they can reach a plane where they are able find each other and create enough 'chemistry' to feel empowered to work jointly on the sustainability challenges they come to share (Wals, 2007). An important first step in social learning towards sustainability is becoming aware of one's views and interpretations of sustainability. Only then can they become aware of their own hidden assumptions, their ideological underpinnings and the resulting blinding insights they provide. When this is done in a collaborative setting, where dissonance is properly cultivated, managed and utilised, participants become exposed to the deconstructed ideas and ways of seeing of others, which will help them rethink their own ideas and ways of seeing and will challenge them to jointly create new ones. This kind of co-creation may well prove to be a central element of moving towards sustainability as it allows for the development of a common vision, a (renewed) sense of community as well as a joint action perspective. In the words of one of the participants in the Eva-Lanxmeer case: "We are all in this process together and as a group we will make things happen even though it is not exactly what I had in mind in the beginning." This joint action perspective, sense of community and a better understanding of the positions of others makes softening one's own individual demands easier.

The Eva-Lanxmeer case shows that 'sustainability' or *duurzaamheid* in Dutch, can be a catalyst for the joint contextualization and exploration of meaning when citizens become engaged in, what we have called, a social learning process. Through dialogue, discourse, negotiation, joint fact-finding, mediation, etc. people can arrive at their own interpretation of sustainable living as contextual and relevant to their own situation. Given that we do not know what comprises the right or best 'sustainable lifestyle', it would be wrong for 'technical experts' or the government to prescribe to citizens how they should behave. Rather governments should support and create space for the development of autonomous thinking and self-determination that will help communities to decide for themselves what counts as sustainable living. This is not to say that policy-makers, scientific experts or other relative outsiders have nothing to contribute. On the contrary, as this case shows they are important resources and stakeholders. Social learning benefits from the collective realization that not all information is available in one's own community and context, and that alternative ways of knowing, acting and valuing, not present at the local level, can provide the necessary imagery to develop new solutions.

Before engaging a community in a process like the one described here, it seems wise to first assess whether there is sufficient room and support to allow for it in the first place. In this preliminary phase the initiators of the change process should reflect on the nature of the change process (Jickling & Wals, 2008; Wals et al., 2008) and the institutional spaces and support available by asking questions such as: Is the kind of change that is desired of a more emancipatory (we have no clear idea of what is needed, how it is done, etc. but we do know it requires the active participation of all involved) or of a more instrumental nature (we do have a clear idea of what is needed, how it needs to be done and have a mandate to implement them)? And: Is there sufficient political and organisational space available for engaging people in a participatory process characterised by high levels of self-determination and autonomy? Such questions need to be asked in order to be able to confidently introduce and enhance social learning as an important vehicle for exploring pathways towards sustainability.

NOTES

[1] Special recognition should go to two former graduate students of Wageningen University: Jitske van Diepeningen and Melanie Brunings whose thesis work provided the base of this study.

[2] For a detailed description of the more technical and environmental design aspects of Eva-Lanxmeer refer to van Timmeren et al., 2007.

REFERENCES

Jickling, B., & Wals, A. E. J. (2008). Globalization and environmental education: Looking beyond sustainable development. *Journal of Curriculum Studies, 40*(1), 1–21.

Monroe, M. C. (1990). Converting "It's no use" into "Hey, there's a lot I can do:" A matrix for environmental action taking. In D. A. Simmons, C. Knapp, & C. Young (Eds.), *Setting the EE Agenda for the '90's.* 1990 Conference Proceedings. Troy, OH: NAAEE.

Noorduyn, L., en Wals, A. E. J. (2003). *Een tuin van de hele buurt* [Creating a Neighborhood Garden]. Wageningen: Wetenschapswinkel Wageningen UR.

Vandenabeele, J., & Wildemeersch, D. (1998). Learning for sustainable development: Examining lifeworld transformation among farmers. In D. Wildemeersch, M. Finger, & T. Jansen (Eds.), *Adult education and social responsibility* (pp. 115–132). Frankfurt am Main.: Peter Lang Verlag.

Wals, A. E. J. (Ed.). (2007). *Social learning towards a sustainable world.* Wageningen: Wageningen Academic Publishers.

Wals, A. E. J., & Heymann, F. V. (2004). Learning on the edge: Exploring the change potential of conflict in social learning for sustainable living. In A. Wenden (Ed.), *Educating for a culture of social and ecological peace* (pp. 123–145). New York: SUNY Press.

Wals, A. E. J., Geerling-Eijff, F., Hubeek, F., Kroon, S. van der & Vader, J. (2008). All mixed up? Instrumental and emancipatory learning towards a more sustainable world: Considerations for EE policy-makers. *Applied Environmental Education and Communication, 7*(4), 55–65.

Wals, A. E. J., van der Hoeven, N., & Blanken, H. (2009). *The acoustics of social learning: Designing learning processes that contribute to a more sustainable world.* Wageningen/Utrecht: Wageningen Academic Publishers/SenterNovem.

Weick, K. E. (1984). Small wins: Redefining the scale of social problems. *American Psychologist, 19*(1), 40–49.

Arjen E. J. Wals
Department of Social Sciences,
Wageningen University, The Netherlands

Leonore Noorduyn
De Schrijfster, The Netherlands

CHARLOTTE CLARK

5. SYNERGY OF THE COMMONS: CO-FACILITATED LEARNING AND COLLECTIVE ACTION

INTRODUCTION

Evidence exists that voluntary measures may achieve environmental gains where regulation or economic incentive or disincentive are less successful (Dietz & Stern, 2002; Gardner & Stern, 1996). Where such voluntary actions are taken by a group (that is, taken "collectively") the resulting action(s), and environmental management improvement(s), may prove synergistically effective compared to the sum of individual actions, because of characteristics such as barrier reduction, social incentive, and normative pressures (Carlson, 2000; McKenzie-Mohr & Smith, 1999). In fact, the use of voluntary collective action in communities as an effective environmental management tool is well documented (Bromley, 1992; McCay & Acheson, 1996; McKean, 2000; Ostrom, 1990). If this is true, the process by which voluntary collective actions form in communities is of particular interest, but this formative process is also not well described or understood. To address this gap, my research described and characterized the formative process of learning and collective action in one U.S. community with a focus on issues with environmental implications.

In this chapter, I examine a community's process in developing a policy on whether or not to allow domestic cats to roam freely outdoors (where they can prey on native wildlife). This narrative illustrates: (a) the process by which a collective action agreement was formed, (b) the challenges faced during its formation, (c) the potential changes to learning and behaviour that may have resulted within the community from this process, and (d) the corollary issues that proceed such an agreement, such as the need to orient newcomers, the need to document and reinforce information for all those to whom the policy applies, and the difficulties in considering revision to an approved agreement.

BACKGROUND

I use the term collective action to refer to actions taken by a group to achieve collective benefit, even at a cost to individuals that may not match the individual gain in the future. An example from the collective action literature will illustrate the dynamic of individual action and group benefit (Berkes, 1992). The setting is a small Turkish fishing village, Tasucu, where the fishermen catch bottom-living species in open-coastal waters. As with many fisheries, the fish are not privately

R. Stevenson and J. Dillon (eds.), Engaging Environmental Education: Learning, Culture and Agency, 77–95.

owned, or even communally held. So, no incentive exists for an individual fisherman to reduce his own catch in order to maintain the overall fishery. "Whatever I don't catch today, my neighbour may catch tomorrow," – the quintessential "tragedy of the commons" plotline (Hardin, 1968). However, starting in 1968, this particular village developed a sophisticated voluntary cooperative that effectively maintained the overall population of marketable fish. The cooperative established rules that members had to follow, such as a ban on dynamite fishing, and organized to fight against other aspiring user groups, such as a pulp and paper mill. In short, individual fishermen in the Tasucu community changed their fishing behaviours collectively, even though the end result was likely to be a lower catch volume for each individual, in order to achieve the (potential) future good of a healthier fishery, and one that was regulated exclusively by members of the collective.

Case studies like Tasucu beg a number of questions about the formative process of these voluntary collective actions, or more specifically of what Ostrom calls the "constitutional rules" that underpin the actions. [1] Did the community as a whole approve each decision (e.g., "Starting on this date, we all agree to ban dynamite fishing.")? Did all the fishermen participate in the decision (or even all the community members whether or not they were fishermen)? What were the difficulties faced during the formative process, and how were they addressed (or not)? In most cases in the literature, the specific formative process of such rules and their intended collective actions were not documented and cannot be determined a priori. Ostrom sums up the situation:

> These cases clearly demonstrate the feasibility (but obviously not the likelihood) of robust, self-governing institutions for managing complex [common pool resource] situations, but the origins of these systems are lost in time. It is not possible to reconstruct how earlier users of Swiss alpine meadows, Japanese mountain commons, the Spanish huertas, or the Philippine zanjeras devised rules that have survived such long periods. We do not know who originated or opposed various proposals, or anything about the process of change itself. (1990, p. 103)

This chapter provides one story of the generation of just such a constitutional rule meant to underpin collective action.

THE STUDY COMMUNITY – WEST BRANCH COHOUSING

In order to follow a contemporary process of collective action formation, I studied a U.S. co-housing community over a 6+ year period; I chose this type of community, because such neighbourhoods traditionally have high levels of social interaction and environmental commitment (Meltzer, 2000).

The study community, West Branch Co-housing, formed over a 6½ year period, from a first meeting of only a few people to assess interest in April 2001 to final move-in of the last of 46 families (about 75 individuals) in December 2007. [2] Over this period, members of the community found land, designed the neighbourhood, constructed their homes, and moved in. Planning meetings of the group typically occurred monthly, and residents also met occasionally for social events or workdays on the property (clearing *Wisteria*, rescuing plants before timbering operations for example). For this chapter, data were evaluated from community inception (April 2001) to on-site residency of the first household in May 2006 (Clark, 2007).

Anyone may choose to buy property in West Branch; no process exists whereby current community members choose or preclude other potential members. Nonetheless, the price and unusual characteristics of the community do result in a membership that is different from a "typical" US community; residents are homogenous in some ways (Caucasian, well-educated, middle to upper class, liberal politically) and heterogeneous in others (religion, sexual orientation, cultural background). From the beginning, a collective values process was undertaken, and the community agreed by consensus on four guiding principles: community, affordability, sustainability, and diversity. West Branch decided that policies (constitutional rules) within the community would be decided by consensus, and therefore the discussion described below is set in the context of knowing that any one community member present for a "consensus check" at a meeting could block passage of a policy.

West Branch is well-suited to provide interesting data for several reasons. First, the fact that prospective members collectively decide on most issues using consensus decision-making means that interaction was high, and I found a high level of social cohesion and collective action. Second, because issues were primarily discussed via email and at meetings, agreement, disagreement, progress, and stalemate were relatively transparent and well documented. This process provided a unique window into the social learning process, even for a relative outsider. Third, from the outset, the community named sustainability as one of its four tenets, ensuring that environmental issues would be prevalent among the issues discussed. Fourth, community members agreed that I could have full access to their listservs, community documents, meetings, and socials. They also agreed that I could solicit community members for personal interviews.

These sources provided a multi-faceted picture of the learning process in West Branch. The four email listservs used by the community yielded over 6,000 emails over the study period; community documents including meeting handouts, bylaws, guidelines, covenants, meeting minutes, policies, marketing materials, etc; observational data from meetings, socials, and workdays; and 45 personal interviews, which were transcribed verbatim from a digital audio recorder. Computer-Assisted Qualitative Data Analysis Software (CAQDAS) was used extensively for data analysis (Nvivo^{TM}).

DOMESTIC CATS AND NATIVE WILDLIFE AT WEST BRANCH

This chapter will highlight the process of deciding on a pet policy at West Branch, and more specifically, deciding on the language to regulate whether domestic cats would be allowed to roam freely outdoors in the community. This was a lengthy and controversial discussion; the debatable underlying premises being that domestic cats, when allowed outdoors, kill significant numbers of native wildlife, such as native songbirds, insects, and rodents, and that therefore, the community should mandate mitigative action.

Although this issue is not one that would have high issue consequence compared to other environmental management activities (Brower & Leon, 1999), it provides a particularly interesting example of teaching and learning within the community for four reasons. First, it has run the course from introduction, through community education and discussion, to consensually approved voluntary collective action (the West Branch Pet Policy). Second, enough time has passed since approval of the policy that secondary education and implementation issues have arisen, such as how to explain the policy to newcomers (orientation), how to document the approved policy for members of any longevity (documentation/reinforcement), and whether and how to modify the approved policy (revision). Third, this is an issue with which many community members were not familiar prior to the discussion (unlike more visible issues such as recycling or energy use). Therefore, members came to the issue with a wide variety of prior knowledge and extent of prior commitment to opinion and action. Fourth, this issue was truly community-driven. Few, if any, external organizations or individuals apply pressure of any kind (i.e., social marketing, related regulatory mandates, financial incentives or disincentives) to promote collective action on this issue (e.g., keeping cats indoors).

As an overview, discussion on the policy spanned two years of meetings and emails from introduction in November 2002 to consensual community approval in October 2004, encompassing three drafts and much community discussion. The result was the following language in the community pet policy.

In harmony with our community's desire to encourage the flourishing of wildlife in and around our community, residents should make every reasonable effort to keep their cats indoors. (West Branch Pet Policy, October 3, 2004)

On two occasions after approval (1½ years and 2 years afterwards), relative newcomers to the community raised the issue again, yielding interesting data on orientation, reinforcement, and revision. The next section will describe the formation of the pet policy at West Branch, including issue introduction and initial discussion; initial community action; cycles of research, negotiation, and consensus check; final approval; and subsequent issues (newcomer orientation, documentation and reinforcement, and revision).

Issue Introduction and Initial Discussion

In November 2002, the issue of pets was raised by the developer, a person spearheading the organization and planning for the new community. He suggested that the community consider developing policies on pets and weapons, based on his experience (as a co-housing resident himself) that these were often contentious issues in co-housing communities. Immediately thereafter, a community member,

Patrick[3], wrote an email to the community, an excerpt of which is provided below. With this email, Patrick established himself as an issue advocate, established some credibility for himself by noting his experience in and expertise with wildlife issues (in point of fact, he was a founder of the local wildlife centre), and used normative pressure by invoking the community tenet of sustainability.

> I would like to consider a no outside cat policy. Cats are devastating to birds, killing hundreds of millions per year in the U.S. (about 70 million pet cats, 100 million cats total in US, so that's only several birds per year per cat.) I volunteered at the wildlife center in [a local town] and cat injuries were second only to automobile injuries. If we are to be environmentally sensitive, then that means respecting the wildlife. (Email, November 9, 2002)[4]

A number of community members responded via email over the next 30 days. Some of the responses reflected pure disagreement.

> I generally have no problems with other cats being allowed to roam free, though I do worry about fights. I ...am fine with the fact that cats hunt. (Email, November 4, 2002)

Others referred to other forms of experts (in this case, a veterinarian).

> I would have to say that not allowing outdoor cats in the neighborhood would make us reconsider whether we want to live in West Branch. ... Our vet tells us that all indoor cats are more prone to behavioral problems than outdoor cats: in other words, they're miserable being locked up all day. Wouldn't you be? (Email, November 10, 2002)

Note that this member also threatened exit from the community over this issue. Thus, from this early communication, the community received the message that the issue could be a polarizing one with significant implications. Another community member saw cat hunting as an environmental good, invoking the community tenet on sustainability from the opposite angle.

> One of the reasons I've had cats has been for rat/mice control - at which they are much more environmentally safe than poisons. (Email, November 10, 2002)

Thus, two diametrically opposed views were expressed, both from the perspective of environmental good. These views highlight the fact that although community members thought of themselves and each other as environmentally-minded, the reality of how that philosophy or belief system was implemented could be fairly heterogeneous, and could have significant implications for consensually-made decisions. Some have suggested that people act in congruence if values and preferences are compatible (Loeber, et al., 2007, p. 90), but this example illustrates how difficult defining compatibility may be in many cases.

A number of people suggested other mitigative actions other than an outright ban.

> I know to keep my bird-feeders high off the ground. (Email, November 11, 2004).

I do not let [my cats] out during peak bird feeding times–i.e., early morning or noon or late afternoon. (Email, November 11, 2002)

One member explicitly called for voluntary collective action on the issue.

I always keep my cat inside during nesting season. At that time, parent birds are very vulnerable because they will put themselves in danger to protect their nests. Could all of us cat-owners agree to some times or seasons when we wouldn't have our cats out? A middle ground between always confined and always able to be out. I'd gladly continue to keep my cat in during nesting season and at night. Maybe we can come up with some good ideas for protecting bird feeding stations? (Email, November 11, 2002)

These mitigative ideas caused someone to ask for information – a request for learning:

When is nesting season exactly and how long does it last? (Email, November 14, 2002)

Patrick immediately answers the question, concurrently documenting that his answer comes from a reputable source. (Note that he also provided data advocating his position that outdoor cats kill significant numbers of wildlife.)

I took a look at the [Animal Protection Society] Wildlife data from 2001 (the last complete year). According to this data the baby birds start coming in April and keep coming until August. Birds start breeding in March and many species make more than one nest per season, so this makes sense. (Email, November 14, 2002)

Action taken: Formation of a Pets Team

The community paused on this issue for a little more than a year with little to no conversation on the topic in meetings or on email. Minutes of several meetings during this period (2003) reflect brief discussion of general pet issues such as the need to schedule further discussion of the pet policy, or the possibility of having a fenced-in dog run on-site. The first official discussion of the pet policy at a meeting took place in December 2003, and in January 2004 two members of the community offered to form a team to draft a policy for community discussion (actually the team was to discuss safety issues, firearms, and pets).

Cycles of Research, Negotiation, and Consensus Check

After formation of a Pets Team, the community entered a phase in the decision-making process that was made up of cycles of research and negotiation within the Team, presentation to the community at a meeting, consensus check, and (at times when the draft was not approved) return to research and negotiation. Interestingly, the leader of the Team (Jacquel) was opposed to an outdoor cat ban.

I would also heartily agree with [Victoria's] comments on outdoor cats. My cat is an outdoor cat, but she stays indoors at night. She is very healthy and I believe the outdoor exercise, more than anything keeps her that way. She would go crazy cooped up inside all day. (Email, November 11, 2002)

Furthermore, although Patrick did not join the Pets Team at this time, he did join at a later date when the Team changed from solely a research mission to both a research and negotiation mission. The Team began to garner input through email and Team meetings.

In February 2004, an email was sent that provided the first documented evidence that Patrick's education and advocacy had changed the intentions for future behaviour of a community member.

I currently have a 14-year-old indoor/outdoor cat whom I hope to keep only indoors/on screened porch when I move into West Branch, although ... it will be challenging. (Email, February 23, 2004)

In March 2004, the Pets Team provided an initial draft to the community for discussion at the meeting. No language was included that discussed the issue of domestic cats and native wildlife; the only requirement was that cats have a collar and identification. The draft pet policy was not approved at the meeting, and discussion continued.

Subsequent to the March 2004 community meeting, a number of people wrote emails stating their difficulties in keeping a collar on their cat. One person connected the need for a collar with bell with the issue of wildlife threat.

I think the concern is that a silent cat is a (potentially) deadly cat. At least as far as the local bird population goes. (Email, March 3, 2004)

More meeting discussion occurred (without binding decision checks) on topics ranging from free-roaming cats to enforcement issues to management of stray/feral cats on community property. One community member was active with a national organization that traps and neuters feral cats, and then releases them again to their original outdoor community. This conversation sparked Patrick, the original issue advocate to re-enter the discussion in an impassioned and informative manner. In the quotation below, he let the community know he would block consensus (i.e., prevent policy approval). He also added a new philosophical basis to the discussion (which had previously been centred on the killing of wildlife) – advocating for a hierarchy of native species over introduced ones.

The pet policy was discussed yesterday at West Branch and it appears the group is headed towards a policy that allows outdoor cats. It seemed that many were familiar with my opinion on this subject, so I didn't reiterate it at the time. I find, however, that if I ask myself if I could consent to such a policy or, at the least, step aside and not object, the answer is no. Simply, the resulting killing of wildlife by these cats is, in my opinion, not an acceptable tradeoff for the enjoyment some receive from owning cats that cannot, or will not, be kept indoors and the enjoyment the cats themselves may receive from that lifestyle. It is my opinion that the life of a native wild animal takes precedence over the presence of an introduced species. (Email, June 7, 2004)

Patrick went on to estimate the number of wildlife that might be killed (based on assumptions on the number of cats from West Branch and data on killings per cat), to restate his argument for a higher priority for native wildlife, to mention (and provide references for) other ills (such as rabies, diseases transmitted through cat feces in children's sandboxes), and to argue his belief that allowing outdoor cats makes bird feeders a cruel trap. He provided websites for outdoor cat enclosures as another possibility.

Several events resulted from this apparent impasse. First, Patrick joined the Pets Team, in acknowledgement that a pet policy must be approved, but that he stood in its way of passage. The community often asked members obstructing progress on a policy to join the research time and resolve their conflicts outside of community meeting time. In this way, research times sometimes took on more of a negotiating purpose (usually interspersed with additional education and research).

In addition, community members discussed their intention to change behaviour. One community member stated not only an intention to change her behaviour (or her cat's behaviour) at a future time in West Branch, but also mentioned an actual real-time pilot behaviour change effort.

It has…been my intention to start keeping [my cat] indoors once I move to West Branch…. For a while now, I have been keeping [my cat] indoors during the day, and letting him out only at night, because I think he can't do as much harm…. I hope we can work this out as a community. I am compelled by your views, by my own animal rights philosophy, and by my experience losing cats to cars to advocate an indoor-only cat policy at West Branch. (Email, June 7, 2004)

Note that this quotation contained a clear expression of the impact of Patrick's influence, of the overall West Branch discussion, and of the complex fabric that mixes new information with current information and experience to contribute to new behaviour.

A third event at this point was that someone suggested yet another mitigative possibility – that of allowing existing cats to be outdoors, but mandating that future cats be kept indoors.

It seems to me to be very hard to take an outdoor cat and make that cat an indoor cat. …. Maybe the best solution is to give people information on the harm that cats can do to wildlife, and hope that folks take this information seriously when they acquire new cats. …Providing information on cats and their effect on wildlife is certainly a good thing. (Email, June 9, 2004)

This came to be known as the grandfathering option in community discussion. Several people wrote emails stating their willingness to agree to this future behaviour in the community.

We have intended to raise our next cat indoor only for all of the reasons [Patrick] mentioned in his email. ...I would happily commit to raising future generations indoors. (Email, June 9, 2004)

The person who originally threatened exit on this issue emailed at this point, appearing willing to not have cats as pets in order to comply with an outdoor cat ban (and was no longer threatening exit).

If, by some chance, outdoor cats at West Branch became prohibited, we just wouldn't have one. As far as preserving various species go, I'm not sure why birds are being singled out as more important than other types of animals— say, earthworms (which birds eat), other bugs, squirrels and mice. (Email, June 14, 2004)

Often along the way in such a developmental process, individuals weighed in with thoughts about the overall process, including an appreciation of a perceived willingness of people to work together.

I have been watching with interest as people share their thoughts and feelings over the past few weeks, starting with the pet policy and now the phasing changes. How we are interacting now is setting a tone and building a base from which our community will grow. I just want to let you know I appreciate all the flexibility, consideration, spirit of cooperation and adventure that we are currently sharing! (Email, July 9, 2004)

In July 2004, a second draft pet policy was provided to the community. The language was little changed from the first draft, and again no mention was made of the issue of outdoor cats and their impact on native wildlife.

Pet Policy Draft 2: Cats should have a collar with identification and a bell if possible or have a microchip. (Draft pet Policy 2, July 22, 2004)

This second draft was discussed for 45 minutes at the community meeting in August 2004. At the meeting, Patrick referenced the community's environmental goals, including the choice of density (46 households on 8 acres), and continued to advocate for his point of view.

We can choose to protect the tapestry of wildlife around us, like we choose landscaping. This decision involves everyone. (Community Meeting Minutes, August 1, 2004)

Attendees discussed 'grandfathering' existing outdoor cats (while mandating that future cats be indoor cats), and a non-binding vote was taken showing that those present would not approve a grandfathering clause, because (a) the issue is not one with a large environmental impact relative to others, (b) the goal may not be realistically achievable for all cats, and (c) fears that such an extremist position would negatively impact real estate re-sale value. Several attendees said that 'a no outdoor cats policy' would cause them to not move into the community. Although this was stated to be a non-binding vote, the issue of grandfathering was dead for all practical purposes, and was not raised again. In essence, this was a consensus check with a number of declared "blockers" where supporters chose not to pursue this aspect of the issue further.

A proposal was made to add strongly suggestive language to the document.

In conformity with our community's desire to encourage the flourishing of wildlife in and around our community, residents should make every reasonable effort to keep their cats indoors. (Community Meeting Minutes, August 1, 2004)

One community member specifically invoked Patrick's efforts in stating that use of the word "should" was to be a serious directive for the community. A cultural norm was clearly expressed here.

As mentioned earlier, [Patrick] has made a good effort to follow consensus process and has compromised; I think it's important that if we use "should" it is an agreement by everybody that we plan to try to implement this decision. (Community Meeting Minutes, August 1, 2004)

This speaker seems to be suggesting that the group acknowledge that Patrick's compromise was not made simply to achieve a consensus, but because he believed that behaviour from the community would be consistent with the language in the policy. When any law or policy is enacted, the resulting behaviour change lies along a spectrum from those who deliberately ignore the requirement to those who follow it to the letter. This speaker infers what is likely a question for many in the community – what are the attributes of a written policy and/or of cultural norms in West Branch that will maximize obedience to community policies like this one?

A subsequent modification to the language substituted the word *harmony* for *conformity* in the above proposal. This change from the harsher more directive word "conformity" to the gentler word "harmony" may illuminate some interesting aspects to this process. Did invoking the spirit of "harmony" infer that conflict avoidance was a goal for this policy decision? Does it infer that harmony at West Branch is the higher goal for this policy over obedience with the policy, and therefore trumps this particular environmental "good"? For some, the cultural principal of harmony may be more persuasive than an environmental principal. When consensus was requested on this issue, was it consensus on having harmony, keeping cats indoors, or perhaps both?

Consensus was achieved at the meeting for this modified text. Although, this was not approval of the entire document, those involved in this discussion understood that it was consensus on the only major stumbling block for approval. The August meeting closed with the note that the Pets Team would make changes to the entire document and bring it back to the community for official approval at a subsequent meeting.

Collective Agreement Approved

In September, Jacquel sent a revised pet policy to the community containing the new language. However, because she did not attend the September meeting, and because there was some confusion as to whether it was in fact the updated version of the policy, the issue was tabled until the meeting in October 2004.

The following West Branch Pet Guidelines were approved by consensus at the community meeting in October 2004 containing the following language relative to cats and wildlife.

In harmony with our community's desire to encourage the flourishing of wildlife in and around our community, residents should make every reasonable effort to keep their cats indoors.

Community Response to Approved Pet Collective Agreement

Patrick believed his efforts made a difference in what people know, and in some cases in what they intended to do. In the end, he contented himself with a willingness to accept a change in knowledge rather than the more preferred outcome of evidence of intent to change in behaviour. (Recognize that actual change in behaviour could not be ascertained yet, as individuals did not yet live on site.)

I thought we came to a good resolution, you know. It wasn't that outdoor cats were banned, but at least somewhere the community says they are not preferred, and they'll make an effort to not have them outside, and at least the community had the discussion, and realized that not only are their wildlife issues, but there are public health issues, and you know even nuisance issues involved with that. You respect their issues, and I think at the very end, I tried to summarize it and was corrected. Some people said OK we're buying into this, we don't agree with it, but we're buying into it. It's a compromise we ended up with. So, I think it came out to a better place than it would have been if I didn't [Patrick trailed off without finishing the sentence.] (Interview with Patrick, May 7, 2002)

It is clear that this process provided information that was new learning to many.

There were quite a lot of people concerned with the bird population, so I learned something about that, because I never thought about that you know. I had pets, and I never thought you know what do they do when they go out. I was more worried they would get run over by a car. So I learned something about that, and how different people can see that. (Interview with Judith, May 4, 2005)

I sort of had a limited understanding of that, and maybe a narrow belief about the desirability of cats or… and it was useful for me to see people holding diverse views way to either side of where my opinion and beliefs were and arrive at a creative solution that accommodates all of those concerns. (Interview with Mike, November 13, 2004)

Some community members articulated that their position was changed by the discussion in general, and more specifically by their exposure to new information and individual passion.

> I was very influenced by that discussion, because Patrick is such a strong voice that I had not heard on that wildlife side. (Interview with Nicole, February 10, 2005)

> I would never have thought of it. Never thought of it. And so, it impacted me in that I would be careful about the wildlife in a way that I would never have thought to be previously. (Interview with Pamela, November 16, 2004)

While other people made clear that their perspective was not changed by the discussion.

> I have a huge amount of compassion for animals being out and doing their work…[what their] biology tells them to do. And for me that really wins out in where my heart is. (Interview with Angela, January 28, 2005)

> The thing about killing animals, my cats kill birds, and they kill grouses, and moles, and stuff like that. I'd rather they didn't, but I feel like that's part of nature. This is how the world is now. Cats are the predators. We don't have the big predators anymore. We have medium and small predators. (Interview with Gloria, April 20, 2005)

> I read the studies that [Patrick] cited, because it's pretty interesting. It's interesting to see the volume of destruction that they were causing. But that did not sway my argument…it really didn't. (Interview with Dennis, February 3, 2005)

These two sets of quotes provide interesting contrast. All five of the individuals quoted here were exposed to similar information and passion from Patrick (although no statement can be made that they were listening at the meeting, or that they read their email). Of course, each came to the discussion with different prior experience and perspective on cats and other wildlife. Therefore, the social learning process must accommodate incremental, and likely not consistent, change.

> "Successful change is grounded in personal transformation, encourages experimentation, and eventually evolves the system as a whole." (Bradbury, 2007, p. 292)

Some people anticipated a change in their future behaviour (i.e. an intent to change behaviour).

> I would consider for example not to let them out in breeding time… (Interview with Judith, May 4, 2005)

> So I think it was Jane and Lori who have cats who are indoor only, and they have made this whole indoor structure for them … and it kind of inspired me, along with the discussions that were going on to try to change my cats from being outdoor cats to indoor cats. (Interview with Nicole, February 10, 2005)

I would say I would want some way of making sure that my cats didn't run rampant in the local wildlife. (Interview with Pamela, November 16, 2004)

When the idea was first presented ... that cats should be confined, I thought, "Uh uh. I'm not doing that." ... And so I was pleased when the result was we will make every attempt to keep our cats indoor cats, but if that's impossible, they'll be outdoor cats....[From that position, it raised my consciousness, because the fact that I had one cat who caught blue-tailed skinks, and another one who caught butterflies on the wing that I started thinking, "Oh, maybe I don't want them to be outdoor cats anymore." And when I moved to town, I had to keep them indoors at least for a month so they wouldn't get lost, and then I just kept them indoors... So, I'm actually hoping I can hang in there through this period ..., and let them be indoor cats, so I shifted from "over my dead body" to all right, this is worth making an effort to do. (Interview with Dorothy, August 17, 2005)

Others clearly state that they do not intend to change their behaviour, and will go their own way regardless of a policy.

Our solution ... was that we're going to do what we need to do, and... we're just not going to worry about it, and if ... the policy as written... doesn't meet our needs, then we're going to break the rules ...and so is everyone else, because those kind of policies are going to become normative over time, and there's no way around it. (Interview with Dennis, February 3, 2005)

One community member, who not only stated her intention to change her behaviour to keep her cat indoors, but also began to try to keep her cat indoors in her current home, talked about the dynamic of flexible community policies.

...I think the trick for me is that if I'm keeping my cats indoors ... to not feel ... self-righteous or to feel indignant that somebody else isn't even trying. There's so much potential to get in other people's stuff and have an opinion about what they should do, so much potential to be self-righteous. (Interview with Dorothy, August 17, 2005)

These quotes exemplify the dilemma between having too many rules (but clear expectations of action) and having fewer rules (but then leaving the door open for normative judgment, or the reverse – guilt or perceptions of judgment from others that may or may not be true).

A number of community members talked about their perspective on Patrick's role. People saw his willingness to take time to provide information and write emails, they saw his passion, his single-mindedness, his tenacity. Several of these quotations show that some saw and valued his ability to compromise (which Patrick himself recognized).

I so admire [Patrick] for... you know he's an outsider on this one. You know...definitely not mainstream, and it affects people in a way. I really admire his willingness to go out there and say ...this is where I am on this, and ... here's why, and I think he understood at some point ...'cause way early on the whole parking space thing and the whole bird issue thing I know these were his issues... and it sounded like they were deal breakers at the time. Like he might leave over those, and you know it sounds like he too has relaxed. He's like OK, I can only move the community this far, and that's as far as we've gotten. (Interview with Angela, January 28, 2005)

Subsequent Topics: Orientation, Reinforcement, Revision

Subsequent to approval in October 2004, relative newcomers inadvertently raised this discussion on two separate times with the community, causing the community to entertain issues of how to orient newcomers to prior community decisions, how to document (and make accessible) officially agreed-upon documents so that current and new members could remind themselves of what was agreed, and whether and/or how revision could be made to policies previously adopted by the community.

First, in October 2005 (one year after policy adoption), Brenda, who was a newcomer to the community sent an email whose topic was actually whether or not guineafowl would be a good idea for the community. At the time of the quotation, she appeared not to have been aware of the policy to discourage outdoor cats for the very reason of their predatory nature.

Brenda: Love 'em. But to eat ticks they need to roam. Will they be OK that near [West Branch] Forest? Or near my sneaky cat?' (Email, October 28, 2005)

This email sparked a number of responses with interesting implications. Some (Angela and Dennis) were from those who were members of the community during the topic discussions, and therefore had the opportunity to know the issue's history and outcome. Some (Henry) were from relative newcomers.

Henry: What is the established policy for cats at West Branch? ....I heard a while back that cats would be required to be indoor cats. Is this still the case? (Email, October 31, 2005)

Angela: ...you know, unfortunately when you see a policy so many different times in so many different forms, I can't actually tell you what we agreed on. (Interview with Angela, January 28, 2005)

Dennis: I don't recall reaching a consensus on cats, although we have discussed it for years. Others have raised your concerns. Still others have pointed out that cats from neighbouring developments are not likely to obey West Branch's policies, whatever they may be. (Email, October 31, 2005)

Patrick took this opportunity to email the community that the pet policy was adopted the year before, to insert the policy itself directly into the email, and to provide a link to the location on the community website where the document was archived. Note that Patrick was not only orienting newcomers with these moves, but was also reinforcing prior decisions to long-time members of the community.

The community was silent for a few months on the issue, but then Henry (the newcomer) wrote again. Although he was not specifically asking for a revision to the policy, his discontent with the current policy was clear. Brenda (the other newcomer quoted above) added her voice to his.

Henry: It's a shame that we are going through all this trouble to ban invasive plants, but we are apparently not banning invasive (outdoor) cats. As a bird lover, I was hoping this was going to be a covenant, but apparently not. (Email, March 23, 2006)

Brenda: I'm not exactly looking for trouble, but am concerned about the banning language here. (Email, March 24, 2006)

Would these *de facto* requests for review of the policy have occurred if the approved policy had been less ambiguous (that is, if it had simply stated that cats were or were not allowed outdoors)? Perhaps the voluntary nature of the approved policy created space for interpretation, which in turn allowed people opposed to its outcome to argue for review.

Some interesting responses resulted. Edward, a long-time member of the community described the adopted policy as proposed, which clearly confused some.

Edward: Henry, I read through the proposed pet policy again, and I think it does indeed give you the right to enjoy your birdfeeders without disturbance from cats. (Email, March 24, 2006)

Nicole: Henry, etc, I can assure you that extensive consensual discussion occurred about the very topic of birds & cats at West Branch, and our decisions about the pet covenant were taken very seriously. (Email, March 24, 2006)

Walter: I am sorry to be a late-coming to the pet policy issue, but could someone bring me up to date? Many hours were spent on this issue years ago and I thought it was resolved. …it is confusing to see that a pet policy is now being called a proposed pet policy. … I'm in favor of reviewing things that need it, but am also wanting to be mindful of reinventing the wheel. (Email, March 24, 2006)

Nicole and Patrick (who had both supported the policy) assured the newcomers that the policy was an *approved* policy, and that its adoption had involved significant discussion and compromise. Walter, another long-time member, expressed hope that review of adopted decisions will not be undertaken lightly. In ensuing discussions, and notwithstanding Patrick's email from only a few months prior providing text and document link, Edward claimed he could not find the document. Patrick again provided specific details about where to find the final policy and took the opportunity to specifically reprint and highlight the phrase about outdoor cats. Further, he noted for newcomers that the wording was the result of much discussion and compromise. This exchange exemplified some of the issues that even a small and tightly-knit community faces ensuring a common understanding (and remembrance) of agreed upon policies, both for newcomers, and as reinforcement for those who are not new to the issue or its evolution.

CO-FACILITATED LEARNING

John Falk states "defining learning is a tricky business.... So slippery is learning as a concept that even the social scientists that study learning for a living... have difficulty agreeing on a single definition" (Falk & Dierking, 2000, p. 9). Describing the complex learning process in West Branch is certainly no exception. Scott and Gough provide a pertinent summary of the traditional ways to distinguish learning: "different types of learner (e.g., primary age children; people with special needs; students in higher education), different settings in which the learning takes place (e.g., museums; field study centres; the gym), different purposes of learning (e.g., assertiveness training; health education, professional practice), or some combination of these" (2003, p. 38). In their book, they propose a fourth way to distinguish learning – three *strategies* that underpin the learning process – information, communication, and mediation (2003, p. 39). These strategies find strong support in the case study data presented here from West Branch.

According to Scott and Gough, information provision is a one-way learning strategy. When Nicole learns how to build an extensive cat play structure in her home from Jane and Lori, or when Patrick provides Jacquel with information on the timing and duration of nesting season, or the number of bird casualties, these are essentially examples of information provision.

> On that webpage is a chart of the causes for injury for the 3073 birds that were brought in 2001 and 2002, 511 were the result of cat attacks. 959 are classified as unknown. ... This is the single largest cause of known injury. (Email, November 14, 2002)

West Branch residents often participated in the strategy Scott and Gough termed communication, whereby learners consider and debate the usefulness of information through interactive engagement and negotiation.

> I don't agree that the community should take such a conservative stance regarding the pets many of us will bring to the neighborhood. ... If I were to get another cat, I would make it an indoor pet. However, I am not willing to go through such a change with my two 10-year-old cats. (Email, June 14, 2004)

However, the strategy that most describes what I have seen in West Branch is what Scott and Gough call mediation – multiple person interactions where "everyone involved may bring what they know to the table, and *everyone* involved should expect to learn" (Scott & Gough, 2003, p. 41). For example, in an interview after policy adoption, Patrick expressed amazement at the heterogeneity of views in the community. He had assumed that many community members were environmentalists, but this experience made him realize the heterogeneity that existed within that apparent homogeneous outlook – heterogeneity that has significant repercussions for community life and policy.

You tend to think people know what you know. And they don't, and also you don't know what they know, so you have to understand it both ways. You're speaking with 23 people who identify themselves as environmentally, socially minded.... There are people in the pets discussion who said... 'I don't care about wildlife. To me cats are the same', or 'a native species is not any better than a non-native species.' That someone after reasoning all this thing...you know, if you see yourself environmentalist, then you hear all the...you know...endangered species, native species, invasive species, and there's a hierarchy, and I was just understanding the appreciation that people have for pets. I've been a pet owner pretty much all my life, but there's always been that hierarchy. (Interview with Patrick, May 7, 2002)

The prevalence of this strategy of learning at West Branch led me to coin a new term, *co-facilitated community learning* to encapsulate four characteristics of this learning strategy when seen in a community setting: a setting in everyday life, a perspective that is shared and constructed, a context that emphasizes the learning process over its product, and roles that are non-hierarchal and flexible (Clark, 2007, p. 73). This term originates from the term "community learning," and it contains my sense of the learning as beyond that "...represented by the sum total of individual abilities and interests" (Wright referenced in Brookfield, 1984, p. 100). However, I did not feel it sufficiently captured the lack of hierarchy in role. Therefore, I added the term "co-facilitated" to recognize this flat and flexible relational structure.

In addition to illuminating aspects of community learning, this case study also highlights the murky nature of applied consensus and of mutual "agreement." Underneath each decision or policy approved by consensus at West Branch is in fact much ambiguity – Who was and wasn't present? Who spoke or was silent (and why)? Whose words truly expressed their agreement or disagreement, and to what extent do those agreeing intend to actively abide by the policy?

CONCLUSION

This narrative illustrates the chronology of one approved collective action agreement with environmental implications – albeit on a small scale. Community members shared information, communicated and negotiated, but most importantly, conducted their learning through co-facilitated mediation processes during development of this policy. Some responses indicate that behaviour has already changed (cats previously allowed outdoors are being kept in), but because the on-site residency in the community is short, time will tell whether the policy has broad implementation in the community, or in what circumstances.

The narrative highlights other interesting aspects to the process. First, the apparent homogeneity of environmentalism among community members was shown to belie a heterogeneous reality of how an individual's environmental ethic would implement this specific action. Second, cycles of research and negotiation were punctuated by consensus checks within the community, and a significant amount of time and shared experience was required to obtain consensual approval of this policy. Jensen and Schnack consider whether common experiences mediate individual to collective action, and similarly development of individual action competence (Jensen & Schnack, 1997).

> Perhaps common experience is the key notion in connection with the qualitative transition from individual to collective action and in that way to development of action competence. (p. 177)

I would heartily agree. Third, even for an issue that maintained a high profile within the community for several years, issues of newcomer orientation, documentation and reinforcement for all community members, and revision to approved policies are of high importance. Finally, the use of a consensus decision-making approach is integral to these findings; a different narrative indeed might result in a community using a majoritarian form of governance.

NOTES

[1] Ostrom terms constitutional-choice rules as those that determine "who is eligible and determining the specific rules to be used in crafting the set of collective-choice rules that in turn affect the set of operational rules" (Ostrom, 1990), p. 52).

[2] The name West Branch is a pseudonym.

[3] All names used throughout this paper are pseudonyms.

[4] Direct quotations from the community, whether email, transcribed interview, or other written document, are formatted in italics and in boxes such as this one to highlight the fact that the words are original data. To that end, any misspellings or typos that are original are not corrected in this chapter (nor did I choose to disrupt the text with edits such as "sic" to indicate that the word is misspelled).

REFERENCES

Berkes, F. (1992). Success and failure in marine coastal fisheries of Turkey. In D. W. Bromley (Ed.), *Making the commons work* (pp. 161–182). San Francisco: International Center for Self-Governance.

Bradbury, H. (2007). Social learning for sustainable development: Embracing technical and cultural change as originally inspired by the natural step. In A. E. J. Wals (Ed.), *Social learning towards a sustainable world* (pp. 279–296). Wageningen, The Netherlands: Wageningen Academic Publishers.

Bromley, D. W. (1992). *Making the commons work*. San Francisco: International Center for Self-Governance.

Brookfield, S. (1984). *Adult learners, adult education and the community*. New York: Teachers College, Columbia University.

Brower, M., & Leon, W. (1999). *The consumers guide to effective environmental choices*. New York: Three Rivers Press.

Carlson, A. E. (2000). *Recycling norms*. Retrieved May 21, 2000, from http://papers.ssrn.com/sol3/papers.cfm?abstract_id=233836

Clark, C. (2007). *The synergy of the commons: Learning and collective action in one case study community*. Unpublished Dissertation, Duke University, Durham.

Dietz, T., & Stern, P. C. (Eds.). (2002). *New tools for environmental protection: Education, information, and voluntary measures*. Washington, DC: National Academy Press.

Falk, J. H., & Dierking, L. D. (2000). *Learning from museums: Visitor experiences and the making of meaning*. Walnut Creek, CA: Altamira Press.

Gardner, G. T., & Stern, P. C. (1996). *Environmental problems and human behavior.* Needham Heights, MA: Allyn and Bacon.

Governing the Commons: The Evolution of Institutions for Collective Action, 280 (1990).

Hardin, G. (1968). The tragedy of the commons. *Science, 162*, 1243–1248.

Jensen, B. B., & Schnack, K. (1997). The action competence approach in environmental education. *Environmental Education Research, 3*(2), 163–179.

Loeber, A., van Mierlo, B., Grin, J., & Leeuwis, C. (2007). The practical value of theory: Conceptualising learning in the pursuit of a sustainable development. In A. E. J. Wals (Ed.), *Social learning towards a sustainable world* (pp. 83–97). Wageningen, The Netherlands: Wageningen Academic Publishers.

McCay, B. J., & Acheson, J. M. (1996). *The question of the commons: The culture and ecology of communal resources.* Tucson, AZ: The University of Arizona Press.

McKean, M. A. (2000). Common property: What is it, What is it good for, and what makes it work. In C. C. Gibson, M. A. McKean, & E. Ostrom (Eds.), *Keeping the forest: Communities, institutions, and the governance of forests* (pp. 23). Cambridge: MIT Press.

McKenzie-Mohr, D., & Smith, W. (1999). *Fostering sustainable behavior: An introduction to community-based social marketing.* Gabriola Island, BC: New Society Publishers.

Meltzer, G. (2000). Cohousing: Verifying the importance of community in the application of environmentalism. *Journal of Architectural and Planning Research, 17*(2), 110–132.

Scott, W., & Gough, S. (2003). *Sustainable development and learning: Framing the issues.* London: RoutledgeFarmer.

Charlotte Clark
Nicholas School of the Environment,
Duke University, USA

95

LEARNING AND AGENCY IN WORKPLACE AND INFORMAL CONTEXTS

ELIN KELSEY AND JUSTIN DILLON

6. 'IF THE PUBLIC KNEW BETTER, THEY WOULD ACT BETTER': THE PERVASIVE POWER OF THE MYTH OF THE IGNORANT PUBLIC

INTRODUCTION

Museums, aquariums, science centres, zoos and other informal science institutions (ISIs) are increasingly committed to engaging the public in issues connected to environmental conservation and sustainability. Although ISIs around the world may hold different views about what information should be shared with the public, they appear to share the belief that 'if the public knew better, they would act better'. They operate within a common authoritative discourse about the power of education to transmit information from those who are knowledgeable to those who are not (Kelsey, 2001).

In this chapter, we explore the implications of this particular discourse on environmental learning, participation and agency within informal science institutions. More specifically, we examine a case study of conversational learning between guests (visitors) and volunteer guides in the galleries of a major U.S. aquarium. This is a particularly timely topic, as the interaction between ISIs and their publics has undergone significant change in recent years. Throughout the 1980s and 1990s, environmental public participation programs operated in a type of 'decide-announce-defend' mode based on a 'one way' transfer of information from experts to the public (Davies *et al.,* 2009). Such programs echoed a deficit model of Public Understanding of Science (PUS) rhetoric, with its tacit assumption of public ignorance (Lehr *et al.*, 2007).

Today, a new emphasis on 'co-determined' decisions and 'two-way' exchanges between experts and the public of both information and values has emerged. As Lehr *et al.* (2007) noted, 'the deficit model has—in theory, at least—been firmly rejected in response to a series of crises in the public trust of science and the government in the 1990s (for example, the BSE and genetically modified foods controversies), and a 'new mood for dialogue' between scientists, policy-makers, and various publics has emerged as its replacement' (House of Lords Select Committee on Science and Technology, 2000, p. 44).

A major response from ISIs to this shift toward more authentic public participation has been the creation of 'dialogue events' (Lehr *et al.*, 2007). Lehr *et al.* define these as face-to-face, adult-focused forums that bring scientific and technical experts, social scientists, and policy-makers into discussion with members of the public about contemporary scientific and socio-scientific issues.

R. Stevenson and J. Dillon (eds.), Engaging Environmental Education: Learning, Culture and Agency, 99–110.

A number of ISIs now host *Café Scientifiques* where members of the public are invited to informal gatherings to discuss current issues of science, environment and/or technology (McCallie *et al.*, 2007). The Dana Centre, which opened in 2003 at the London Science Museum, for example, is a purpose-built venue which describes itself as 'a place for adults to take part in exciting, informative and innovative debates about contemporary science, technology and culture' (Dana Centre, 2008).

Rather than focusing on special 'dialogue events', which occur in specialized areas and/or at scheduled times, this paper deals with another highly complementary locus for environmental learning, participation and agency in ISIs, that is, the interactions between volunteer guides and visitors in the public galleries of ISIs, and the potential they hold for learning through conversations.

THE VALUE OF LEARNING THROUGH CONVERSATIONS

A growing body of research in out-of-school contexts recognizes that people learn in museums through conversations (Leinhardt, Crowley, & Knutson 2002). Indeed, much attention has been paid to research on conversations between visitors at recent annual conferences of the Visitor Studies Association, the Association of Science-Technology Centers, the National Association for Research in Science Teaching (NARST) and the American Educational Research Association (AERA) (see for example the AERA 2002 symposium entitled *Learning conversations for all: Explanation, reflective reasoning, thematic content and significant events*). There is also a well-articulated awareness within the research literature of the importance of conversation to enhancing and changing knowledge, attitudes and values (Baker, Jensen, & Kolb, 2002; Jickling, 2004; Laurillard, 1993; Lave & Wenger, 1991).

In terms of environmental learning, Rennie (2003) finds that conversation promotes engagement in environmental awareness or action projects. A number of authors highlight the role of conversation in increasing public participation in politics and in real-world issues (Bobbio, 1987; Bohman & Rehg, 1997; Chambers, 1996; Cohen, 1989; Elster, 1998; Fishkin & Luskin, 2005; Gutmann & Habermas, 1996; Keane, 1991; Public Conversations Project, 2008; Zeldin, 1998).

Much of the literature on the role of language in learning fits within a Vygotskian/sociocultural paradigm (as explicated by Wertsch, 1991) in which it is the social plane that is so critical to development, through interaction, primarily through talking. Indeed, a growing body of literature emerging from research in schools points to the key role of 'exploratory talk' (Barnes, 1976), discussion, dialogic teaching, dialogic inquiry, collaborative reasoning (Chinn and Anderson, 1998) and argumentation, as playing critical roles in developing conceptual understanding and changes in mood and emotion (Rojas-Drummond & Mercer, 2003; von Aufschnaiter *et al.*, 2008). At the heart of the debate is language which, as Halliday (1993) points out, 'has the power to shape our consciousness; and it does so for each human child, by providing the theory that he or she uses to interpret and manipulate their environment' (p. 107).

Mercer and Littleton (2007) characterise exploratory talk (Barnes, 1976) as being:

dialogue which involves partners in a purposeful, critical and constructive engagement with each other's ideas. Statements and suggestions are offered for joint consideration. These may be challenged and counter-challenged, but challenges are justified and alternative hypotheses are offered. Partners all actively participate, and opinions are sought and considered before decisions are jointly made. 'Exploratory talk' has some similarities with the notions of 'accountable talk' (Resnick, 1999) and 'collaborative reasoning' (Chinn and Anderson, 1998). (Mercer, 2008, p. 357)

Now, many of these ideas may not be supported by rigorous empirical research but they act as powerful lenses through which to see how discussion and dialogue impact on learning in its broadest sense. In terms of dialogue, Mercer (2008) notes that:

It is our natural habit to express our ideas in dialogue, to test our views against those of others, and to attempt to persuade other people to share the conceptual understandings that we believe are the best. It is of course also normal that we resist changing our minds, if the views we hold are bound up with aspects of our social identities. But, nevertheless, most of us proceed as if we believe that one of the most important ways of changing someone's mind is to talk with them. (p. 355)

Many environmental issues, as they impact on the interface between science and society, are controversial. To help make sense of these controversies, we would argue that the public would benefit from a deeper understanding of the ways in which scientific understanding develops. One of the ways in which young people may come to understand the nature and development of science is by engaging in the processes of argumentation, that is, building knowledge through purposeful weighing of evidence and analysis of warrants for 'truth'. We know something about how argumentation, a foundation of the ways in which science works can be taught to young people. Much of the work of Osborne and colleagues points to the fact that teachers can be taught to develop higher order argumentation given enough time (see, for example, Simon, Erduran, & Osborne, 2006).

Rather than teaching the 'neutral' skills of argumentation or dialogic talk, ISI programs, such as the Monterey Bay Aquarium's Seafood Watch initiative, endeavor to use these formats to engage visitors and persuade them to change their actions. But human decision-making is hard to affect, as Eiser and van der Pligt (1988) argue:

[evidence suggests] that the conscious thought preceding a decision may be of a relatively simple nature, given the difficulty of processing complex information. People seem to rely on simple heuristics for making probability judgements and hardly seem to think about more complex combinations of probabilities and values or utilities involved in a decision [...] In other words, people's decision processes seem relatively inarticulated and are hardly compatible with the sort of rigorous, systematic thinking required by normative decision models. (p. 181)

So, given these limitations, how can ISIs play an active role in promoting conservation using conversations? The potential to do so is very high: every year, for example, more than 143 million people visit zoos and aquariums (Falk *et al.,* 2007). Furthermore, there is evidence that visitors seek opportunities to converse about issues of societal importance during their visits. Cameron (2003) found that 95% of people surveyed in an Australian sample wanted museums to provide *more* opportunities for visitors to have their say about topics; to converse; to exercise their democratic right to be heard in a publicly funded institution. Fortunately, volunteer educators (guides or docents) already exist as a well-established part of the operation of ISIs in many countries and rather than static exhibits, these volunteers represent a tremendous opportunity to engage the public in personally relevant conversations about current environmental issues.

THE PREVALENCE OF MINI-SCRIPTS

Despite the potential value of conversational learning, dialogue and exploratory talk in theory, a multi-year study of a major USA aquarium reveals that such conversations are rarely observed in practice. Instead, guides typically default to a one-way transfer of information to visitors in the form of 'mini-scripts' (Kelsey, 2004). Kelsey defines mini-scripts as predetermined statements which guides tend to pair with specific animals or props. Although not officially scripted, these statements are repeated so frequently that they take on the appearance of standard scripts, and are sometimes shared across shifts and individuals. At the touch pools, for example, at least one tenth of the aquarium's 500 volunteer guides say 'sea cucumbers and chitons are the vacuum cleaners of the sea' and 'sea urchins feel like a hairbrush' even though no formal script actually exists. Rather than engage in conversations, guides tend to create longer engagement sequences by moving from one prop to another, stringing together mini-scripts for each specimen or piece of apparatus.

Though no other study of mini-scripts has yet been conducted, their presence appears to be well-recognized by professional educators working in ISIs. Each time they are mentioned at presentations at AERA, NARST and the North American Association for Environmental Education (NAAEE), professional colleagues have been quick to acknowledge their existence at their own host institutions. Sanders, for example, describes the tendency for Explainers at the Natural History Museum in London to favor particular entry points, or "opening gambits" in their interactions with students (personal communication).

In 2006, an opportunity to explore the tenacity of mini-scripts presented itself at the same aquarium where they were first identified. The aquarium had just established a new 'Take Action' temporary exhibit on marine protected areas (MPAs) to coincide with a major initiative to grant further conservation protection to MPAs along the California coast. The exhibit provided information on the issues and names and addresses of elected officials. It invited guests to become more engaged and explore issues in more detail by inviting them to sign up for an email listserve operated by the aquarium.

The exhibit was located in close proximity (approximately 5 metres) from a guide station called the 'Ocean Advocacy Station'. The station takes the form of a large cart equipped with props such as cans of seafood, a computer screen and 'Seafood Watch' cards. Guides use the station as a base from which to interact with visitors or "Guests" as they are referred to at the aquarium. Each guide shift was given specific training and enrichment sessions about the issue of MPAs and asked to engage guests in conversations about the issue. It is important to note that these training sessions deliberately used a conversation-based instruction style that invited guides to share their own thoughts about and experiences with MPAs in a facilitated group format. The MPA campaign was timely, local, clearly endorsed by the aquarium and supported by the new exhibit. It was hypothesized that guides would readily engage guests in conversations about MPAs as a result of:
- overt institutional support;
- specific guide training; and,
- specific gallery location (guide cart in close proximity to 'Take Action' exhibit)

However, during 15 half-hour observation sessions by one of the authors (EK), guides did *not* engage guests in conversations about MPAs even when presented with the opportunity. Instead, they stuck to their mini-scripts associated with the Ocean Advocacy Station.

Further analysis of the guides' actions revealed the following findings:

1) *Guides adhered to mini-scripts that were prop-driven.* Rather than discuss MPAs, the guides talked about Seafood Watch using the cards, video clips and cans of seafood on their cart.

2) *Guides were 'glued' to their cart, even in circumstances where there were no guests at the cart and there were guests at the Exhibit.* Only one guide in the 15 observation sessions left the guide cart to engage guests at the 'Take Action' exhibit.

3) *The 'Mini-scripts' used at the carts lacked context and created confusion.* Mini-scripts at the guide cart existed as a series of simplified sentences that were strung together and repeated frequently. The problem here is that many important concepts that served to make the complexity of the ideas understandable were lost in the repetition. For example, some guides were so eager to advocate the consumption of wild caught salmon that when a guest picked up a can of tuna and asked which kind of tuna is dolphin safe, the guide responded with a mini-script about the benefits of wild caught salmon.

4) *The 'Mini-scripts' used were not personalized.* In responding to visitors, the guides tended to draw on a number of favourite phrases and linked them together in response to guest questions or comments, creating the impression that a conversation was happening. However, the sentences themselves remained the same no matter who the guide was speaking with or what the guest asked/answered. For example, one guide asked every guest who stopped at the station if they had seen the movie *A Perfect Storm*. None of the guests answered in the affirmative, yet each time, the guide proceeded to explain how well the movie depicted a certain kind of fishing practice.

5) *The 'Mini-scripts' used were not age appropriate.* In the observation sessions, guides were very friendly to children but did not change their 'mini-scripts' when children were present. Thus, in a number of encounters preschool and early elementary school aged children were asked if they liked to eat tuna and then told about the dangers of high mercury levels or the entrapment of dolphins and their babies during tuna purse seine fishing. The lack of age sensitivity on the part of the guides is worrying, not least because there is mounting evidence from researchers such as Sobel (1996, 2008) of the dangers of presenting children with examples of environmental problems before they are emotionally and developmentally (around age eight years old) equipped to deal with them.

Subsequent discussions with a focus group of eight guides revealed that they had a different perception of their interactions with visitors in that when asked specifically how they transferred the experiences of their MPA training to their conversations with guests, most guides answered decisively that this readily occurred. As one guide expressed: 'Many, probably most (guides), are highly educated here so they are able to integrate that information into the other stuff that they know and to present it at different locations.' Yet, from observations, the transfer did not happen. Guides did *not* share information they learned at the MPA enrichments with guests at the guide cart during any of the observation sessions. Instead, they adhered to the familiar mini-scripts associated with the Seafood Watch program.

SO WHY ARE MINI-SCRIPTS SO PERVASIVE?

The evidence above demonstrates the pervasiveness of mini-scripts in these volunteers' practice. It appears that the guides' own experiences of schooling and, perhaps, the traditional lecture approach become so ingrained that they are hard to shake despite a training format that modelled conversational learning and an explicit request to engage the guests in conversation. It suggests that this transmissionist model on learning, teaching, and communicating is the default, despite interest in the field (both researcher and practitioners) and the aquarium leadership to act and believe otherwise.

We see an answer, partly, in the work of Mortimer and Scott who have researched the difficulties faced by schoolteachers trying to move from what they call authoritative teaching to more dialogic teaching. Mortimer and Scott have identified 'Four Classes of the Communicative Approach' (Scott, Mortimer, & Aguiar, 2006):

a. *Interactive/dialogic*: Teacher and students consider a range of ideas. If the level of interanimation is high, they pose genuine questions as they explore and work on different points of view. If the level of interanimation is low, the different ideas are simply made available.
b. *Noninteractive/dialogic*: Teacher revisits and summarizes different points of view, either simply listing them (low interanimation) or exploring similarities and differences (high interanimation).

c. *Interactive/authoritative*: Teacher focuses on one specific point of view and leads students through a question and answer routine with the aim of establishing and consolidating that point of view.

d. *Noninteractive/authoritative*: Teacher presents a specific point of view.

Table 1 indicates the four classes of communicative approach model schematically.

Table 1. Four classes of communicative approach

INTERACTIVE NON-INTERACTIVE

	interactive/ authoritative (e.g., teacher-led discussion)	non-interactive/ authoritative (e.g., teacher lecture)
AUTHORITATIVE		
DIALOGIC	interactive/ dialogic (e.g., teacher/student collaboration)	non-interactive/ dialogic (teacher summarises students' views)

Source: (Adapted from Mortimer & Scott, 2003, p.35)

What the model points to is a tension between the talk associated with authoritative science knowledge and the kind of knowledge built by students engaged in dialogic activity. While Mortimer and Scott suggest a need to have a balance of approaches, they argue that interactive dialogic is preferable for exploring ideas and facilitating their engagement. Wells (1997) argues that dialogic discourse does not necessarily mean an equal discourse. From this perspective the guides would be seen to have a responsibility to shape the exchange. Yet the prevalence of mini-scripts suggests that the transition from authoritative communication to dialogic communication fails to occur.

Furthermore, McCallie (2008, personal communication) makes a distinction between teaching in contexts in which there is a preordained set of information to be learned – 'learning for mastery' – as opposed to a more open learning agenda in which what is to be learned is not yet known or codified. In other words, what is to be learned is yet to be figured out. The question of whether or not to establish MPAs, for instance, is a socio-scientific issue that fits in the latter category. Guides could engage in discussions about what could be done, for example, 'The Aquarium thinks this, what do you think?'

Yet we believe that these teaching and learning considerations are only part of the answer. The idea of a common discourse that prevents ISIs from realizing their stated aim with respect to public engagement is supported by the notion of 'structure' as described by Sewell (1992) and Giddens (1991). According to Sewell (1992, p. 3) structure is an elusive and difficult to describe a notion that reflects 'something very important about social relations: the tendency of patterns of relations to be reproduced, even when actors engaging in the relations are unaware of the patterns or do not desire their reproduction.'

The degree of guide *agency* meanwhile, that is the capacity of individuals to act independently of the *structures* imposed by social systems, remains a question of debate. In his theory of structuration, for example, Giddens (1991) argues that it is a mistake to pose social systems and individual agency as separate from one another because neither exists except in relation to the other. In this sense, there is what Giddens calls a *duality of structure,* which is to say the structure of a system provides individual actors with what they need in order to produce that very structure as a result. Structures, says Giddens, are both the medium and the outcome of the practices that constitute social systems. Structures shape people's practices, just as people's practices constitute and reproduce structures.

One of the hallmarks of structures, according to Sewell (1992), is that it is often difficult for one engaged in a pattern to be aware of it. Thus, it is possible that ISIs operating within a common structure—in this case, a common discourse about scientific knowledge, the public and education—will be unaware of it even while their actions serve to sustain and reproduce it.

The power of discourses to shape public life, whether or not individuals engaged within these discourses are aware of them, forms the basis of Foucault's (1988) work on the connections between language, knowledge, power and social control. Foucault argues that language and knowledge form a basis for power in their role in the social construction of reality. The modern mode of domination, he claims, is based on a combination of scientific disciplines and professional and administrative practices which penetrate each and every socialised subject of society. How we talk and think about the world shapes how we behave and the kind of world we help to create. Discourses are powerful because they both define and limit the ways in which we conceptualise reality (Gee, 1999).

Blades (1997) provides an example of Foucault's theory in action in a formal education setting through his case study of curriculum change in secondary school science. According to Blades (1997, pp. 2–3):

> attempts to change secondary school science education curricula are defined and thus limited by the positivistic, technical-rational assumptions of the discourse of modernity. So en-framed, curriculum change seems destined to technicality, to a view of change as a problem to be solved once all the factors are elucidated; a search for the correct method and generalisable technique.

SO, WHERE NEXT?

The prevalence of mini-scripts indicates a worrisome disconnect between the stated intention of ISIs to serve as sites for public engagement and the realities of the interactions between guides and guests. The use of mini-scripts has the unintentional effect of treating the visiting public as if they are ignorant and/or as if they don't know what questions to ask or what information they need. This disconnect is further mirrored in volunteer guide training programs and enrichments which are typically structured as information dissemination sessions where guides are *told* by an expert staff member (often in a friendly though authoritative, non-interactive manner) how they should interact and engage in dialogue with visitors. Adding a few conversational learning sessions is not sufficient to help guides learn how to transition between authoritative information giver and dialogic discourse promoter.

A major issue with dialogue is that it is not 'secure' or 'consistent.' It is far more challenging than following mini-scripts. In order to engage in argument (or dialogue in general) one must have a much stronger command of the information in order to think and be flexible with it. It is the difference between 'knowing something' 'and being 'literate' in the sense of being able to apply information and skills in a variety of contexts.

Failure to create and model a conversational learning environment for guides serves to reinforce the status quo and to undermine the guides' participation and agency in engaging guests in conversational learning in the public galleries. Yet changing the structure of guide training sessions is not an easy task. Training sessions are a mainstay of most volunteer guide programs and both staff and volunteers have strong, well-established expectations about how training should be conducted. Volunteers at the aquarium described in this paper, for example, speak in proud terms about having survived 'training boot camp' wherein they mastered scientific names of marine invertebrates and challenging concepts of ocean geomorphology.

For many ISIs, including the one mentioned in this paper, the corps of volunteers is even more stable than its staff. These long-term, experienced guides serve an important 'gate-keeping' role in inspiring and maintaining a high level of professionalism. Though keenly committed to remaining 'cutting edge', a number of these individuals are of the opinion that the existing system of guide training and guest/guide encounters is working well and needs little change. The fact that experienced guides mentor new guides at the stations further perpetuates the traditional discourse of guide as information giver rather than dialogist.

Furthermore, many volunteers are seniors who attended school at a time when the teacher was the unquestioned source of expertise and authority. Beginning attempts to create training sessions that challenge this norm by facilitating learning through conversations have been met with enthusiasm by some volunteers but not-unexpectedly, with confusion and scepticism from others.

Nevertheless, this aquarium and a growing number of ISIs (see for example Osborne and Rodari's work regarding training programs for museum educators across Europe) are interested in improving and developing their training programs, especially with regards to learning literature.

Perhaps the greater barrier to progress is the institutional identity of ISIs. ISIs have a distinguished history as a 'trusted source of information' with respect to science (Astor-Jack et al., 2006). This identity as a purveyor of science authority and expertise further reinforces a transmission-based learning culture in both guide training programs, and the ways in which guides interact with the public in exhibit galleries. Yet as the past decades of conservation initiatives attest, the issues are rarely straightforward. Nor are they exclusively confined to problems answered by science. As Johnson et al. (2001) note, conservation issues are defined as much by socio-cultural values and political and economic factors as by the biophysical dimension. Indeed, the complexity of conservation issues is evidenced by the multiple roles that ISIs are increasingly adopting (information source, habitat protector, political advocate, role model, etc.) with respect to conservation action.

The ideas put forward in this paper recognize the importance of learning models that openly encourage and value multiple ideas and perspectives (Layton *et al.* 1993; Larochelle, Bednarz, & Garrison, 1998). Such models challenge the belief that facts speak for themselves and, instead, emphasize the active role of the learner and the contextual nature of learning. Clarifying messages and transmitting ISIs positions on key conservation issues is one important institutional role. Yet, the goal of engaging the public in conservation demands that ISIs continue to expand their identity as a scientific authority to more fully embrace their identities as a forum and facilitator of a conversational learning culture.

REFERENCES

Astor-Jack, T., Balcerzak, P., & McCallie, E. (2006). Professional development and the historical tradition of informal science institutions: Views of four providers. *Canadian Journal of Science, Mathematics, & Technology Education, 6*(1), 67–81.

Baker, A., Jensen, P., & Kolb, D. (2002). *Conversational learning: An approach to knowledge creation.* Westport, CT: Quorum.

Barnes, D. (1976). *From communication to curriculum.* Harmondsworth: Penguin Books.

Blades, D. W. (1997). *Procedures of power and curriculum change: Foucault and the quest for possibilities in science education.* New York: Peter Lang.

Bobbio, N. (1987). *The future of democracy: A defence of the rules of the game.* Cambridge: Polity.

Bohman, J., & Rehg, W. (Eds.). (1997). *Deliberative democracy: Essays on reason and politics.* Boston: MIT Press.

Cameron, F. (2003). Transcending fear - engaging emotions and opinion – a case for museums in the 21st century. *Open Museum Journal, i,* 1–46. Retrieved December 24, 2008, from http://archive. amol.org.au/omj/volume6/cameron.pdf

Chambers, S. (1996). *Reasonable democracy: Jurgen Habermas and the politics of discourse.* Ithaca, NY: Cornell University Press.

Chinn, C. A., & Anderson, R. C. (1998). The structure of discussions that promote reasoning. *Teachers College Record, 100,* 315–368.

Cohen, J. (1989). Deliberation and democratic legitimacy. In A. Hamlin & P. Pettit (Eds.), *The good polity.* New York: Blackwell.

Dana Centre/Science Museum. (2008). *Dana centre: About us.* Retrieved December 24, 2008, from http://www.danacentre.org.uk/aboutus

Davies, S., McCallie, E., Simonsson, E., Lehr, J., & Duensing, S. (2009). Discussing dialogue: Perspectives on the value of science dialogue events that do not inform policy. *Public Understanding of Science, 18*(3), 338—353.

Eiser, J. R., & van der Pligt, J. (1988). *Attitudes and decisions.* Routledge: London.

Elster, J. (Ed.). (1998). *Deliberative democracy.* Cambridge: Cambridge University Press.

Falk, J. H., Reinhard, E. M., Vernon, C. L., Bronnenkant, K., Deans, N. L., & Heimlich, J. E. (2007). *Why zoos and aquariums matter: Assessing the impact of a visit.* Silver Spring, MD: Association of Zoos and Aquariums.

Fishkin, J. S., & Luskin, R. C. (2005). Experimenting with a democratic ideal: Deliberative polling and public opinion. *Acta Politica, 40*(3), 284–298.

Foucault, M. (1988). *Politics, philosophy, and culture: Interviews and other writings, 1977–1984.* In M. Morris & P. Patton (Eds.). New York: Routledge.

Gee, J. (1999). *An introduction to discourse analysis: Theory and method.* New York: Routledge.

Giddens, A. (1991). *Modernity and self-identity. Self and society in the late modern age.* Cambridge: Polity Press.

Gutmann, A., & Thompson, D. (1996). *Democracy and disagreement.* Cambridge, MA: Belknap Press of Harvard University.

Habermas, J. (1996). *Between facts and norms.* Boston: MIT Press.

Halliday, M. A. K. (1988). On the language of physical science. In M. Ghadessy (Ed.), *Registers of written English: Situational factors and linguistic features.* London: Frances Pinter.

House of Lords Select Committee on Science and Technology. (2000). *Third report: Science and society.* Retrieved December 24, 2008, from http://www.parliament.the-stationery-office.co.uk/pa/ld199900/ldselect/ldsctech/38/3801.htm

Jickling, B. (2004). Making ethics an everyday activity: How can we reduce the barriers? *Canadian Journal of Environmental Education, 9,* 11–30.

Keane, J. (1991). *The media and democracy.* Cambridge: Blackwell.

Kelsey, E. (2001). *Reconfiguring public involvement: Conceptions of 'education' and 'the public' in international environmental agreements.* Unpublished PhD thesis, King's College London, UK.

Kelsey, E. (2004, April 1–3). *From science learning to conversations about conservation: A study of guide training at the Monterey Bay Aquarium.* Paper presented at the annual meeting of the National Association for Research in Science Teaching, Vancouver, British Columbia, 2004.

Larochelle, M., Bednarz, N., & Garrison, J. (Eds.). (1998). *Constructivism and education.* Cambridge: Cambridge University Press.

Laurillard, D. (1993). *Rethinking university teaching: A framework for the effective use of educational technology.* London: Routledge.

Lave, J., & Wenger, E. (1991). *Situated learning. Legitimate peripheral participation.* Cambridge: Cambridge University Press.

Layton, D., Jenkins, E., Macgill, S., & Davey, A. (1993). *Inarticulate science? Perspectives on the public understanding of science and some implications for science education.* Nafferton: Studies in Education Ltd.

Lehr, J. L., McCallie, E., Davies, S., Caron, B. R., Gammon, B., & Duensing, S. (2007). The value of "dialogue events" as sites of learning: An exploration of research and evaluation frameworks. *International Journal of Science Education, 29*(12), 1467–1487.

Leinhardt, G., Crowley, K., & Knutson, K. (2002). *Learning conversations in museums.* Mahwah, NJ: Lawrence Erlbaum Associates.

McCallie, E., Kollmann, E. K., Simonsson, E., Chin, E., & Dillon, J. (2007). *Visitors and engagement: Findings from research and evaluation studies of discussion forums on controversial issues.* Paper presented at the 20th Annual Visitor Studies Association conference. Columbus, OH: Visitor Studies Association. Retrieved from http://www.informalscience.org/research/show/3574

Mercer, N. (2008). Changing our minds: A commentary on 'Conceptual change: A discussion of theoretical, methodological and practical challenges for science education' by D.F. Treagust and R. Duit. *Cultural Studies in Science Education, 3*(2), 351–362.

Mercer, N., & Littleton, K. (2007). *Dialogue and the development of children's thinking: A sociocultural approach.* London: Routledge.

Mortimer, E. F., & Scott, P. H. (2003). *Meaning making in secondary science classrooms.* Maidenhead, UK: Open University Press.

Public Conversations Project. (2008). *Public conversations project.* Retrieved December 24, 2008, from http://www.publicconversations.org/pcp/pcp.html

Rennie, L. (2003). *The Australian Science Teachers Association science awareness raising model: An evaluation report.* Canberra: Department of Education, Science and Training. Australian Government.

Resnick, L. B. (1999). Making America smarter. *Education Week, 18*(40), 38–40.

Rojas-Drummond, S., & Mercer, N. (2003). Scaffolding the development of effective collaboration and learning. *International Journal of Educational Research, 39,* 99–111.

Scott, P. H., Mortimer, E. F., & Aguiar, O. G. (2006). The tension between authoritative and dialogic discourse: A fundamental characteristic of meaning making interactions in high school science lessons. *Science Education, 90*(4), 605–631.

Sewell, W. F. (1992). A theory of structure: Duality, agency, and transformation. *American Journal of Sociology, 98*(1), 1–29.

Simon, S., Erduran, S., & Osborne, J. (2006). Learning to teach argumentation: Research and development in the science classroom. *International Journal of Science Education, 28*(2&3), 235–260.

Sobel, D. (1996). *Beyond ecophobia: Reclaiming the heart in nature education.* Great Barrington, MA: Orion Society.

Sobel, D. (2008). *Childhood and nature: Design principles for educators.* Portland, ME: Stenhouse Publishers.

von Aufschnaiter, C., Erduran, S., Osborne, J., & Simon, S. (2008). Arguing to learn and learning to argue: Case studies of how students' argumentation relates to their scientific knowledge. *Journal of Research in Science Teaching, 45*(1), 101–131.

Wells, G. (2008). Learning to use scientific concepts. *Cultural Studies in Science Education, 3*(2), 329–350.

Wertsch, J. V. (1991). A sociocultural approach to socially shared cognition. In L. B. Resnick, J. M. Levine, & S. D. Teasley (Eds.), *Perspectives on socially shared cognition.* Washington, DC: American Psychological Association.

Zeldin, T. (1998). *Conversation: How talk can change your life.* London: Harvill Press.

Elin Kelsey
Royal Rhodes University, Canada

Justin Dillon
King's College London, UK

JEPPE LÆSSØE AND MONICA CARLSSON

7. LEARNING AND PARTICIPATION IN DEVELOPMENTAL PROJECTS DIRECTED TOWARDS SUSTAINABLE DEVELOPMENT IN CONFERENCE CENTRES

INTRODUCTION

Interest in workplaces as settings for sustainable development has intensified over the last two decades, and a range of government and branch organisation driven initiatives have sought to encourage competence development and change in relation to sustainable development. In this sense, a general societal interest in sustainable development has been linked with another general societal emphasis - lifelong learning and competence development.

A review of literature indicates that although there is a sound basis of knowledge and experience related to workplace learning in general (cf. Billett, 2001; Clematide *et al.*, 2004; Ellström, 1992; Illeris, 2004), there are few studies in the area of workplace learning related to sustainable development, especially not studies based on a participatory learning approach. In the Danish context there are only two studies on experiences with participatory learning related to sustainable development efforts at work places (Høyrup & Bottrup, 2004; Lorentzen & Remmen, 2000). However, Høyrup and Bottrup minimize the outer environment aspects of sustainable development, and the study of Lorentzen and Remmen has a restricted focus on big enterprises with polluting production and participation embedded in formal organisational structures. Therefore compelling reasons exist to gain a better understanding of applied participatory learning approaches related to sustainable development at other types of workplaces.

This chapter is based on a recently concluded case study, involving participatory learning projects on sustainable development at three conference centres in Denmark. The focus here is, in other words, on service companies. Furthermore, these service companies are rather small; each of them with around 50 employees of whom only a little more than one half typically are at work at the same time. In the Danish hotel and restaurant branch they have for some years tried to support efforts to reduce energy consumption and promote environmental improvements. Many of these initiatives have been based on a technical, quality assurance or marketing rationale (such as eco-audit schemes and the hotels' green key quality branding). Essentially these efforts are founded in pragmatic concerns about reducing costs, linked to a decrease in the branch's economic turnover. But in order to take another step, some of the hotel managers have realized that they need to

R. Stevenson and J. Dillon (eds.), Engaging Environmental Education: Learning, Culture and Agency, 111–127.

involve their employees in the efforts to reduce the consumption of energy. This is where this study takes its point of departure. In co-operation with the Danish hotel and restaurant branch organisation, HORESTA, we followed and interacted with managers and employees at five hotels who have tried to apply participatory learning approaches to development projects on the reduction of electricity consumption. Grounded in the empirical material from three of these five hotels – all conference centres – the focal point of this chapter is the shaping of and experiences with employee involvement, more or less directly related to energy and environmental issues at these conference centres. The aim is to discuss examples of learning and participation in relation to sustainable development and, as part of this, to identify potentials, constraints and dilemmas that influence the process of participatory learning.

METHODOLOGICAL APPROACH

The study has been developed through an abductive process, that is by alternating between observations and reflections related to the specific empirical cases and broader conceptual and theoretical sources of inspiration (Coffey & Atkinson, 1996, p. 156). During this process our own theoretical approaches to participation, learning and sustainable development in this setting gradually have been elucidated and elaborated.

The project was conducted from November 2003 to July 2005. Each enterprise has set up their own development projects in cooperation with a team consisting of one researcher, an energy consultant and a Green Key consultant from HORESTA. We have applied an interactive research approach which implies that we have been playing an active part in defining the framework for the involved hotels, and by following and discussing their development projects with them during the one and half year process. Additionally, the generation of data has been based on transcribed individual and focus group based interviews with leaders and employees, during visits at three different times at intervals of every half year, producing in total 36 interviews.

A narrative analysis framework, which situates leaders' and employees' voices within the processes and products involved in making changes related to energy consumption and sustainable development in each work place, has been used to gain an understanding of how participants identified with the participatory learning and change processes involved. An analysis across cases has aimed at identifying synergies, dilemmas and tensions in relation to central elements in sustainable development in the hotel and restaurant area, as well as identifying different perspectives on participation and learning.

KEY CONCEPTS

As noted in the previous section we did not start with a clarified theoretical construct. It was explicated and elaborated during the process. In order to present the results it may, however, be appropriate to start with a brief introduction to our approach to the concepts of participation and sustainable development.

Participation

The idea of involving employees in development projects is indeed not new, and in the social sciences there exist two rather distinct and different discourses on staff participation at workplaces:

The learning approach: This approach has its roots in the social learning tradition (cf. Friedmann, 1987) and in Lave and Wenger's (1991) situated learning approach, where participation is related to learning. In the field of management and working life studies, a number of theoretical schools such as the human resource school (Argyris, 1994), learning organization theory (Senge, 1990), as well as theories of workplace learning (Billett, 2002), form part of this approach. Together these management and working life theories can be identified as part of a 'soft' management approach. In brief, they conceive a participatory process as a matter of facilitating creative co-operation in which the employee is a potential resource. The perspective is consensual as the participatory development process is expected to improve the quality of the employees' working life, their competence development and, thus, the productivity of the company (Clausen & Kamp, 2001, p. 75).

The democratic influence approach: In contrast to the learning approach, this approach is focused on power relations and thus on participation as a matter of democratic influence. As with Arnstein's well known 'ladder of participation', this approach differentiates between different types of participation and critiques the top-down way of organising 'token participation'; that is without any real influence (Arnstein, 1969). But even the genuine involvement of employees has been criticized because the direct involvement of the individual employee risks undermining the collective and formal democratic structures with unions who are negotiating rights and responsibilities with managers (Lambrecht Lund, 2002).

Basically, our project is located within the learning approach to participation. Participation implies, as we conceive it, a potential for learning through practices (experiences generated from observations of consequences) and through social interaction and reflections on these immediate experiences (cf. e.g., Dewey, 1938; Lave & Wenger, 1991; Negt *et al.*, 1974). In order to promote these processes in workplaces we have stressed the potential of involving employees in development projects; that is, in identification of tasks and organisation of spaces for learning and action that facilitate creative reflections and problem solving related to their own work practices. As the potential learning outcome we have used the concept 'action competence' (Jensen & Schnack, 1997; Carlsson & Jensen, 2006) by which we, in this case, refer to the competence of the employees to reflect on and work towards sustainable development. Some of the important aspects of the development of action competences are the facilitation of the use of one's own experiences, the exchange of experiences, the development of and reflection on new experiences, the facilitation of creativity (sociological imagination), the use and elaboration of existing knowledge, skills, habits, commitment, and the ability to operationalize reflection-in-action (cf. Schön, 1983; Læssøe, 2006).

On the other hand, the participatory learning approach does not imply a rejection of the relevance of the power relation discourse. Clausen and Kamp (2001) have argued that it is possible to integrate the two discourses on participation: on the one

hand, competence development and engagement, and on the other hand, political participation. In concordance with this view, we argue that the two approaches do not imply an either-or choice. Even with an interest in participatory learning processes power relations are important as:
- conditions that influence the time and space for learning;
- dynamics that influence the degree of involvement and the social dialogue;
- something that may create resistance and thus influence the process and learning outcome; and
- not least, something that works as implicit in all kind of social relations and thus risks counteracting the explicit intentions (Kothari, 2001).

Sustainable Development

Like participation, sustainable development is an ambiguous concept (Dryzek, 1997: 123ff). In the original definition it was related to global development and global relations (WCED, 1987). Sustainable development has, however, as Dryzek shows, been elaborated into a discourse which also makes it possible to apply it to local settings. The key intentions are to apply a holistic view on development that integrates environmental, economic and social considerations, takes responsibility for avoiding deteriorations in long term perspectives, and transgresses a narrow local perspective by emphasising the interdependence and common interest in equally shared resources. These characteristics – the wishful thinking about holism, peaceful development, long term orientation, and about avoiding risks that by definition are uncertain - makes the concept extremely comprehensive and diffuse. As a subject for learning this might be regarded as a problem. However, we find it reasonable to approach it like Scott and Gough who stress the incomplete and process-oriented character of the concept (Scott & Gough, 2003). The subject of learning (sustainable development) and the learning process are not divided. Sustainable development is not a measure, but is constructed through a process that implies learning. Our ambition has been to describe this process as it happened at the conference centres and to discuss the limits and qualities of this learning-about-sustainable-development process.

After this introduction to our topic and approach, we present four thematic analyses. The first focuses on the different approaches to participation that were revealed during the development projects. The second exposes the power aspect that influenced some of the participatory processes as well and, thus, became a condition for the promotion of participatory learning. The third analytical part is about key elements and concerns in sustainable development in similar service workplaces to the research sites. While the first theme distinguishes between incorporative, delegate oriented and dialogue oriented approaches, we make another theoretical distinction in the fourth and final analysis by focusing on the relationship between a technical oriented and pedagogical oriented approach. Then we summarize and discuss our findings. We conclude by discussing our approach in the presented empirical project as an example of educational research in the public interest.

THREE APPROACHES TO PARTICIPATION

Incorporative Oriented Approach

Centre A is a technologically advanced conference centre with around 35 employees and 30 casual labourers. The management style is modern with an emphasis on social activities, team spirit and quality assurance systems. They have for some years tried to save resources by means of green technology innovations such as timer regulated electrical light. Through these and other initiatives they have turned a period of recession into a time of prosperity. Their motives for participation in the project on electricity consumption and the development of competences was primarily economic.

The way centre A chose to approach the involvement of their employees in energy-saving improvements could be characterized as a top-down incorporation. By this we mean that the process was organised by the technical manager who regarded participation as the involvement of employees in generating ideas for energy-saving improvement. Afterwards, when the managers had decided what to do, employees were involved in the implementation by means of incentives such as control systems and rewards. Hence, the employees were only trained in the creation of ideas based on their experiences and in an instrumental rule-following behaviour, while they did not take part in the investigation of the ideas, in pro and con dialogues, in decision making or in evaluation.

Delegate Oriented Approach

Centre B is a very modern and 'development oriented' conference centre. The size is almost the same as centre A and like centre A they have already been working with technical energy-saving innovations for some years. Especially by renewing the technical installations in the kitchen, they have been able to reduce their electricity consumption pretty much. As part of these efforts they have some experiences with involvement of employees. The manager has been the key person in the innovative projects, but as the centre recently became a member of a chain of hotels, they are now expected to implement the total philosophy of this chain during the coming years. It might give the impression of centralisation and it partly is. However, one of the key principles of this concept is delegation of responsibility. As the manager says, this, in ideal terms, means that:

> Everybody should be able to think about all necessary factors....If somebody is creating an idea, they should elaborate into a project themselves. That is, look at the consequences: Pros and cons.

In order to support this delegation of responsibility one of the employees is trained as a coach who should inspire and facilitate the competence development of the other employees.

This idea of approaching participation and competence development as a matter of delegation of responsibility also characterised the centre B manager's ambitions for a development project on electricity savings. This strategy creates the opportunity for more comprehensive participatory learning processes than the incorporative approach. However, this case also shows important mediating steps between the ideal concept and the real practice. First, the manager admits that as his personal character is being engaged and dynamic, he opposed the delegation of responsibility. One of the section leaders added that her staff members hesitated to take responsibility because they are used to passing it over to the dynamic manager. Another problem is that the structural conditions for employees at hotels makes it difficult for them to find time and space to meet and conduct projects, and sometimes the required improvements are simply too technically complicated to pass it over to them. These obstacles mean that a transformation of the principles is taking place during practice which, consequently, means that there is no direct relationship between the principles and the competence development among the employees. However, the case includes some good examples where employees were allowed to research their own ideas for improvements and take part in the decision-making. For example, a technical labourer had an idea to change some light fittings. He presented the idea, got it accepted and conducted it himself. The staff in the cleaning section were in the same way involved in the replacement of an old washing machine and the choice of a new machine. In this case, the process also implied a dialogue with the manager about the quality standards of the new product.

Dialogue Oriented Approach

Centre C is a conference and holiday centre with 14 employees who, in the summer season, are supplemented by almost the same number of casual labourers. Unlike the previous two centres, where modern management methods are prevalent, formal hierarchies are not as prevalent in this centre. Rather the green attitude here is part of a basic value orientation which implies an egalitarian and community-like social orientation.

In this setting, the participatory learning approach is primarily a matter of dialogue. They have organised four groups of employees to investigate possibilities for improvements and, among them, one group focuses on energy savings. The experiences have been rather disappointing partly because of external obstacles for their projects and organisational problems owing to different working hours and different periods with business. Another explanation, formulated by the manager, is that the members are practical people who lack competence in chairing meetings. In this sense participatory learning methods do not necessarily produce new competencies, they are dependent on a certain level of competencies in order to be successful. A trial to involve the young casual staff members in order to raise their commitment and responsibility had a more positive outcome. Dialogue meetings where the manager listened to their problems and ideas for improvements and explained her expectations to them showed that especially the teenager group were good in coming up with ideas and taking responsibility afterwards. These kinds of meetings were supplemented with very brief daily section meetings where the younger casual staff members and the permanent staff members were evaluating their work during the previous day. This can be characterized as a way of organizing mimetic workplace learning. But, at the same time, it is a powerful social control system as well.

Based on the discussion of the three approaches we want to outline some analytic points regarding participatory learning approaches to sustainable development issues in this type of setting:

– Participation is interpreted in different ways. In a learning perspective it makes an important difference whether it is approached in an incorporative, delegate oriented and/or dialogue oriented way.

– Even though the choice of approach is important, it does not guarantee the result. The ideas will always be mediated. As illustrated in our presentation of the process in conference centre B, the approach is interpreted by the manager and the section leaders, and they will add their personal touch and combine it with other experiences and sources of inspiration.

– There will be differences between these actors' ideas and what actual happens in practice. General changes in workplace culture and organization, the specific situation at the conference centre (e.g., lack of resources such as time), and its social dynamics influence the process. This process of mediation from idea to practice is something that has been emphasised by post-structuralists who have warned against the 'romantic participation orthodoxy' (Cooke & Kothari, 2001). There are good reasons to listen to their critique, even though there is no reason to abandon the whole idea of participation. Another and more constructive route will be to develop theories that identify general dilemmas and dynamics in participatory processes on sustainable development issues in order to qualify the management of these processes (cf. Hvid, 2003).

POWER AND PARTICIPATORY LEARNING

In the introduction we stressed the importance of combining a social learning perspective on participation with a perspective on participation, as a matter of power and influence. Even though participation aims at democracy it does not exclude power. We mentioned Kothari who argues that power will always be part of participatory processes. This does not only imply bias in manifest power like the power relation between an employer and employees. It is also something which is embedded in the applied discourses and constructed into the social relations during participative projects (Kothari, 2001). We will now look at participatory processes at the three conference centres from this perspective.

At conference centres A and B (both marked by a modern management approach), the employees were, in general, pleased with the invitation to participate and take responsibility for the resource consumption and economy of the centre. But there was resistance too. At both places some of the older waiters were not willing to take part because they felt that the process was going to undermine their collective negotiated formal agreement about their duties and rights. This is in accordance with Lambrecht Lund who, based on other studies of participatory methods at workplaces, warns against this risk (Lambrecht Lund, 2002). At conference centre B the resistance among the employees became even more visible when the restructuring of the organisation caused a reduction in staff members. In this situation it became impossible for the manager to involve anybody in energy-saving projects for a longer period of time. As these examples indicate, participation approached only as a matter of consensual co-operation and learning might cause problems. From a learning perspective it may be argued that the replacement of consensus with conflict may create an even better situation for learning. However, if it undermines the trust in participation among the employees it blocks further learning. Both conference centres emphasize good social relations, but the way they are trying to facilitate such good social relations, among other things by means of participatory projects, are contradictory. On the surface they construct what seems to be something similar to a traditional community but, as a part of a hyper-modern strategy, it implies a commitment to flexibility and willingness to accept changes. When this demand becomes a reality for the employees it risks undermining their basic feeling of stability and acceptance (Bovbjerg, 2004; Åkerstrøm Andersen & Thygesen, 2004). Hence, this cocktail of green idealism and new management risks provoking serious resistance.

We also observed power as an integral component of the social relations between the employees. At centre B, one of the employees has a special responsibility for security issues. She told us that it was crucial for her to be aware of cliques among her colleagues and about the informal leaders: "There is always somebody who acts as spokesman".

> If you can get in touch with this person and explain it to him and hear what he thinks of it, then there are no problems.

This is obviously ordinary group psychology. However, it is important to be aware that these informal power relations work and influence the participatory learning projects. At centre C, we met another aspect of the power relations between the employees. As mentioned, the young casual labourers took part in brief daily meetings where the work during the previous day was evaluated. In one sense this was an opportunity for these youngsters to influence their workplace. In another sense it was a manifest control system, where they were socialised by the senior employees.

Power cannot be excluded and power relations imply potential for learning. At service enterprises of the size of these conference centres, participation can easily be approached as a matter of consensus and a community-like spirit. As we have emphasized in this section, this may appeal to the employees, but there is a risk that it will cause a neglect of tensions that may block further learning and involvement in sustainable development processes. A conscious integration of conflicting issues in the participatory approach might be a better way to cope with the power issue.

KEY ELEMENTS AND CONCERNS IN SUSTAINABLE DEVELOPMENT

As noted in the introduction, the concept of sustainable development has been interpreted in many different ways. How is it constructed in our cases? What is included and what is excluded? Environmental, economic, social and service aspects seem to be essential elements and concerns in relation to energy consumption and sustainable development at the conference centres:

Environmental aspects: responsibility for reducing the energy and environmental related consumption out of consideration for global sustainable development;

Economic aspects: related to business existence and development;

Social aspects: the social responsibility of the workplace, including employee well-being and possibilities for development;

Service aspects: guest satisfaction and safety issues.

The case study develops new perspectives on conflicts and potential synergic relations between these aspects, and of dilemmas related to coping with these dynamics. The environmental aspects are indicated as subordinated to the service aspects, and the latter are indicated as closely related to economic aspects of survival as a business. Dissatisfied customers lead to poor profits, and asking the customers to save energy is therefore unthinkable, as described by the AV-mid level manager at conference centre A:

> We would like them to use the dimmer while teaching, if they can, because it saves the bulb and energy. But we cannot dictate to the customers what to do. We would not get satisfied customers, and it would be a mortal sin if we did, because then we cannot live up to the objective we have formulated.

It is not only the managers who underline the conflicting relation between environmental aspects at the centres and aspects of economic survival and development. At conference centre B, an employee discussed the visibility effect of using lights, including in areas of the centre that are not used directly, such as the corridors related to the teaching facilities. The advantage of having the lights off is that it saves energy, which is good, but the disadvantage is signalling a closed centre that can mean a potential restaurant customer won't step inside, which is obviously bad for business.

At conference centre C the manager could not think of an example where the kitchen would produce food of lower quality or the guests would have to wait longer because of an interest in saving energy. The service must be maintained. One of the employees at the centre is actually presenting an example where food product quality and the energy saving interest might collide:

> I was quite alarmed by the 42% in the kitchen [the kitchen's share of the total electricity consumption at the centre]. Of course it costs to make food, and some of our machines are very old. But then again – we have this old potato-peeler, but we cannot throw it out since it is the best peeler in the world – one cannot see that it is a machine that has peeled those potatoes.

A key aspect of service is safety, stressed by the conference centres as an imperative factor. Automatic switch-off mechanisms regulated by light sensors are common and essential in regulating electricity consumption in the big spaces at the conference centres. But in the entrance area at conference centre C, the light cannot be turned off by a sensor:

> ...If it is dark, when a guest is going down the stairs, there is a risk.

We find that it is the 'ecological modernistic' (Hajer, 1995) way of approaching sustainable development, with its emphasis on economic conditions and modern management methods, that characterizes the case studies. Development is seen as a basic condition for these workplaces and as a demand directed both to the organisation as a whole and the employees as subjects. The motto is 'if not development then dismantling'. A mid-level manager at conference centre C formulates the motto as follows:

> We tell them from the day they are employed: You cannot hide in this workplace, we want you to develop and we want you to take part in developing the workplace. Because that's the way we survive as a business.

APPROACHES TO SUSTAINABLE DEVELOPMENT

Like many other places, the key agents who are responsible for environmental improvements at the conference centres are people from the technical department and from the management, drawing on technical and management approaches to change. This 'environmental centred' and rational approach has implications for the way competence development of the staff is organised. In our project this approach has been contested by our emphasis on sustainable development as a comprehensive approach, including a participatory pedagogical approach which implies much more than just informing and motivating the staff. In this section we describe examples and discuss opportunities and barriers related to each approach, as well as the overlaps between the approaches.

Technical and Management Approaches to Sustainable Development

The conference centres already had many experiences with technical and management approaches to sustainable development when the project started up, and the project led to more experiences. The technical potential for energy-savings were more often than not a focus of attention and the following questions organised the approach: Where can we save (energy)? How? Who does what?

The main approaches were:

Technical mapping of energy consumption:
The centres identified saving potentials through the technical mapping done by an external energy consultant, and thereafter developed technical or behaviour oriented solutions.

Checklists:
The results from the mapping were used in checklists, either by the manager, or in collaboration with the employees. The lists are used in inductions of new employees to the introduction of new technologies, or new organisations of work.

New equipment:
The results from the mapping are also used in decisions on investments in, for example, new freezers or kitchen machines or new technologies for the control of light and heating. This approach is related to and supported by quality control systems, since they reward investments in new technology and facilities.

Quality steering:
Performance monitoring, customer audits of perceived quality of service, and technical facilities, etc., are a part of quality assurance and control systems such as the 'five-star-system' used in the conference centres in Denmark. The technical mapping in the centres revealed new possibilities for energy savings - even in centres that had worked previously with energy savings. But in some centres the information from the mapping never reached the employees. A mid-level manager at centre A emphasized the need for a combination of new technology and use of checklists:

> ... they have really used the checklists. At the same time we have used thousands of *kroner* on new light switches. [...] so the consumption is reduced, it is not only people, technology is also needed.

The checklist is seen as a tool that helps the employees to practice a new routine until it is a habit. Habits save time, but also constrain us to certain ways of thinking and acting, which can be less of an advantage if development is needed. One of the employees at the same centre regards the quality steering system as a positive factor:

> It is good because you don't stagnate but have to perform better. It means something that there is a positive development, because when you get recognition you run faster. The stars are a carrot and a motivational factor – you have to hold on to it.

Socio-Cultural and Pedagogical Approaches to Sustainable Development

This approach to sustainable development is seen in the study as implemented in the centres through interaction with the pedagogical development work initiated by the project. The approach is characterized by taking its starting point in the employees and in the organisation of work, and in the following questions: Why is the work organized as it is? Which are the reasons for a high energy-consumption? How can the barriers for reduction be overcome?

The main approaches were:

External Pedagogical Consultancy:
We organized an idea and experience generating workshop for all the participating conference centres and hotels, visited the centres and participated in staff meetings, talked with managers and employees about involvement of the employees and about hotel culture, aims and strategies, provided suggestions for methods and activities, and developed resource materials, such as an inspiration folder for project start-up methods.

Internal technical expert:
In general the centres had an internal technical expert, an employee responsible for the energy area in the centre and who therefore had experience in involving the other employees in energy-saving.

Internal educational facilitator:
One of the centres had appointed an employee to organize and promote competence development and involvement at the workplace in relation to the principles of their business concept, where broader environmental issues were one of the key aspects.

Self-initiated and implemented idea and dialogue meetings:
In one of the centres, the manager initiated an idea and dialogue meeting with the younger and causual workers in the kitchen and restaurant with the aim to find solutions to issues regarding responsible environmental behaviour in this group.

Work-teams:
In two of the centres the employees worked in teams where the aim was to initiate a dialogue with the managers and other employees about the energy consumption. The energy team was responsible for using the external energy consultants' report and involving the other employees at the centre in issues on how to save energy.

The centres emphasised that an external pedagogical consultant can inspire and motivate the centres to work with energy savings. A learning/pedagogical approach was often understood as motivating the employees to save energy, and as one of the managers (from centre A) expressed – the motivation bit is not enough:

> The idea is good. But I think it demands a lot from the manager, to motivate the employees. And I don't think it is enough in itself, but other initiatives that have economic premises, have to be taken, like, e.g., installing light sensors.

The internal technical experts have developed high level competences in energy saving and environmental revision processes, through internal workplace-based collaboration and use of external technical experts in problem-solving related to energy consumption. One of the challenges stressed by the technical experts was the tendency of the other employees to put the responsibility on the technical expert and to react negatively towards instructions on how to save energy.

The role of the internal educational facilitator is described by the manager at centre B:

> He will be an 'inspirator', motivator, 'whipper', in all areas of work. He is qualified to be an expert, in the areas you find necessary.

The educational facilitator stressed the importance of the informal department leaders in change processes; that in some case they had to be 'won over' in order to make a change. The difference between the technical experts and the educational facilitator is that the latter is employed to promote competence development and involvement in all areas of work, while the technical experts' field of competence is more narrowly related to the energy and environmental areas of the workplace.

The Meeting between Technical and Pedagogical Approaches

A combination of the technical and pedagogical approaches in change processes directed at sustainable development can be an advantage, but the two approaches can also be conflicting. The technical mapping of energy consumption can promote learning in change processes, if the information from the mapping is distributed. But they can also lead to negative consequences, if the information is used without consideration for the centres' culture, and isolated from the other aims in the centres, such as service and social aims.

On the one hand, a starting point in the employees' conditions and learning can improve the effect of the technical approach, such as the use of checklists, by utilizing the employees' thoughts on the organisation of work and their suggestions for changes. On the other hand, technical approaches, such as checklists and quality steering tools may, if they are experienced as predefined, abstract, time-consuming and with a strong element of control, undermine the motivation and involvement of employees and create a resistance to change. An example in the case study is one of the waiters filling in the checkpoints and signing the checklist without checking the points.

Just as an 'environmental centred' approach can be inappropriate by neglecting all but environmental aims, a pedagogical approach can be inappropriate by emphasizing the pedagogical development project and learning as an aim in itself. We tried to avoid the worst culturally biased pitfalls in our pedagogical consultancy by researching and taking into consideration the hotels' culture, aims and strategies. But there was a significant distance between the direction we suggested that they should go in the project – competence development - and change through the involvement of the employees. And the conference centres usually found ways to make energy savings, which were based on the technical and management approaches described above. The centres' general conditions (e.g., time constraints, their aims and ongoing general development) are making a change approach based on learning and employee involvement vulnerable. Furthermore, it was a challenge for the centres to work with another focus on learning in change processes than motivation and behaviour modification. The pedagogical development project was understood as a way to motivate the employees to save energy, which was seen as a useful and 'economic' approach.

The quality assurance strategies and related technical artefacts, such as registration forms and checklists, seemed to set the stage for the pedagogical development strategies, emphasising dialogue and room for reflexivity. The case study is giving an opportunity to explore the relation (or the boundaries) between, on the one hand, technical and management elements in approaches to sustainable development and, on the other hand, pedagogical elements. A social learning perspective has much to offer in understanding this relation, by directing our attention to the influence of everyday work practices, regulatory frameworks, such as the use of managerial and technical strategies and artefacts, and collegial relationships. Wenger's concept of communities of practice is an often used perspective in workplace learning projects and describes groups that interact to achieve a shared purpose (Wenger 2001). Billett (2002) questions the benign nature of communities of practice, pointing out that the nature of one's role in the practice will limit the participatory learning opportunities available. He argues that workplace hierarchies, group affiliations and personal relations are some of the factors influencing opportunities to act and interact in workplaces. Opportunities for learning at the conference centres are influenced by the stressful nature of work in small-scale service branch workplaces. Employees emphasise that the lack of time limits their opportunities for learning, while managers and mid-level managers seem to have both access to learning opportunities and a role in 'distributing' learning to the employees.

Even though technical and management approaches represent the same kind of rationality, we find it important to establish a more differentiated view on their relations to the participatory pedagogical approaches. Technical mapping of energy consumption, for example, may serve as a useful tool in combination with participatory methods, since it provides information that can be utilized in relation to both technical changes and the organisation of work (although it normally is a management tool, and not an employee one). In contrast, environmental management systems and other types of quality assurance tools with systematic use of registration schemes, risk undermining the motivation of the employees and result in resistance because it is experienced as predefined, abstract, time-consuming and with a strong element of control.

CONCLUDING DISCUSSION

The three conference centres shared an interest in applying a participatory approach to electricity savings and, more generally, to the development of a sustainable workplace. As we showed in our first thematic analysis, this gave rise to different development projects with different interpretations of the participatory approach. We made a distinction between 'incorporation', 'delegation' and 'dialogue orientation' as different principles for participatory involvement. They have consequences for when and how the employees are involved during a project and, thus, for the development of their action competences. In practice, at the conference centres, these principles were combined, but with different weightings due to different cultures and key agents. This was, however, not the only way to conceptualise potential differences of involvement of employees in sustainable workplace innovations. In our third thematic analysis we made a distinction between technical management oriented and socio-cultural pedagogical oriented approaches. They risk being contradictory but we also showed that combinations are possible.

The choice between the different principles and approaches, as well as the possibilities and constraints for sustainable development, is intimately connected with the 'workplace culture' of the conference centre, including values and social organisation in terms of distribution of roles of managers and employees. At two of the conference centres, the workplace culture was marked by a modern management orientation. On the one hand, this support attempts to involve employees in order to improve their action competences and facilitate resource-saving innovations. On the other hand, as we have showed in the second and fourth thematic analysis, this orientation does include some serious constraints as well. First, it creates a tension between participation as a matter of individual learning and as a matter of collective influence. At both 'modern management' conference centres, this tension gave rise to resistance among the employees. Second, at the modern conference centres, sustainable development is approached from the local perspective; it is about their own sustainable development. In a way this is to turn the concept of sustainable development upside down; to give priority to your own existence and neglect the concern for 'the other at another place at another time (Læssøe, 2006). The situation at our third, and less modern, conference centre was a bit different. They do, indeed, give priority to their own survival as well. However, their workplace culture and values are essentially more egalitarian and green.

EPILOGUE: EDUCATIONAL RESEARCH IN THE PUBLIC INTEREST?

The quest for taking the living conditions of the coming generations and the consequences of our actions for other people and species into account, even in other parts of the world, makes it obvious to state that sustainable development must be 'in the public interest' in the most comprehensive sense. And research committed to support these ambitions, not least research on education for sustainable development (ESD), must be the same. For this reason it seems reasonable to conclude this chapter by reflecting on the implication of conducting educational research in the public interest. We do so by, first, briefly introducing the way we conceive our role as researchers and our scientific approach and, afterwards, by reflecting on our experiences from the project presented in this chapter.

The kind of research, we have conducted, belongs to what Nowotny *et al.* have characterised as 'mode 2 research' (Nowotny *et al.,* 2001). Among other things it implies that it is problem-based, change-oriented, interactive, dynamic and concerned with the production of contextual embedded knowledge.

As we all know, ideal thoughts seldom come through in practice. When we are talking about mode 2 interactive research this is perhaps especially true because you, as a researcher, are not able to design the research process in a systematic way or, at least, a way that you will find optimal. You have to negotiate already before the project is started, and further on, during the project, the other partners can change their minds and practices. When you are doing this kind of project you are always trying to find a path that still makes sense from a research point of view. However, there is always a risk that it fails. In the research and development project with HORESTA (The Hotel and Restaurant Branch Organisation) and the three conference hotels, we already had to adapt seriously in order to get a grant. The foundation from which we received the grant has a narrow scope of interest on electricity savings, which made it necessary for us to focus the whole project on this issue, even though we found it rather arbitrary to develop a participatory approach with this narrow scope.

Another issue was the rather technocratic-instrumental approach that characterized the demands from the foundation. We had to develop a model that would aim at supporting hotels and restaurants in involving and developing their employees' energy-saving competences. We found, however, that we still had the opportunity to influence the participatory approach and open it up to other aspects and competences during the process. In retrospect we partly succeeded in that endeavour. In small workplaces it does not make sense to divide everything into small separated bits. On the other hand, we were not prepared for the very narrow limits regarding the time and economy that characterize private companies as a space for learning, and we were not prepared either for the unforeseeable character of hotel work that made it very difficult to apply the idea about development projects. Things we had planned to do, not least a number of interviews with employees, were obstructed by this limitation. For this reason we find that we only got part of the story. This is not to say that our material is poor. We got a lot of interesting interviews and generated a number of points, actually much more than we are presenting in this chapter. It is difficult to say how much we influenced the three conference hotels but their response was what we pushed them to reflect and act upon.

Furthermore we succeeded in developing a model that, from our point of view, contains an important new development for the hotels. According to the response we have received from the hotel branch and from energy advisors, it has opened up the concept of participation to a number of different approaches and different phases. Our differentiation of hotel cultures that affect the choice of participatory strategy and methods is another aspect that we presume will open their minds for a less instrumental approach. At the same time we have been adaptive and fulfilled the demands for operational knowledge, we have also collected material that we now are allowed to analyse from a more detached and critical position. These analyses can, as in this chapter, be directed towards the academic world and, hopefully, give rise to critical comments that will allow us to elaborate on them. But, later, it is our plan as well to contribute on this basis to the public debate on participation, learning and sustainable development.

REFERENCES

Åkerstrøm Andersen, N., & Thygesen, N. T. (2004). Styringsteknologier i den selvudsatte organisation. (Steering technologies in the selfexposed organisation) *Grus*, *25*(73), 8.

Argyris, C. (1994). *On organizational learning*. Cambridge, MA: Blackwell.

Arnstein, S. R. (1969). A ladder of citizen participation. *Journal of the American Planning Association*, *35*(4), 216–224.

Billett, S. (2001). Learning through work: Workplace affordance and individual engagement. *Journal of Workplace Learning*, *13*(5), 209–214.

Billett, S. (2002). Toward a workplace pedagogy: Guidance, participation and engagement. *Adult Education Quarterly*, *53*(1), 27–43.

Bovbjerg, K. M. (2004). Selvets disciplinering - en ny pagt i arbejdslivet. (The disciplination of the self - a new pact in working life.) *FOFU-nyt*, *6*(3), 37.

Carlsson, M., & Jensen, B. B. (2006). Encouraging environmental citizenship: The roles and challenges for schools. In A. Dobson & D. Bell (Eds.), *Environmental citizenship*. Cambridge, MA: The MIT Press

Clausen, C., & Kamp, A. (2001). Forandringer i arbejdslivet. Mellem læring og politik. (Changes in working life. Between learning and politics.) *Tidsskrift for arbejdsliv*, *3*(2), 73.

Clematide, B., Andersen, V., & Høyrup, S. (2004). *Arbejdspladsen som læringsmiljø*. (The workplace as a learning environment.) Frederiksberg: Roskilde Universitetsforlag.

Coffey, A., & Atkinson, P. (1996). *Making sense of qualitative data. Complementary research strategies.* Thousand Oaks, CA: SAGE Publications.

Cooke, B., & Kothari, U. (Eds.). (2001). *Participation - the new tyranny?* London & New York: Zed Books.

Dewey, J. (1938). *Experience and education.* New York: Simon and Schuster

Dryzek, J. S. (1997). *The politics of the earth: Environmental discourses.* Oxford: Oxford University Press.

Ellström, P.-E. (1992). *Kompetens, utbildning och lärande i arbetslivet. Problem, begrepp och teoretiska perspektiv.* (Competence, education and learning in working life. Problems, concepts and theoretical perspectives) Stockholm: Fritzes.

Friedmann, J. (1987). *Planning in the public domain. From knowledge to action.* Princeton, NJ: Princeton University Press.

Hvid, H. (2003). Dilemmaer knyttet til medarbejderdeltagelse i "partnerskaber". (Dilemmas related to employee participation in "partnerships") *Tidsskrift for arbejdsliv, 5*(2), 7.

Høyrup, S., & Bottrup, P. (2004). *Bæredygtighed på arbejdspladsen - refleksion og læring i arbejdet:* (Sustainabaility in the workplace - reflection and learning at work) LO.

Illeris, K. (2004). *Learning in working life.* Roskilde: Roskilde University Press.

Jensen, B. B., & Schnack, K. (1997). The action competence approach in environmental education. *Environmental Education Research, 3*(2), 163–178.

Kothari, U. (2001). Power, knowledge and social control in participatory development. In B. Cooke & U. Kothari (Eds.), *Participation - the new tyranny?* (pp. 139–152). London, New York: Zed Books.

Lambrecht Lund, H. (2002). Integrerede ledelsessystemer og arbejdspladsdemokrati i et bæredygtighed sperspektiv. (Integrated systems of steering and workplace democracy in a sustainability perspective) *Tidsskrift for arbejdsliv, 4*(4), 39.

Lave, J., & Wenger, E. (1991). *Situated learning: legitimate peripheral participation.* Cambridge: Cambridge University Press.

Lorentzen, B., & Remmen, A. (2000). Medarbejderdeltagelse i miljøindsatsen - læreprocesser i miljøgrupper. (Employee participation in contributions for the environment - learning processes in environmental groups), *Tidskrift for arbejdsliv* (2000, årg. 2, nr. 1), 63.

Læssøe, J. (2006). Participation and sustainable development: the role and challenges of mediating agents. In A. Reid, B. B. Jensen, J. Nikel, & V. Simovska (Eds.), *Critical international perspectives on participation in environmental and health education.* Copenhagen: The Danish University of Education Press.

Negt, O., Kluge, A., & Reitan, R. (1974). *Offentlighet og erfaring. Til organisasjonsanalysen av borgerlig og proletarisk offentlighet.* [S.l.]: Nordisk Sommeruniversitet.

Nowotny, H., Scott, P., & Gibbons, M. (2001). *Re-thinking science. Knowledge and the public in an age of uncertainty.* Oxford: Polity Press.

Schön, D. A. (1983). *The reflective practitioner. How professionals think in action.* New York: Basic Books.

Scott, W., & Gough, S. (2003). *Sustainable development and learning. Framing the issues.* London: RoutledgeFalmer.

Senge, P. M. (1990). *The fifth discipline. The art and practice of the learning organization.* London: Century.

Svensson, L. (2002). *Interaktiv forskning. För utveckling av teori och praktik.* (Interactive research. For development of theory and practice.) Stockholm: Arbetslivsinstitutet.

WCED. (1987). *Our common future* (No. 019282080x). Oxford: Oxford University Press.

Wenger, E. (2001). *Communities of practice. Learning, meaning, and identity.* Cambridge: Cambridge University Press.

Jeppe Læssøe and Monica Carlsson
Research Programme for Environmental and Health Education,
The Danish School of Education,
University of Aarhus,
Denmark

LEARNING AND AGENCY IN A MEDIA CULTURE

MARTIN STORKSDIECK AND CATHLYN STYLINSKI[1]

8. THE ROLE AND INFLUENCE OF NEWS MEDIA ON PUBLIC UNDERSTANDING OF ENVIRONMENTAL ISSUES

INTRODUCTION

Across a variety of studies over the last 20 or so years, the public has exhibited mixed performance on knowledge tests about science and environmental topics (e.g., Coyle, 2005; National Science Board, 2008; European Commission 2001). These studies raise concern about the public's ability to respond to environmental challenges or contribute to current science debates. However, the results may be somewhat misleading, as they focus on what the public does not know rather that what it does. Mostly limited to fewer than 20 multiple-choice questions, the validity of a "test" of public knowledge depends on the degree to which one believes that (a) these questions represent a valid indicator of operationalizable knowledge and (b) an immediate recall of facts provides a good measure of knowledge and understanding outside the structured learning environment of formal schooling; both of these notions have been criticized. The testing of "public knowledge" or "public understanding" by a set of multiple-choice questions has been likened to a "deficit model" of knowledge and understanding, since it does not allow individuals to express what they do know or provide an appropriate learning context for that knowledge (Falk, Storksdieck & Dierking, 2007). The alternative asset-based model of knowledge and understanding suggests that much can be learned in adult life through informal, or free-choice, learning and that tests should focus on (a) what an individual does know and (b) be tied to the way we construct our knowledge and understanding outside of formal schooling (Falk *et al.,* 2007). Free-choice learning is the basis for this knowledge construction; it is voluntary, non-assessed, self-directed and under the control of the learner. It is based on an individual's own interest and motivation and builds on his/her prior knowledge. It occurs wherever a person encounters information: in a conversation with others, during a museum visit, while watching TV, reading the newspaper or surfing the Internet. A recent study by the National Research Council (2009) summarized what is known about learning science in informal settings. While the report represents a milestone in documenting the role of informal learning on scientific literacy, it also makes it clear that currently we know little about what people learn from these settings and the degree to which this information corrects or reinforces misconceptions, particularly with regard to learning from media.

R. Stevenson and J. Dillon (eds.), Engaging Environmental Education: Learning, Culture and Agency, 131–146.

Several studies have indicated that mass media, particularly the news media, play a potentially important part in free-choice learning about science and the environment (e.g. National Science Board, 2008; Falk *et al.,* 2007; European Commission, 2001). However, few researchers have attempted to determine the direct influence of the news media on learning about environmental topics and issues. In this chapter, we try to indirectly assess environmental learning from the news media by examining the way in which environmental stories enter the news (including the forces that shape how they are reported) and then relating this reporting to national surveys and case studies of public understanding of environmental issues.

HOW IS ENVIRONMENTAL KNOWLEDGE DIFFERENT FROM GENERAL SCIENCE KNOWLEDGE?

No major distinction is typically made between public understanding of science, history or civics in general and public understanding of environmental issues, evolution or stem cell research. We postulate that, while some of the factors that influence the public's understanding of any issue may be universal in nature, issues touching on morality, questions of right and wrong, and potential changes in individual, collective, or even institutional behavior are of a different nature. Whether someone will learn the intricacies of organic chemistry or material science might be influenced by a variety of factors, including a knowledge base stemming from formal schooling, interest in and attentiveness to the subject matter, and opportunities to learn. One's beliefs and morality are likely not among these factors. However, in areas where value judgments and belief systems influence even whether we want to know, or where knowledge implies subsequent action that may contradict beliefs and personal values, knowledge acquisition itself is influenced by additional factors. We argue that this is the case for environmental topics ranging from global climate change to local issues of pollution. These additional factors serve as "perceptional" filters, which are beliefs, attitudes and values that validate or invalidate information *a priori* (Storksdieck, 2006). Information is deemed reliable or believable if it fits into one's personal worldview.

Schema also influence how we process information. Schema are mental devices of prior knowledge and experiences that help store or organize new knowledge. Miller *et al.* (2006) note schema can act as filters of new information and that an individual is not likely to assimilate a news story if it does not align with an existing schema. For instance, if a viewer is not familiar with the concept of a "greenhouse gas," then a television news story on the significant contribution of methane to global warming may not draw their attention. The news media can create a new schema or expand an existing one by introducing new terms and concepts, but subsequent exposure is necessary to solidify the assimilation of information. However, audiences primarily seek and select news that supports their existing schema, and they judge the source of information (bias, quality, reliability) by the degree to which the source's information fit preconceived notions. Only genuinely trusted sources can challenge the orthodoxy otherwise the information will be rejected. For example, Eveland and Shah (2003) found that political orientation (i.e., being Republican, strong partisan or politically involved) and interpersonal discussions with like-minded friends have a significant role in shaping perceptions of media liberal bias.

WHERE DOES THE PUBLIC GET THEIR ENVIRONMENTAL INFORMATION?

Very few surveys have captured what the public knows about issues related to the natural world and how they acquire this information. Much more has been written about the public's understanding of science and technology (e.g., National Science Board, 2008). As noted, perceptional filters rarely limit the information exchange in science learning; however these science/technology literacy findings can still serve as a proxy to the public's understanding of environmental issues.

Traditional news media provide a key form of free-choice learning about environmental issues and science topics in general. As Nelkin (1995, p. 2) notes,

[The public understands science] less through direct experience or past education than through the filter of journalistic language and imagery.

Among the myriad of media sources, television news (newscasts, news magazine programs, and documentaries) stands out as the main source of science and environmental information for Americans and Europeans (e.g., National Science Board, 2008; Coyle, 2005; European Commission, 1999, 2001). Of these, local newscasts are the most widely-used TV news medium with half of U.S. adults regularly watching local news (Pew Research Center for the People and Press, 2006).

The Internet is a close second for audiences seeking general science and technology information and is the primary source for those interested in specific scientific issues (National Science Board, 2008). It is not well understood how the Internet impacts public understanding of environmental issues. Much of the world has access to the Internet (including about 70% of the North American population[2]), and consequently much information gathering happens online. For example, U.S. college students recently reported using non-newspaper Internet sources and cable news almost equally (Harvard University Institute of Politics, 2008). However, the switch from traditional mass media sources to those provided on the Internet may not be a radical change *per se*. According to Nielson Online in May 2008, the dominant news websites with more than 10 million unique visitors are, in decreasing order of importance, Yahoo News, MSNBC sites, CNN sites and Time.com, AOL News, NYTimes.com, Tribunes Newspapers, Gannett Newspapers, Google News, ABC News sites, USAToday.com and Fox News sites. All contain content generated by traditional news media (MSNBC, CNN, New York Times, etc.) or by traditional journalists (Yahoo, AOL) and thus follow the typical newsroom "rules." "Citizen journalism" and "crowdsourcing" may eventually alter these rules, as the public is given an opportunity to drive story development[3] but this practice is relatively new and not typically used by most established news organizations. Another consideration is the secondary news consumption by young adults who increasingly rely on comedy and satire news shows; emailed newslinks from friends and other "personal sources of trust;" personal network sites; and YouTube hypes and blogs. For example, 84% of 18–24-year-olds in the U.S. are familiar with two popular late-night television political satirists (Jon Stewart and Stephen Colbert), and over a third of 18–24-year-olds use their Facebook accounts to promote a political candidate or issue (Harvard University Institute of Politics, 2008). In the future, information that has been selected and reported through the traditional mechanisms of news media will likely get increasingly filtered and editorialized by interpretive sources of trust (friends, satire shows); the long-term consequences of this additional filtering and selection process is difficult to predict.

We can conclude from the public understanding of science literature that some unknown portion of the public's understanding and perception about environmental issues stems from the media. The question, however, is what kind and what quality of understanding and perception does the public derive from the media? We believe that an in-depth examination of news media practices will shed some light on this question. In the next sections, we explore how information about environmental issues is created and distributed; how the media's coverage influences knowledge; and how future research needs to provide more solid information on the role of the media in educating the public about environmental issues.

WHAT DRIVES COVERAGE, DEPTH AND ACCURACY OF ENVIRONMENTAL NEWS STORIES?

While news organizations differ in their goals and audiences, we have identified five common news room characteristics that play a key role in determining which environmental stories receive airtime or print space and the coverage, depth and accuracy of these stories. Topping the list is "news value," a moving target determined by the newsroom editor based on his/her review of competitors' news coverage, often-conservative assessment of what is current, and intuition about audience taste and expectation. A chasm can exist between what scientists and environmentalists think is important and what editors perceive as important. As cited by Smith (2005, p. 1474), one BBC media decision maker noted,

[A]n issue may be important as you say…but that doesn't make it news.

For example, while climate change research began in earnest in the 1960s, it did not reach "news value" until 1988 when a particularly hot dry summer allowed reporters to make concrete links to people's daily lives.

Related to news value, reporters do not perceive their task to present issues—environmental or otherwise; rather they must translate complex science concepts, policy issues, and political debates into public-interest stories with clear compelling visuals (even for radio broadcasts). As Carvalho (2007, p. 223) noted,

[S]cience is reconstructed and not merely mirrored in the media. Depictions of the world in the media result from a series of choices such as whether an issues will make the news, the highlight it will be given, and who is going to speak for it.

As an example, Anderson (2002) found that news stories on oil spills lacked information on structural or institutional causes such as marine transportation and alternative energy sources; instead they centered on the melodrama (disruption of normalcy, investigation of mystery and restoration of normalcy, suffering of wildlife) and visual aspects of the story. Wilkins and Patterson (1987, p. 14) suggested,

> Perhaps the most fundamental problem in the way the mass media report risk is the necessary reliance upon images to cover a story.

Apparently, most news editors and journalists do not seem to understand the science fundamentals that underlie environmental issues. In surveying members of the Society of Environmental Journalism, Wilson (2000) found that many did not understand the basic science of climate change (e.g., only 48% knew that the greenhouse effect is a scientifically accepted theory) and those who lacked this knowledge tended to exaggerate the climate change debate. From discussions with news decision makers and scientists, Smith (2005, p. 1478) concluded,

> [T]he confident assumption that there are facts to be found and communicated leaves editors poorly equipped to understanding and negotiating the character of uncertainty within climate change science and policy.

Perhaps not surprisingly, scientifically-literate reporters often leave mainstream news media for other communication outlets (books, documentaries, magazines) that allow for the depth in reporting often necessary to cover complex environmental issues (Archibald *et al.,* 1999).

Exacerbating the problem, many reporters working on environmental stories typically limit their sources to other journalists (Wilson, 2000; Antilla, 2005) or established economic, political and government sources (e.g. Corbett, 1998). As Logan *et al.* (2000, p. 7) noted,

> Instead of providing readers with an educational context or background, or seeking fresh angles, journalists are often found to follow a compelling news story by relaying the results of continuing, daily news conferences or relying on news releases generated by major governmental agencies, large companies or well-organized public interest organizations.

The result is stories that lack detailed exploration of underlying issues (Logan *et al.,* 2000). Climate change began as a science story in the late 1980s with researchers as the primary sources; but focus soon shifted to politicians and interest groups, as the topic become more politicized (Trumbo, 1996; Boykoff & Boykoff, 2004). Some commentators suggest reliance on special interest groups (such as oil and coal companies) promotes confusion about the probability of climate change (e.g., Gelbspan, 1998; Williams 2001).

Together, the use of limited sources and weak scientific understanding lead to the final significant characteristic of science and environmental reporting— journalistic balance. Journalists often give equal weight to competing perspectives even if one side lacks merit or is a minority position (Dearing, 1995; Stocking, 1999; Mooney, 2004). McComas and Simone (2003, p. 396) suggest that,

Arguably, for a media that thrives on human interest and intrigue, conflict of interest stories offer dramatic energy and intrigue to more mundane science stories.

However, as noted, journalists rarely have the science literacy to scrutinize different viewpoints—a much easier task for political or economic stories where size often matters. The impact of "balanced" reporting is readily observed in climate change reporting, where, despite widespread scientific consensus (IPCC, 2007), media stories regularly depict a divided science community and emphasize a perceived uncertainty (e.g., Corbett & Durfee, 2004; Antilla, 2005; Carvalho, 2007). Boykoff and Boykoff (2004) found just over half of the stories on global warming in the New York Times, Washington Post, Wall Street Journal and Los Angeles Times did not reflect scientific consensus, and they concluded,

> [The press provides] informationally biased coverage of global warming... hidden behind the veil of journalistic balance (p. 134).

Trumbo (1996) found that scientists were often associated with stories that emphasized problems and causes, while politicians and special interests were associated with stories that emphasized judgments and remedies. However, as cited by Smith (2005, p. 1479), news editors prefer to stay clear of prescriptive ideas:

> We're not here to tell the public how to behave—we're there to tell them what's happening.

Smith (2005) counters that some feel such guidance is offered for other topics such as human rights and terrorism, where the news media feel far safer taking sides, if only because of a clear consensus of the moral underpinnings of the issues.

The effect of "balanced" reporting in the media on readers and viewers became apparent in a recent, unrelated study at three science museums/centers in Seattle, Albuquerque and Lancaster (Institute for Learning Innovation, unpublished data). Visitors were asked by researchers to rate their interest in learning about current science (i.e., recent scientific findings regularly discussed in the scientific community) and to explain their rating. About 19% of the 258 respondents spontaneously referred to the need for balance—to hear both or all sides of the argument and to provide unbiased perspectives. These visitors were apparently influenced by the media's framing of science as a conflict between opposing sides rather than a process to propose, test and refine evidence-based explanations about the natural world.

MEDIA COVERAGE AND THE APPARENT NARRATIVE FOR THE PUBLICS— FRAMING OF NEWS

News generation and news consumption are linked in a complex feedback loop of perceived demand and real supply (Perse, 2001). Societal factors have a strong influence on news reporting. For example, Griffin and Dunwoody (1997) found community structure affects how reporters tell pollution stories: media in larger, diverse communities were more likely to link pollution to health risks compared to smaller, more homogenous communities. Media also depend on agenda-building efforts of various established news sources (e.g., large companies or well-organized public interest organizations) (Curtin & Rhodenbaugh, 2001).

News media can themselves play a large role in shaping both the agenda for public debate and political action (so-called agenda-setting) and the way in which the public perceives an issue by the selected "framing" of news stories (Nitz, 1999; Scheufele & Tewksbury, 2007). Agenda-setting works largely through increased exposure; a topic becomes more visible and is therefore perceived to be of greater importance by the public (and other news makers, editors and reporters). Agenda-setting can influence public opinion and ultimately policy-making (Shanahan & Good, 1999 as cited in Nitz 1999; Scheufele & Tewksbury, 2007). TV reporting, with its imagery and immediateness, is particularly effective when coverage of an issue is intense and repeated across stations and news segments (Brosius & Kepplinger, 1990). Constant local reporting, particularly on environmental stories that are linked to health risks ("we bring you more on this emerging story at 11...") has the potential to resonate strongly with the public and with decision-makers. Indeed, the news media has been called the "Great Mentioner" (Nitz, 1999) because of its power to influence public discourse and public attention.

"Framing" refers to the way the news media report on issues. While any issue can be reported from multiple angles, the preferred reporting narrative determines how the public understands the nature of an issue (rather than the importance of it). The preferred narrative is a function of the news room characteristics cited earlier. The resulting "frames" focus on certain aspects and angles of a topic while ignoring or minimizing others (Nisbet & Mooney, 2007). As mentioned above, science and technology (and environmental issues) are often discussed in the mass media with frames that focus on conflict and controversy (e.g., Gamson & Modigliani, 1989; Nisbet & Lewenstein, 2002). As noted, climate change began as a science story defined by scientists and primarily drawn from scientific literature; but the narrative quickly shifted from consensus to controversy (Trumbo, 1996; McComas & Shanahan, 1999; Boykoff & Boykoff, 2004; Carvolho, 2007). As cited by Carvalho (2007, p. 236), even scientists' abilities and ideologies were questioned with one London *Times* reporter asking,

If climatologists can't get the present right, how can we trust them with the future?

Now, thanks to the success and broad appeal of Al Gore's *An Inconvenient Truth* (2006) and mounting scientific evidence, coverage of climate change has significantly increased, permeating the front, business, political and even travel pages and shifting the framing from asking "if " to examining how we should respond (Kennedy School Bulletin, 2008). Overall, through the process of agenda-setting and framing, the media has the power to set the tone and the agenda for environmental issues as broad as environmental protection and as specific as the nuclear reactor meltdown in Chernobyl (Nitz, 1999).

HOW DOES MEDIA COVERAGE OF ENVIRONMENTAL ISSUES IMPACT PUBLIC KNOWLEDGE, ATTITUDES AND BEHAVIOR

As noted earlier, the impact of environmental news stories on public knowledge, attitudes and actions is not well understood. Some reject the idea that media affect knowledge, let alone behavior, as suggested by Clark (1983, p. 445),

> [M]edia are mere vehicles that deliver instruction but do not influence student achievement any more than the truck that delivers our groceries causes changes in our nutrition.

However, some studies point to enhanced awareness and knowledge. For example, there have been small increases in the number of Americans stating they understand global warming "very well," agreeing that we are already feeling the effects, and feeling that most scientists support this view (Saad, 2006; Nisbet & Myers, 2007). As the media are the primary source of science information for the public, any increase in understanding could be attributed to reporting on climate change (interestingly, a recent study notes no significant change in global warming worries over the last 19 years (Newport, 2008)). Other studies have even directly linked media stories with changes in public knowledge or opinion. The NSF-funded program *ScienCentral* found a small but significant portion of their overall audience of about 12 million viewers were able to recall science content from three or more stories (Miller *et al.,* 2006). Brothers *et al.* (1991) reported that a news broadcast on the Great Lakes environment significantly increased viewers' knowledge and concluded that television can serve as an effective means to inform the public about the environment. Hong Kong students were more knowledgeable about environmental issues regularly reported in television news programs and less knowledgeable about issues that had low priority in the media (including details of causes and consequences) (Chan, 1999). From their research, Holbert *et al.* (2003, p. 191) concluded,

> [The] use of television news, even with its episodic and overly dramatic coverage of the environment, has a positive influence in creating a greater desire within individuals to recycle, purchase products that are environmentally friendly, and being more energy efficient in their daily routines.

Stamm *et al.* (2000) also found both media (TV, newspapers, magazines, books) and interpersonal channels (family/friends) helped study participants make connections between climate change, fossil fuel consumption, and environmental behavior (driving less; reducing home energy use; using more energy-efficient technologies). However, because news stories often focus on impeding but rare or unlikely disasters, behavior changes may be based on fear rather than "cognitive information transition" (Holbert *et al.,* 2003) and thus may not be sustained. The media also create and perpetuate science and environmental misconceptions (Logan *et al.,* 1997; Stamm *et al.,* 2000; Nisbet *et al.,* 2002). Moreover, many stories lack context and inflate controversy, which can cause audiences to question the certainty of environmental issues such as climate change (Corbett & Durfee, 2004).

Of course, viewers do not receive news media reporting in a vacuum. As reported earlier, various filters (including prior knowledge, attitudes and metacognition) shape what they hear and see and ultimately learn. Education, socioeconomic status, gender and age may also influence science perceptions, learning and behavior. For example, Kahlor *et al.* (2004) found socioeconomic status was a significant predictor of the public's understanding of how a parasitic outbreak impacts drinking water, while Nisbet *et al.* (2002) showed better-educated individuals typically chose more in-depth coverage of newspapers over television. Wilson (2002) found that weathercasters (often the most scientifically literate member of a local newscast) hold many misconceptions about basic climate change science; these misconceptions could be directly connected to their values and beliefs about climate change. Chan (1999) points to a possible link between male students' environmental knowledge and their television viewership. Horbett *et al.* (2003) found age was correlated with television public affairs and nature documentary viewing, which in turn were strong predictors of pro-environmental behavior. Overall, individual factors seem to influence what and how news is consumed and how individuals are impacted by their news media consumption.

PUBLIC UNDERSTANDING OR PUBLIC CONFUSION?

Since the news media have limited time or space to delve deeply into the root causes of environmental issues or to explain the scientific underpinnings of environmental problems, there is concern that the language, imagery and metaphors used in news stories to "explain" complex environmental issues may misinform and confuse the public (American Opinion Research Inc., 1993; Boyes & Stanisstreet, 1997; European Commission, 1999; Lehmann, 1999; National Science Board 2008). Thus, we need to consider not just if the public learns from the news media but what it is that the public may learn from the media. To do this, it is important to distinguish between not knowing or incorrectly memorizing isolated facts (tested in most national and international surveys) and not understanding entire concepts. For instance, whether one believes that the U.S. emits 10 or 20 tons of carbon dioxide annually per person may not matter as much as if that person cannot identify carbon dioxide as an important greenhouse gas or fails to realize that burning fossil fuel leads to increased concentrations of carbon dioxide in the atmosphere (Storksdieck, 2006). The concern that emerges from misconception studies is that the news media may have successfully conveyed that carbon dioxide is connected to climate change (a simple fact) but failed to communicate how it impacts the climate, where it comes from, or how it can be reduced, all of which are tied to a learner's mental model about carbon dioxide and its effects on the environmental and climate.

Like Miller *et al.* (2006), Roschelle (1995) suggests that, if a learner's deeper understanding of a topic conflicts with an "expert's" explanation, that deeper understanding is almost impossible to change. A new understanding may actually require a total reconstruction of the learner's schema or mental models—a process that so-called misconception studies prove can be extraordinarily difficult to accomplish (Strike & Posner, 1985; Stanisstreet & Boyes, 1997). Incorrect mental models are so robust and resistant to modification because they have been constructed and are therefore "owned" by the individual learner; they are particularly resilient when linked to an individual's other ideas and concepts (Ausubel, 1968). Knowledge construction, in this perspective, is conservative and strives to uphold the status quo, making learners reluctant to challenge existing fundamental understandings. Misconception studies serve as a sober reminder that, as (Palmer (1997, p. 5) noted,

> learning that requires changes in students' concepts about scientific issues is very difficult to accomplish.

Various studies on environmental misconceptions were conducted in the early/mid-1990s. They showed that the public knew little about global warming and ozone layer depletion or strategies to mitigate them. More importantly, the studies revealed that the public lacked a basic understanding of the underlying scientific processes behind global warming and ozone layer depletion, and thus they provide insight on how news reporting might contribute to public confusion rather than understanding, of an environmental issue (Kempton, 1991; Bostrom, Morgan, Fischhoff, & Read, 1994; Read, Bostrom, Morgan, Fischhoff, & Smutts, 1994; Kempton, Boster, & Hartley, 1995Diekmann & Franzen, 1996;). For example, visitors to the Franklin Science Museum in Philadelphia were familiar with the greenhouse effect and global warming; however, there was considerable confusion about the relationship between ozone depletion and global warming with two-thirds believing that the ozone hole was the cause of global warming (Ramberg, 1990). In a larger study, only about a third of U.S. adults knew that burning fossil fuels is the primary method for generating electricity (National Environmental Education and Training Foundation/Roper Starch Worldwide, 1998). Consequently, even though most Americans conceded that climate change might pose a threat, they failed to distinguish between effective and ineffective preventive measures (Bostrom et al., 1994; Read et al., 1994). For example, many adults felt that they could combat global warming by eliminating aerosol cans and replacing Styrofoam with paper; they neglected to identify energy-saving measures as the most effective solution to the problem (Bostrom et al., 1994). These studies may not exemplify the public's current level of environmental science knowledge (though the aforementioned annual studies by NEETF/Roper Starch indicate little change since). However, as often occurs in news stories, they do show that misconceptions can easily arise when scientific processes are complex and when information is presented out of context, emphasizes minority viewpoints, and directly or indirectly reinforces existing misconceptions.

A mental model that linked the ozone hole to global warming, prevalent in adults in the early 1990s, was also found to dominate 13- and 14-year-old students' perspective of global warming in England (Boyes & Stanisstreet, 1993; Boyes & Stanisstreet, 1997). From these studies, Stanisstreet and Boyes (1997, p. 308) concluded,

> [S]tudents will gain much of their information from out-of-school sources. Even if the information given is correct and balanced, there is no opportunity for students to interact with colleagues or peers to determine that they have

not misunderstood the information. Furthermore, there is a danger that environmental problems suffer from over-exposure, that students develop 'environmental fatigue.'

In other words, free-choice learning, if it occurs without a chance for feedback and correction, can lead to partial misconceptions. Furthermore, Boyes and Stanistreet (2001) found that students who learned from media sources showed greater knowledge but also held more misconceptions than those who learned primarily in school; they also suggested that learning from TV and the Internet might be limited in scope and quality, unless these sources are able to challenge pre-existing or newly-generated misconceptions. Likewise, Henriksen and Jorde (2001) found that most 16-year-old Norwegian students could understand concepts such as the greenhouse effect, global warming and the ozone layer in a museum setting if this learning included pre- and post-visit explorations. However, students who held strong misconceptions did not change their mental models, presumably because museums, and possibly the news media, are not ideal places to address misconceptions and because students are not trained to transfer knowledge from one situation to another.

CONCLUSIONS

The public still relies on the traditional news media to learn about environmental issues; however, few studies have quantified the media's impact on these free-choice learners. An analysis of how news media select, report and frame environmental stories; how they influence the public agenda on environmental issues; and what the public understands about the environment suggests that learning from the news media leads to mixed results. We found that the public's perception, attitude, attentiveness, and (mis-)understanding of environmental issues are potentially influenced by the news media. It seems that, while the public is aware and informed about environmental issues, the preferred narrative of reporting, with its lack of context and over-emphasis on controversy, can lead to learning isolated, decontextualized facts and can influence attitudes and perceptions. But it fails in developing deeper understanding of key concepts. This is certainly true for news stories that are reported in the general news media (e.g., local newscasts) and target the general public. We did not analyze the more specific and in-depth reporting in print and broadcast magazines for audiences interested in science and nature; these will likely have a different impact and are worthy of further investigation.

Despite its apparent limitation in influencing the public's mental models or schema on environmental issues, evidence suggests that the media's role in informing the public is significant. News stories serve the important role of raising awareness and alerting the public about new, underappreciated or immediate environmental issues and, in that function, can provide solutions to non-controversial problems and threats. In this kind of "detection narrative" journalism, reporters tend to rely on scientists as a source of trusted and unbiased information, as illustrated by early reporting of climate change. However, over time, these narratives of detection and revealing of information often shift to a conflict format. Journalists give equal weight to competing (and not necessary equal) perspectives, and issues move from the scientific to the political realm. This shift causes the public to question the certainty of the issue and even scientific findings in general and may reinforce perceptional filters and existing schema about bias in science and other related concerns. Once the media moves to the next stage of the narrative (reporting on consequences and responses to an issue rather than whether it exists), environmental news stories may offer more sustenance and support for more in-depth understanding of the topics.

Free-choice learning from the media is highly fragmented and depends on the environmental topic, the reporting, and the personal characteristics of the learner. A large-scale study linking public understanding and news media consumption in a causal way will be necessary to truly understand the news media's influence on environmental literacy. However, as reported in the latest Science & Technology Indicator Study by the National Science Board (2008),

> [S]tudies that seek to isolate the effects of mass media face numerous challenges.

Controlled experiments that isolate the effect of news media on learning may not reflect the real-life situation in which the public deliberately chooses its consumption of news media or simply happens to come about it. In addition, laboratory-like media learning research will likely miss long-term effects that would include subsequent reinforcing experiences (Falk & Storksdieck, 2005) or follow-up learning (Storksdieck, 2006) and would ignore the cumulative effect of multiple resources in a person's lifelong practice as free-choice learners. Personal beliefs and other perceptional filters influence not only what people focus on in the news but also how they perceive and integrate the information into existing schema and mental models. Thus, an effective study of media impacts needs to seek information about subjects' prior knowledge, values, attitudes and beliefs, and it needs to consider important contextual factors that could influence public perception on an issue (e.g., the release of the Academy Award winning and commercially successful documentary on global warming *An Inconvenient Truth* changed the public discourse on global warming considerably in the United States). To determine the impact of news media on the public's understanding of environmental issues, a new approach is needed that blends ethnographic and naturalistic methodologies using a longitudinal design and large-scale samples of news media consumers in clearly-defined media markets. It should integrate deficit- and asset-based models to conduct an in-depth assessment of ecological and environmental literacy and directly link learning to media reporting. Such a comprehensive approach should also provide overall insight into factors that contribute to lifelong environmental learning.

NOTES

[1] Both authors contributed equally to this chapter.
[2] See http://www.internetworldstats.com.
[3] See http://www.beatblogging.org.

REFERENCES/BIBLIOGRAPHY

Anderson, A. G. (2002). The media politics of oil spills. *Spill Science & Technology Bulletin, 7*(1–2), 7–15.

Antilla, L. (2005). Climate of skepticism: US newspaper coverage of the science of climate change. *Global Environmental Change-Human and Policy Dimensions, 15*(4), 338–352.

Archibald, E. (1999). Problems with environmental reporting: Perspective of daily newspaper reporters. *Journal of Environmental Education, 30*(4), 27–32.

Ausubel, D. P. (1968). *Educational psychology: A cognitive view*. New York: Holt, Rinehart, and Winston.

Bostrom, A., Morgan, M. G., Fischhoff, B., & Read, D. (1994). What do people know about global climate change? 1. Mental models. *Risk Analysis, 14*(6), 959–970.

Boyes, E., & Stanisstreet, M. (1993). The greenhouse effect: Children's perceptions of causes, consequences and cures. *International Journal of Science Education, 15*, 531–552.

Boyes, E., & Stanisstreet, M. (1997). Children's models of understanding of two major global environmental issues (ozone layer and greenhouse effect). *Research in Science and Technological Education, 15*(1), 19–28.

Boykoff, M. T., & Boykoff, J. M. (2004). Balance as bias: Global warming and the US prestige press. *Global Environmental Change-Human and Policy Dimensions, 14*(2), 125–136.

Brosius, H.-B., & Kepplinger, H. M. (1990). The Agenda-Setting function of television news: Static and dynamic views. *Communication Research, 17*(2), 183–211.

Brothers, C. C. (1991). The impact of television news on public environmental knowledge. *The Journal of Environmental Education, 22*(4), 22–29.

Carvalho, A. (2007). Ideological cultures and media discourses on scientific knowledge: Re-reading news on climate change. *Public Understanding of Science, 16*(2), 223–243.

Chan, K. K. W. (1999). Mass media and environmental knowledge of secondary school students in Hong Kong. *The Environmentalist, 19*, 85–97.

Clark, R. E. (1983). Reconsidering research on learning from media. *Review of Educational Research, 53*(4), 445–459.

Corbett, J. B. (1998). The environment as theme and package on a local television newscast. *Science Communication, 19*(3), 222–237.

Corbett, J. B., & Durfee, J. L. (2004). Testing public (Un) certainty of science: Media representations of global warming. *Science Communication, 26*(2), 129–151.

Coyle, K. (2005). *Environmental literacy in America: What ten years of NEETF/Roper research and related studies says about environmental literacy in the U.S.* Washington, DC: The National Environmental Education and Training Foundation.

Curtin, P. A., & Rhodenbaugh, E. (2001). Building the news media agenda on the environment: A comparison of public relations and journalistic sources. *Public Relations Review, 27*, 179–195.

Dearing, J. W. (1995). Newspaper coverage of maverick science: Creating controversy through balancing. *Public Understanding of Science, 4*(4), 341–361.

Diekmann, A., & Franzen, A. (1996). *Einsicht in ökologische Zusammenhänge und Umweltverhalten.* Bern, Switzerland: Verlag Paul Haupt.

European Commission. (1999). *What do Europeans think about the environment? The main results of the survey carried out in the context of Eurobarometer 51.1.* Luxembourg: Office for Official Publications of the European Communities.

European Commission. (2001). *Europeans, science and technology: Eurobarometer 55.2 (December 2001).* Luxembourg: Office for Official Publications of the European Communities.

Eveland, W. P. J., & Shah, D. V. (2003). The impact of individual and interpersonal factors on perceived news media bias. *Political Psychology, 24*(1), 101–117.

Falk, J. H., Storksdieck, M., & Dierking, L. D. (2007). Investigating public science interest and understanding: Evidence for the importance of free-choice learning. *Public Understanding of Science, 16*(4), 455–469.

Gamson, W. A., & A., M. (1989). Media discourse and public opinion on nuclear power: A constructionist approach. *American Journal of Sociology, 95*(1), 1–37.

Gelbspan, R. (1998). *The heat is on: The climate crisis, the cover-up, the prescription.* New York: Perseu.

Griffin, R. J., & Dunwoody, S. (1997). Community structure and science framing of news about local environmental risks. *Science Communication, 18*(4), 362–384.

Harvard University Institute of Politics. (2008). *The 14th Biannual Youth Survey on Politics and Public Service.* Retrieved May 2, 2008, from http://www.iop.harvard.edu/Research-Publications/Polling/Spring-2008-Survey

Henriksen, E. K., & Jorde, D. (2001). High school students' understanding of radiation and the environment: Can museums play a role? *Science Education, 85,* 189–206.

Holbert, R. L., Kwak, N., & Shah, D. V. (2003). Environmental concern, patterns of television viewing, and pro-environmental behaviors: Integrating models of media consumption and effects. *Journal of Broadcasting and Electronic Media, 47*(2), 177–196.

IPCC. (2007). *Climate change 2007: Synthesis report. Contribution of working groups I, II and III to the fouth assessment report of the intergovernmental panel on climate change.* Geneva, Switzerland: IPCC.

Kahlor, L., Dunwoody, S., & Griffin, R. J. (2004). Predicting knowledge complexity in the wake of an environmental risk. *Science Communication, 26*(1), 5–30.

Kempton, W. (1991, June). Lay perspectives on global climate change. *Global Environmental Change,* 183–208.

Kempton, W., Boster, J. S., & Hartley, J. A. (1995). *Environmental values in American culture.* Cambridge, MA: The MIT Press.

Kennedy School Bulletin. (2008). *Man bites planet: News coverage of climate change* [Electronic Version]. Retrieved May 2, 2008, from http://www.hks.harvard.edu/ksgpress/bulletin/08winter/charles/russell.html

Lehmann, J. (1999). *Befunde empirischer Forschung zu Umweltbildung und Umweltbewußtsein* (Vol. 4). Opladen, Germany: Leske + Budrich.

Logan, R. A., Fears, L., & Wilson, N. F. (1997). *Social responsibility in science news: Four case studies.* Washington, DC: The Media Institute.

Logan, R. A., Zengjun, P., & Wilson, N. F. (2000). Science and medical coverage in the Los Angeles times and The Washington Post: A six-year perspective. *Science Communication, 22*(1), 5–26.

McComas, K., & Shanahan, J. (1999). Telling stories about global climate change: Measuring the impact of narratives on issue cycles. *Communication Research, 26*(1), 30–57.

McComas, K. A., & Simone, L. M. (2003). Media coverage of conflicts of interest in science. *Science Communication, 24*(4), 395–419.

Miller, J. D., Augenbraun, E., Schulhof, J., & Kimmel, L. G. (2006). Adult science learning from local television newscasts. *Science Communication, 28*(2), 216–242.

Mooney, C. (2004). Blinded by science: How 'balanced' coverage lets the scientific fringe hijack reality [Electronic Version]. *Columbia Journalism Review.* Retrieved May 2, 2008, from http://cjrarchives.org/issues/2004/6/mooney-science.asp

National Environmental Education and Training Foundation/Roper Starch Worldwide. (1998). *The national report card on environmental knowledge, attitudes, and behaviors: The seventh annual survey of adult Americans.* Washington, DC: NEETF/Roper Starch.

National Research Council. (2009). *Learning science in informal environments: People, places, and pursuits.* Committee on Learning Science in Informal Environments. In P. Bell, B. Lewenstein, A. W. Shouse, & M. A. Feder (Eds.), *Board on science education, center for education, division of behavioral and social sciences and education.* Washington, DC: The National Academies Press.

National Science Board. (2008). *Science and engineering indicators.* Arlington, VA: National Science Foundation.

Nelkin, D. (1995). *Selling science*. New York: Freeman.

Newport, F. (2008). *Little increase in Americans' global warming worries*. Retrieved May 2, 2008, from http://www.gallup.com/poll/106660/Little-Increase-Americans-Global-Warming-Worries. aspx

Nisbet, M. C., & Lewenstein, B. V. (2002). Biotechnology and the American media: The policy process and the Elite press, 1970 to 1999. *Science Communication, 23*(4), 359–391.

Nisbet, M. C., & Myers, T. (2007). The polls—trends: Twenty years of public opinion about global warming. *Public Opinion Quarterly, 71*(3), 444–470.

Nisbet, M. C., & Mooney, C. (2007). Framing science. *Science, 216,* 56.

Nisbet, M. C., Scheufele, D. A., Shanahan, J., Moy, P., Brossard, D., & Lewenstein, B. V. (2002). Knowledge, reservations, or promise? A media effects model for public perceptions of science and technology. *Communication Research, 29*(5), 584–608.

Nitz, M. (1999). *The media as a tool for communication on the environment and sustainability.* Paper presented at The Millennium Conference on Environmental Education and Communication. Retrieved from http://www.projekte.org/millennium/

Palmer, J. A. (1997). Beyond science: Global imperatives for environmental education in the 21st century. In P. Thompson (Ed.), *Environmental education for the 21st Century* (pp. 3–12). New York: Peter Lang.

Perse, E. (2001). *Media effects and society*. Mahwah, NJ: Lawrence Erlbaum Associates.

Pew Research Center for People and the Press. (2006). *Online papers modestly boost newspaper readership*. Retrieved August 12, 2008, from http://www.people-press.org/reports

Ramberg, J. S. (1990). *Greenhouse earth (unpublished technical report)*. Philadelphia: Franklin Institute Science Museum.

Read, D., Bostrom, A., Morgan, M. G., Fischhoff, B., & Smutts, T. (1994). What do people know about global climate change? 2. Survey study of educated laypeople. *Risk Analysis, 14*(6), 971–982.

Roschelle, J. (1995). Learning in interactive environments: Prior knowledge and new experience. In J. H. Falk & L. D. Dierking (Eds.), *Public institutions for personal learnin*. Washington, DC: American Association of Museums.

Saad, L. (2007). *Environmental concern holds firms during the past year*. Retrieved May 2, 2008, from http://www.gallup.com/poll/26971/Environmental-Concern-Holds-Firm-During-Past-Year.aspx

Scheufele, D. A., & Tewksbury, D. (2007). Framing, Agenda Setting, and priming: The evolution of three media effects models. *Journal of Communication, 57*(1), 9–20.

Smith, J. (2005). Dangerous news: Media decision making about climate change risk. *Risk Analysis, 25*(6), 1471–1482.

Stamm, K. R., Clark, F., & Eblacas, P. R. (2000). Mass communication and public understanding of environmental problems: The case of global warming. *Public Understanding of Science, 9*(3), 219–237.

Stanisstreet, M., & Boyes, E. (1997). Vehicles: Metaphors for environmental education. In P. Thompson (Ed.), *Environmental education for the 21st century* (pp. 301–310). New York: Peter Lang.

Stocking, S. H. (1999). How journalists deal with scientific uncertainty. In S. M. Friedman, S. Dunwoody, & C. L. Rogers (Eds.), *Communicating uncertainty: Media coverage of new and controversial science* (pp. 23–41). Mahwah, NJ: Lawrence Erlbaum.

Storksdieck, M. (2006). *Field trips in environmental education*. Berlin, Germany: Berliner Wissenschafts-Verlag.

Strike, K. A., & Posner, G. L. (1985). A conceptual change view of learning and understanding. In L. H. T. West & A. L. Pines (Eds.), *Cognitive structure and conceptual change* (pp. 211–231). New York: Academic Press.

Trumbo, C. (1996). Constructing climate change: Claims and frames in US news coverage of an environmental issue. *Public Understanding of Science, 5*(3), 269–283.

Wilkins, L., & Patterson, P. (1987). Risk analysis and the construction of news. *Journal of Communication, 37,* 80–92.

Williams, J. L. (2001). *The rise and decline of public interest in global warming: Toward a pragmatic conception of environmental problems*. Huntington: Nova Science.

Wilson, K. M. (2000). Drought, debate, and uncertainty: Measuring reporters' knowledge and ignorance about climate change. *Public Understanding of Science, 9*(1), 1–13.

Wilson, K. M. (2002). Forecasting the future: How television weathercasters' attitudes and beliefs about climate change affect their cognitive knowledge on the science. *Science Communication, 24*(2), 246–268.

Martin Storksdieck
Institute for Learning Innovation, USA

Cathlyn D. Stylinski
University of Maryland Center for Environmental Science, USA

MARCIA MCKENZIE, CONSTANCE RUSSELL, LEESA FAWCETT
AND NORA TIMMERMAN

9. POPULAR MEDIA, INTERSUBJECTIVE LEARNING
AND CULTURAL PRODUCTION

When we think about our own experiences as learners and teachers, it is the catalysts we mostly recall: embeddedness in community, deep friendship, fear of loss, startling beauty, rootedness or dislocation in place, cultural difference, the stories we hear and tell. These are not experiences of learning about bioregional zones or narrative structure or the more regular curricula of secondary and post-secondary contexts of schooling. Rather, these are experiences of learning understood as eliciting a sense of one's location in relation to others and the world, and indeed, as enabling different ways of knowing and being human.

This chapter represents part of a larger interest in investigating a culturally embedded understanding of experience in relation to socioecological learning and cultural formation (e.g., McKenzie, 2008, 2009; Fawcett, 2009). In considerations of experiences of place, community, art, friendship, literature, cultural difference, media, and a range of other sources of catalytic or transgressive experience, it becomes clear that what they share is their intersubjective or relational nature. That is, learning can be considered to occur in interactions with "others," broadly conceived. The intersubjective – be it with other people, places, species, ideas, images - is the location where the learner "comes into presence" (Biesta, 1999, p.34).

In what follows we explore how forms of media can be engaged as inter-subjective pedagogical experiences that enable student learning in relation to the social and ecological. These media can be engaged as pre-existing artifacts, as products in creation, and/or as interactive spaces; and may take the form of fiction and non-fiction, zines and comics, photography and visual art, film and documentaries, various Internet-based interactive venues, and a range of other forms that cross-over or join these and other genres. We outline a framework for understanding engagements with media as intersubjective experiences that involve both the sensory and the cognitive, and suggest that a collective context can support or intensify this learning. Following the introduction of this framework we elaborate on a range of media genres using examples from our own pedagogical practices. With media as mediating influences through which the students we work with already see and imagine their own lives and those of others around the world (Appadurai, 1996), we have found it important and useful to critically and educatively engage students in a range of intersubjective media experiences.

R. Stevenson and J. Dillon (eds.), Engaging Environmental Education: Learning, Culture
and Agency, 147–164.

INTERSUBJECTIVITY, COLLECTIVE SPACES, AND MEDIA ENGAGEMENT

As suggested above, intersubjective engagements, including those with popular media, can entail emotionally embedded experiences – of humour, irony, empathy, discomfort, and/or belonging. As we will detail below, experiencing a film, making a home-made magazine or "zine," or participating in an online community can be emotionally powerful. When creating dissonance with our habitual or expected understandings and ways of being – causing the strange to become familiar or the familiar strange - these types of experiences can contribute to learning and cultural change. As cultural theorist Raymond Williams (1977) articulates, sensory experiences of lived "practical consciousness" can be considered to rub up against the previously thought, or our "official consciousness," and thus become potential catalysts for, and locations of, personal and cultural formation. Likewise, Elizabeth Ellsworth (2005) suggests the ways that "'knowings' arise from a place more elemental than intellectualisation" (p. 8). She suggests they derive from the "frisson" of the physical encounter and the corresponding sensory response, which then migrates in some form into thought. This sort of orientation to learning is itself difficult to conceptualize, but essentially is concerned with how experiences that provoke and support the sensory can translate into, and coexist with, cognitive learning that would not otherwise have been possible. Representing part of a larger shift away from positioning feeling and thought in opposition in educational scholarship (e.g., Boler, 1999; Zembylas, 2007), Ellsworth asks: "What environments and experiences are capable of acting as the pedagogical pivot point between movement/sensation and thought?" (p. 8).

It is also important to recognize the role that media can play in establishing and perpetuating official consciousness - or that which can be thought, and through which status quo culture is perpetuated or manipulated. Within education, much work has focused on the critique and deconstruction of forms of media for what they perpetuate in and through culture, for example in the "close readings" of popular films, in the deconstruction of popular new sources, or in examinations of the negative implications of technology for face-to-face and embodied interactions with the world (Mitchell & Weber, 1999; Bishop *et al.,* 2000; Payne, 2003). However, rather than focusing on pedagogical activities that begin with "critique" and reside more centrally in the cognitive realm, we instead here turn our attention to engagements with media that take place amidst both the lived or sensory, and the knowable or cognitive (Buckingham, 2003). Or in other words, we focus on those engagements with media that occur between and amidst "being sensate" and "making sense" (Ellsworth, 2005), and which can afford possibilities for difference, learning, and change. Such experiences can centre on media as *artifacts* or pre-existing cultural forms, may involve processes of media *creation*, and/or may entail alternative engagements through media as interactive *spaces*. That is, learners may experience media products, create their own media, or engage with others using media. These are not appropriations of media used as hooks to gain students' attention, but rather engagements that hope to elicit greater consideration of social and ecological issues through sensory and cognitive learning.

Creating opportunities that enable students to engage in collective inter-subjective experiences can support the de- and re-familiarisation that occurs as a result of intersubjective media engagements. These are collective spaces in which students can jointly challenge common sense, and engage in ways that can be counterhegemonic or that "push the boundaries of what 'would be'" personally as well as culturally (Weis & Fine, 2003, p. 97). Enabling individuals and groups to get to know themselves through cultural activity, these social interactions and communities can support the reformulation of identities and culture (Hey, 2002). As John Weaver and Karen Grindall (1998) have proposed, this opens up possibilities of teachers developing pedagogy based on an understanding that students do construct their identities in relationship to each other and the cultures in which they are embedded, including those perpetuated in and through popular media. They and others suggest it is the task of teachers to construct a classroom that allows for the collective exploration and development of these identities, knowing that it is also taking place elsewhere in other ways through other means (Buckingham, 2003).

In a wonderful study of "youth learning on their own terms," Leif Gustavson (2007a) explores these same themes in detail. Through ethnographies of the lives of three youth who are engaged in forging their identities in relation to the creation of zines, graffiti, and turntable music Gustavson highlights the critical importance of the communities of practice in which these youth are embedded. Essential to the deep personal, artistic, historical, and political learning of these youth, are the productive collaborative interlinking communities in which their learning practices take place, including through online and face-to-face interactions and collaborations with peers and mentors. Gustavson writes (2007b),

> What keeps [these] communities of practice together is a belief that the work they are doing is purposeful and meaningful as well as a sense that the work connects them to possibilities of meeting new people, exploring new places, and progressively getting better at what they do. Imagine if these qualities of work were the driving force behind curriculum. (p. 110)

Before turning to specific examples of uses of media in our own teaching, we want to suggest in more detail how students can engage in learning – including socioecological learning - through media artifacts, media creation, and media spaces. We turn first to media artifacts and look at two more specific means of intersubjective engagement: the uses of pre-existing media as testimonial experience and as opportunity to imagine "what if?"

Media Artifacts

The paired events of traumatic testimony of oneself or another and a willingness to face or *witness* that testimony ideally lead to a re-orientation to an ethics of relation and connection and a developing commitment to contribute to social change (Eppert, 2009). Electronic oral histories, films, online art, and other varieties of media that tell the stories of traumatic historical and socio-political events or lives

149

led, can all serve to initiate this sort of reorientation. In the literatures on testimony and witnessing we see an emphasis on the emotional aspects of these sorts of pedagogical experiences. For example, discussing her use of filmed interviews with Holocaust survivors as pedagogical catalysts, Shoshana Felman (1992) writes,

> I want my students to be able to receive information that is dissonant, and not just congruent, with everything that they have learned beforehand. Testimonial teaching fosters the capacity to witness something that may be surprising, cognitively dissonant. The surprise implies the crisis. Testimony cannot be authentic without that crisis, which has to break and to transvaluate previous categories and previous frames of reference. (pp. 53–54)

Through the use of testimonial texts and other media, Megan Boler (1999) likewise suggests that the resulting "pedagogy of discomfort" can move students to question their assumptions and understandings; while Deborah Britzman and Alice Pitt (2003) highlight the possibilities of learning this sort of "difficult knowledge." Essential to educative outcomes of these sorts of engagements are attentive listening, critical questioning, careful facilitation, and a supportive context. Boler (1999), for example, explores how members of a collective can engage each other in examining or "witnessing" responses to testimonial experiences and exploring the implications of their personal and collective lives in social and ecological issues in ways that avail rich opportunities for learning not otherwise possible.

Another variety of intersubjective engagement with popular media as artifacts are those experiences that elicit the possibility of imagining "what if?" As fiction that offers a world clearly discontinuous from the one we know, yet returns to confront that known world in some cognitive way (Scholes, cited in Gough, 1993), forms of media as "fabulation" have been discussed elsewhere as thought experiments, or works of practical imagination which make it possible to think differently about identity and community. For example, Noel Gough (2009) has written about the novels of science fiction author Ursula Le Guin and her capacity to invent alternative societies and environments which can offer the reader visions of "strange places, people, and customs that disrupt assumptions about what is standard, settled, and normal" (p. 77). Gough identifies this sort of defamiliarization as a recurring feature of art and other creative activities where it is intentionally used as a tool towards intellectual breakthrough. He draws on Deleuze and Guattari (1994) to suggest that what is important is not a knowing "inspired by truth" which acts to promote sameness and marginalize difference, but rather how experiences of dissonance and imagination can productively be used to intervene in how we understand and respond to local situations and real lives. Similarly, media experiences of parody or irony (e.g., *The Yes Men, The Daily Show*) can also act in powerful ways to de-familiarize the familiar and elicit the conceptualization of other possible ways forward (Boler, 2008).

Media Creation

A second realm of use of media as potential pedagogical catalysts for socio-ecological learning is through engaging students themselves in forms of media creation. This type of intentional pedagogical engagement has become increasingly common in recent years, with a range of participatory and action-oriented uses of media evident in related literatures (e.g., Goldfarb, 2002; Lamont Hill & Vasudevan, 2007; Stack & Kelly, 2006). Allowing for the "nonrational, the bodily, and the erotic" (Buckingham, 2003, p. 317), experiences of media production also exists in the borderlands of being sensate and making sensate, both in terms of the emotional engagements of creativity as well as in those elicited through meaningful participation in a community. Excerpts from Gustavson's (2007a) study provide a vivid sense of this, such as these late night online chats between a 15-year-old zine-maker, Ian ('Rebelfunk'), and two of his friends:

Slpunk34: what's up
Rebelfunk: hey. I'm in the midst of finishing a zine.
Slpunk34: sorry for botherin u
Rebelfunk: no, it's cool. I can talk and assemble at the same time. I just meant like... like I'm sure you know, assembling a zine is a great feeling, it's like being on stage...I think it's better than being drunk.
...
Rebelfunk: i'm in that place, ya know? Like I might not sleep tonight and my hands are covered with glue and I'm actually happy or at least...I expect you understand this but maybe not
MarxNSparx: kind of, I assume your talking about zine makery?
Rebelfunk: it might be done by the morning...mebe not, I'll try and copy it tomorrow afternoon or Friday morning...
MarxNSparx: cool, do you still have notes [for permission to copy the zine at school]?
Rebelfunk: I don't have any notes, I'll either sneak in or ask [his history teacher] for a note...i don't know if I should work tonight, copy tomorrow afternoon, or sleep tonight so I'll be able to take math final, work tomorrow and copy Friday morning...I don't know if i can sleep when i'm trying to work...then I'm isolated
MarxNSparx: yeah, screw that whole zinester thing, it's not going anywhere, you should find a career in math
Rebelfunk: yes, math is real, emotions are arbitrary (pp. 2–3)

Absorbed in zine-making and the creation of spoken word poems as intersubjective meaning-making and political activity, Ian spends weeks compiling zines for distribution to his peers and organizes a poetry slam (a spoken word poetry contest) at his school. Gustavson (2007a) suggests that in order to make classrooms into youth spaces where students can engage in meaningful learning experiences such as those of Ian, teachers need to take an ethnographic orientation to determining what their students are passionate about and what sorts of "ownable dilemmas" students might be presented with. Presenting this approach to pedagogy as a variety of inquiry based learning, he proposes that it must allow for multiple forms and venues of performance or creation, for idiosyncratic ways of working, and for teachers to work alongside their students. These uses of media ideally involve students developing reflexivity through the production of media texts, and in the process furthering their understandings and practices of themselves and their cultural contexts.

In addition to the intersubjective experiences of students engaging with the personal, historical, political, cultural through their research and creative work, Gustavson (2007a) paints a clear picture of the means through which collaborative community is critical. A community of practice, broadly defined, is essential to enabling experimentation, reflection, interpretation, and evaluation in relation to one's individual or collective work, and to the associated development of individuated and shared cultural identities.

Buckingham (2003) highlights the ways in which play and parody often figure in youth-created media representations, and how youth challenges to dominant conventions and teacher-driven interpretations can create instructor dilemmas. As an opportunity to live out desires or speak the unspeakable, the defining and enacting of social identities can occur in the context of collaboratively created media such as the image *Indian Cowgirl Warrior* created by an ethnically diverse group of 7 and 8-year old girls (Cohen, 1998) or the mock magazine entitled *Slutmopolitan* created by 17-year old girls (Bragg, 2000). Facilitating these sorts of media engagements is more complicated than instructor-led critique of norms perpetuated through existing media, and can require a willingness to negotiate student transgressions of the conventions of schooling and society, as well as instructor comfort zones. The lines between the consumption and production of media and culture are indeed blurred as descriptions of these projects suggest, indicating the difficulties and yet value of collective back-and-forth exploration of the ground between the felt and the thought in relation to categories such as body, gender, class, race, and the ecological (Willis, 2003; Kenway & Bullen, 2008).

Media Spaces

In discussing a new form of cultural citizenship, Nadine Dolby (2003) suggests how youth are increasingly negotiating and engaging participation in public spheres through spaces outside of the formal structures of the political arena. Suggesting that it is not that youth are apolitical, but that the definition of political needs to shift, Dolby (2003), Gustavson (2007a), and others have traced the ways in which youth are increasingly using media as spaces of collective political engagement.

In particular, a range of new media capabilities supporting an "architecture of participation" suggest the possibilities of a shift in forms of democratic engagement and political resistance (e.g., Boler, 2008; Pickerill, 2006): for example, "social writing" or "open source" software that enables user-generated content and editing (e.g., wikis); content management tools that facilitate easily updatable online diaries (e.g., blogs); podcasting, vodcasting, and streaming video services (e.g., YouTube); social bookmarking and collective tagging capabilities for use in informally assigning and aggregating user-defined keywords or "tags" (e.g., del.icio.us); web-content distribution and syndication protocols used by news sites and blogs to share and aggregate content (e.g., RSS feeds and content "mashups"); social networking services which connect people with shared interests (e.g., Facebook); and online social microworlds (e.g., Second Life). Taking neither an anxiety or celebration approach to these developments in popular culture (McCarthy *et al.,* 2003), we rather see them as already playing an enormous role in the everyday lives of our students – their, and our, identities and communities are indeed being formed and reformed in everyday ways through these intersubjective media spaces. These technologies are by no means necessarily political or educative in scope (Livingstone, Bober, & Helsper, 2005), yet it is clear that in some cases they can act to support the development of political identity and collective mobilization (Garrett, 2006; Gordon & Koo, 2008).

As Brian Wilson (2006) indicates, examining the use of interactive web-based media spaces in relation to youth resistance and political action remains relatively undeveloped, particularly in relation to education. Many existing related studies on youth focus on the role of web-based spaces in the negotiation of identity (e.g., Mazzarella, 2005; Bryson *et al.,* 2006), and with increasing numbers beginning to explore the everyday uses of web-based media spaces and their influence on the political mobilization of youth. Initial studies suggest the importance of demographic factors of access, culture, place, class, and gender in who takes up technology use and in what ways (Loader, 2007; Kehily & Nayak, 2008). As the online chat excerpts from Gustavson's (2007a) study epitomize, youth "communities of practice" also commonly involve both offline and online components, though this is not always the case. Discussing the development of Riot Grrrls – a geographically dispersed feminist network which developed in U.S. underground music communities and spread to zine-making and online fora in the 1990s – Marion Leonard (1998) quotes:

> Girls are not girls, but grrrls, super kewl (cool) young women who have the tenacity and drive to surf the net, network with other young women on-line and expand the presence of young women in new and emerging technologies (Friendly Grrrls Guide to the Internet, Leonard, 1998, p. 111).

Exploring the web as operating as both private and public space – "I consider the WWW my political home" (p. 113) – Leonard offers one snapshot of the shifting spatial arrangements and possibilities of youth subcultures and communities (Massey, 1998). In a more recent and intentional pedagogical use of media spaces, Caitlin Cahill (2007) chronicles the participatory learning entailed in "a project for and by young womyn of colour," which used a web-based site as well as other media as part of reshaping their own and their local community's practices of stereotyping women of colour (http://www.fed-up-honeys.org/mainpage.htm).

EXAMPLES OF PRACTICE

In the following section, we provide specific examples of popular media that we have used in our own practices as educators in post-secondary and informal education settings. We selected these examples because we have found them pedagogically rich and because they suit our particular contexts well. The character and outcomes of intersubjective experiences are not easily predicted however (Ellsworth, 2005), and these examples should not be approached as recipes for teaching. We also want to restate that engagements with popular media as described below do not begin or end with individual students' responses, but usually entail collective sharing and co-creation of new understandings of oneself and the various communities and cultures to which one belongs. We have included a combination of examples of uses of media as artifacts and as means of creation.

Fiction and Non-Fiction

The creative representation of characters, worlds, and issues in fiction can offer readers a distance from reality and an emotional connection that can be difficult to find in traditional academic writing. Works of fiction can act as portals between diverse places, actors, past, future, and imagined scenarios and thus can provide sources for imagining "what if." For example, Ursula Le Guin's (1987) short story collection, *Buffalo gals and other animal presences*, is rich with the pedagogical possibilities of questions of "what if?" In the title story, for example, we read about the hybridized life of a human girl who comes to live for a while with Coyote and a range of other species. With two different eyes – one original and one given to her by her new companions - the girl who sometimes goes by Myra and sometimes by Gal, gains a different perception of the world. In reflecting on the story, Karla Armbruster (1998) writes,

> Ultimately, Le Guin's story provides us with a sense in which we can each act as conscious agents of political change. Through an openness to viewpoints and communities outside dominant human cultural experience, Myra... holds the potential for subverting dominant ideologies because her divisions and contradictions allow her to connect without oversimplifying her identity in ways that reinscribe those ideologies in new forms (p. 115).

Through this story, we can collectively explore and imagine our own various hybrid identities and how these affect our understandings of and relationships with our socio-ecological contexts. We have found that students love, hate, and feel angry and disturbed by Le Guin's work; it is simultaneously a means of connective and disruptive pedagogy.

Barbara Gowdy's (1998) novel, *The White Bone,* is an imagining of life from the perspective of a female African elephant. Thoroughly researched and well written, this book provides students with a fictional example of an attempt to give voice to another being. Encouraging readers to leave the comfort of the world as viewed through human eyes, *The White Bone* acts as fabulation by propelling readers into the *umwelt* (life-world) of an elephant. Our class discussions have ranged across such divergent themes as our implicatedness in the challenges facing elephants both in the wild and in zoos, empathy with other species, the roles of "heroes" in animal preservation, group leadership, intergenerational knowledge, and the potential of anti-homophobic, eco-centric learning materials. One trio of students responded to the book by creating and presenting a three-part visual representation of the plot, characters, language translations, and tensions in the novel. They then transposed their graphic representation onto a website for comment by the class and the author.

Figure 1. Drawing by students at York University

Adbusters Magazine: Journal of the Mental Environment (www.adbusters.org) examines intersections of media, technical and scientific change, consumer society, social justice, and environmental issues. The magazine's trenchant critique of capitalism through visual images and textual representations has, in our experience, been both shocking and refreshing to students. The magazine's exploration of current issues and advertising campaigns is often testimonial in function and creates a possible space for discussion of our implication in various social and ecological issues. In conjunction with students' experiences of reading this magazine we have discussed the impacts of consumerism on identity and desire, advertising's perpetuation of sexism, racism, classism, ableism, heterosexism, and anthropocentrism, and possible means of culture jamming as a form of cultural subversion and political action. As an example of culture jamming, Adbusters' "Buy Nothing Day" campaign is an opportunity to not only examine how we are all implicated in cycles of consumerism, but suggests a means of potentially counter hegemonic collective action.

Zines and Comics

Zines and comics have long been associated with countercultural movements. Given the form's usual juxtaposition of images and text, they regularly provide accounts that rub up against official consciousness. Gary Larson's illustrated comic book, *There's a Hair in My Dirt! A Worm's Story* (1998) is a hilariously twisted take on the differences between idealized views of nature and the reality of life for the birds, bees, worms, and humans. It points not only to human implicatedness in the lives of other creatures, but also to the importance of ensuring intersubjectivity does not stop at the human.

Typically low-budget home-spun publications that are often quite radical in their politics, zines originated in the punk scene and are often used by youth and other collectives as a forum for the discussion of ideas, issues, politics, and emotions through a pastiche of art, poetry, and prose. A provocative example of a zine that blends exploration of social and ecological justice was created by one of our students with a group of friends and fellow workers at the Michigan Womyn's Festival (see Figures 2 and 3) (Sarick, 2001; Russell, Sarick & Kennelly, 2002). Concerned about the treatment of transgendered people at the women-only event and about culturally limited constructions of female beauty as informed by fat theory, the group created a zine filled with provocative images and text that questioned and purposely destabilized what counted as "man," "woman," "nature" and "beautiful." The cultural production was not only useful for the individuals working on the zine in that particular intersubjective space, but also for those who purchased or read the zine at the next summer's Festival and engaged in further conversation about the issues raised.

Figures 2 and 3. Zines by students at York University

Photography and Visual Art

Roland Barthes (1980), writing in *Camera Lucida*, says the non-verbal effect of images is "not a question (a theme) but … a wound: I see, I feel, hence I observe, and I think" (p. 21). Alexander Wilson, writing in *The Culture of Nature*, says that most popular representations of nature are organized around the eye, an organ that is itself surrounded by ideologies encouraging a separation of the human individual from the natural world. (1991, p. 121)

Our multifaceted reactions as visual creatures make these forms of media particularly useful as intersubjective pedagogical catalysts. In the current western culture of consumption, images are ubiquitous in the selling of equivalencies (e.g., beer = sex). In contrast, artist Chris Jordan has used photography in disruptive ways in his 2006–2007 show, *Running the numbers: An American self-portrait* (www. chrisjordan.com). With large-scale photographic compilations, he examined issues of consumption based on recent statistics from the United States; for example, images portray various quantities such as 15,000,000 sheets of office paper (five minutes of paper use) or 106,000 aluminum cans (thirty seconds of can consumption), using thousands of smaller images compiled into one large cohesive image. Striking in their size, message, and implication, Jordan's art is a useful and creative classroom tool to demonstrate the dangerously obscene consumption practices in North America and elsewhere. Referring to the show, Jordan wrote that his "hope is that images representing these quantities might have a different effect than the raw numbers alone...My underlying desire is to emphasize the role of the individual in a society that is increasingly enormous, incomprehensible, and overwhelming."

The production of photography can also yield surprising pedagogical discoveries. For example, in a class on ideas about nature and society, Leigha Abergel took photographs of lines of hydro towers with a solitary dead tree stuck in the middle to explore affinities between skylines in urban nature and cyborgs (combinations of organisms, machines and lived social realities) (Haraway, 1991). Based on work begun in an environmental education class, Sinith Sittirak's (1998) autobiographical photo-story revealed her mother's abundant, sustainable living skills in their Thai context, including hand-made kitchen implements and tools, and a bowling game made from coconuts. In the process of interviewing her mother and producing the photo-story, Sinith confronted colonial meanings of "development" and recaptured a pride in her own family's sustainable lifestyle.

The production of other visual art forms can also be pedagogically generative. For over a decade, York University's Faculty of Environmental Studies students have collaborated with other students in the Faculties of Fine Arts, and Communications and Culture to design and implement a university–wide Eco-Art and Media Festival, focusing on student-generated themes such as globalization and food, placelessness and community politics, and embodiment and resistance. The festival is usually a week in length and includes art gallery showings, video installations, performance art, poetry readings, dance performances, and a final cabaret. The interlacing of the students' theoretical studies with performance arts is one of the most remarkable pedagogical strengths of the festival, and offers opportunities for students to engage more publicly in cultural critique and production through media engagement.

Figure 4. Image by Purwa Kuncora, student at York University

Film

Through the combination of the visual and the aural, films can offer an evocative entrée to potentially unfamiliar worlds or the experiences of other humans and the more-than-human. The clay animation (claymation) short, *Creature Comforts* is a "mockumentary" (director Nick Park, 1989) based on interviews with zoo animals about their living conditions, and can be found on *YouTube*. Using interview data from conversations with people living in seniors' homes, housing developments, and hotels, the animators gave voice to the data through their claymation creatures. The film provides a humorous yet often poignant glimpse into the everyday lives of zoo animals, and seniors, and generates good discussion about our role and implicatedness in creating these environments for others.

Documenting the striking stories of Argentinian *cartoneros* - people who make their living from gathering, sorting, and selling garbage - the film, *Cartoneros* (director Ernesto Livon-Grossman, 2007) problematizes the too-often valorized practice of recycling. Watching the film, students see a variety of irreconcilable relationships formed by the production, regulation, recycling, and dumping of garbage. The testimony of the *cartoneros* pushes us into uncomfortable emotional spaces as we realize our simultaneous implicatedness in the production of such vast quantities of "waste," and also the dependency of a large underground population of people who rely on this very waste for their income. Though this film focuses on a Latin American context, *cartoneros* are not limited to Central and South America.

The documentary *Grizzly Man* (director Werner Herzog, 2005) follows the life and death of Timothy Treadwell, an activist who believed he could speak for and protect a group of grizzly bears in Alaska. This film has evoked highly emotional and diverse responses in our students, provoking powerful debates about how, if at all, Treadwell contributed to grizzly conservation. We have used the film to initiate exploration of environmental etiquette, inter-species empathic encounters, harm through over-caring, animal tolerance of humans, animal rights, environmentalist identity, and what constitutes effective and ethical environmentalism. A range of other excellent films, many created by youth, can be found at www.mediathat mattersfest.org.

The Web

Figure 5. Teaching resources sharing site found through www.otherwise-ed.ca (McKenzie & Timmerman, 2008)

Offering access to a multitude of different forms of media, the world-wide-web provides many avenues for intersubjective experience. With the widespread use of blogs, wikis, discussion boards, the identity-bending playfulness of Avatars, and other interactive technologies, users of the web are given increasing access to creative control. Because there are so many different ways in which to create one's own media on the web, the potential to Do It Yourself (DIY) on the web is significant, as are opportunities for the creation of and participation in online communities. We encourage our students to question the degrees of experimentation stimulated by the web, and both the hegemonic constraints it establishes as well as the potential "cracks in consent" that it allows (marino, 1997). In addition to issues of privacy and consent, information on the web is also subject to concerns about accuracy and validity (Garrett, 2007). One web-based media space we have begun to experiment with in our own teaching is the use of a web-based forum for resource sharing and discussion (www.otherwise-ed.ca). With opportunities to add and comment on teaching resources under a range of social and ecological justice categories, the site investigates the potential of participatory venues for teaching and learning.

Cross-Genre

Critical ethnographies or other forms of student research involve the pedagogical use of mixed-media production, often in a peer group. Framed as investigations into teaching and learning as cultural practices, our teacher education students have researched topics such as the construction and use of school spaces, the congruence between the rhetoric and reality of "green" labeled schools, the impact of housing shortages on aboriginal students, the health and environmental issues associated with school cafeteria food, and a range of critical topics related to the socio-ecological. "Data collection" has involved interviewing students, teachers, and community members; soliciting information via wiki or email; filming communities and school spaces; and taking or gathering photographs of school spaces. Final ethnography products have included films, websites, visual art, constructed models, slideshows, and textual analyses. Talking to aboriginal student parents about housing issues or documenting problems with the accessibility of school spaces, processing the material gathered through the creation of a film or website, and sharing it with classmates in end of term presentations can be a powerful introduction to research and its potential for creative learning. For other examples of the engagement of various populations in research, visit the Participatory Action Research Collective website at www.web.gc.cuny.edu/che/start.htm.

INTERSUBJECTIVE LEARNING AND AGENCY

Understanding the individual or "subject" as functioning within the bounds of a formative history, sociality, and corporality, investigating possibilities for political responsibility and action then becomes a matter of asking 'How are we formed within social life, and at what cost?' (Butler, 2005, p. 136). Here we respond by suggesting that we and our students are formed and reformed in part through the influences of media and our engagements with them. Intersubjective experiences that elicit sensory responses and forms of consciousness and thus culture, media can be powerful locations of learning and cultural production, as well as modern forms of governance and surveillance (Kehily & Nayak, 2008). Drawing on understandings which take a "more distributed view of agency" in which the self is inseparable from the influences of the social and the spatial (Mannion, 2007), we remain necessarily optimistic about the collective socioecological learning experiences we seek to create with our students. Endeavoring to support or provoke "docta-spes" or an "educated hope" that contributes to more mature daydreams and actions (Bloch, 1986), these are pursuits that explore agency and productive cultural change, whether at the scale of the individual subject or in ensemble performances of the collective (Lovell, 2003).

They said, "You have a blue guitar,
You do not play things as they are."
The man replied, "Things as they are
Are changed upon the blue guitar."

(Stevens, 1937 in Greene, 1995, p. 19)

REFERENCES/BIBLIOGRAPHY

Appadurai, A. (1996). *Modernity at large: Cultural dimensions of globalization.* Minneapolis, MN: University of Minnesota Press.

Armbruster, K. (1998). "Buffalo gals, won't you come out tonight": A call for boundary-crossing in ecofeminist literary criticism. In G. Gaard & P. Murphy (Eds.), *Ecofeminist literary criticism: Theory, interpretation and pedagogy.* Chicago: University of Chicago Press.

Barthes, R. (1980). *Camera lucida: Reflections on photography.* New York: Hill and Wang.

Biesta, G. (1999). Radical intersubjectivity: Reflections on the "different" foundations of education. *Studies in Philosophy and Education, 18,* 203–220.

Bishop, K., Reid, A., Stables, A., Lencastre, M., Stoer, S., & Soetaert, R. (2000). Developing environmental awareness through literature and media education: Curriculum development in the context of teachers' practice. *Canadian Journal of Environmental Education, 5,* 268–285.

Bloch, E. (1986). *The principle of hope.* Cambridge, MA: MIT Press.

Boler, M. (2008). *Digital media and democracy: Tactics in hard times.* Cambridge, MA: MIT Press.

Boler, M. (1999). *Feeling power: Emotions and education.* New York: Routledge.

Bragg, S. (2000). *Media violence and education: A study of youth audiences and the horror genre.* Unpublished Doctoral Thesis, University of London, Institute of Education.

Bryson, M., MacIntosh, L., Jordan, S., & Lin, H. L. (2006). Virtually queer?: Homing devices, mobility, and un/belongings. *Canadian Journal of Communication, 31*(3), 791–815.

Buckingham, D. (2003, Fall). Media education and the end of the critical consumer. *Harvard Educational Review, 73*(3), 309–327.

Cahill, C. (2007). The personal is political: Developing new subjectivities in a participatory action research process. *Gender, Place, and Culture, 14*(3), 267–292.

Cohen, P. (1998). Tricks of the trade: On teaching arts and "race" in the classroom. In D. Buckingham (Ed.), *Teaching popular culture: Beyond racial pedagogy* (pp. 153–176). London: UCI Press.

Deleuze, G., & Guattari, F. (1987). *A thousand plateaus: Capitalism and schizophrenia* (B. Massumi, Trans.). Minneapolis, MN: University of Minnesota Press.

Dolby, N. (2003, Fall). Popular culture and democratic practice. *Harvard Educational Review, 73*(3), 258–284.

Ellsworth, E. (2005). *Places of learning: Media architecture pedagogy.* New York: Routledge.

Eppert, C. (2009). Remembering our (re)source: Eastern meditations on witnessing the integrity of water. In M. McKenzie, P. Hart, H. Bai, & B. Jickling (Eds.), *Fields of green: Restorying culture, environment, and education* (pp. 191–210). Cresskill, NJ: Hampton Press.

Fawcett, L. (2009). Feral sociality and (un)natural histories: On nomadic ethics and embodied learning. In M. McKenzie, P. Hart, H. Bai, & B. Jickling (Eds.), *Fields of green: Restorying culture, environment, and education* (pp. 227–236). Cresskill, NJ: Hampton Press.

Felman, S. (1992). Education and crisis, or the vicissitudes of teaching. In S. Felman & D. Laub (Eds.), *Testimony: Crises of witnessing in literature, psychoanalysis, and history* (pp. 1–56). New York: Routledge.

Garrett, R. K. (2006). Protest in an information society: A review of literature on social movements and new ICTs. *Information, Communication, and Society, 9*(2), 202–224.

Goldfarb, B. (2002). *Visual pedagogy: Media cultures in and beyond the classroom.* Durham, NC: Duke University Press.

Gordon, E., & Koo, G. (2008, August). Using virtual worlds to foster civic engagement. *Space and culture*, *11*(3), 204–221.

Gough, N. (2009). Becoming transnational: Rhizosemiosis, complicated conversation, and curriculum inquiry. In M. McKenzie, P. Hart, H. Bai, & B. Jickling (Eds.), *Fields of green: Restorying culture, environment, and education* (pp. 67–84). Cresskill, NJ: Hampton Press.

Gough, N. (1993). Neuromancing the stones: Experience, intertextuality, and cyperbunk science fiction. *Journal of Experiential Education, 16*(3), 9–17.

Gowdy, B. (1998). *The white bone*. Toronto: Harper Collins.

Greene, M. (1995). *Releasing the imagination: Essays on education, the arts, and social change*. San Francisco: Jossey-Bass.

Guvstavson, L. (2007a). *Youth learning on their own terms: Creative practices and classroom teaching*. London: Routledge.

Guvstavson, L. (2007b). Influencing pedagogy through the creative practices of youth. In M. Lamont Hill & L. Vasudevan (Eds.), *Media, learning, and sites of possibility* (pp. 81–114). New York: Peter Lang.

Hamilton, C., & Flanagan, C. (2007). Reframing social responsibility within a technology-based youth activist program. *American Behavioral Scientist, 51*(3), 444–464.

Haraway, D. (1991). *Simians, cyborgs and women: The reinvention of nature*. New York: Routledge.

Hey, V. (2002). Horizontal solidarities and molten capitalism: The subject, intersubjectivity, self and the other in late modernity. *Discourse: Studies in the Cultural Politics of Education, 23*(2), 227–241.

Kehily, M. J., & Nayak, A. (2008, September). Global feminities: Consumption, culture and the significance of place. *Discourse: Studies in the cultural politics of education, 29*(3), 325–342.

Kenway, J., & Bullen, E. (2008). The global corporate curriculum and the young cyberflâneur as global citizen. In N. Dolby & F. Rizvi (Eds.), *Youth moves: Identities and education in global perspective* (pp. 17–32). New York: Routledge.

Lamont Hill, M., & Vasudevan, L. (2007). *Media, learning, and sites of possibility*. New York: Peter Lang.

Larson, G. (1998). *There's a hair in my dirt! A worm's story*. New York: Harper Perennial.

Le Guin, U. (1987). *Buffalo gals and other animal presences*.

Leonard, M. (1998). Paper planes: Traveling the new grrl geographies. In T. Skelton & G. Valentine (Eds.), *Cool places: Geographies of youth cultures* (pp. 101–118). London: Routledge.

Livingstone, S., Bober, M., & Helsper, E. J. (2005). Active participation or just more information?: Young people's take-up of opportunities to act and interact on the Internet. *Information, Communication & Society, 8*(3), 287–314.

Loader, B. (2007). *Young citizens in the digital age: Political engagement, young people and new media*. London: Routledge.

Lovell, T. (2003). Resisting with authority: Historical specificity, agency and the performative self. *Theory, Culture & Society, 20*(1), 1–17.

Mannion, G. (2007, September). Going spatial, going relational: Why "listening to children" and children's participation needs reframing. *Discourse: Studies in the cultural politics of education, 28*(3), 405–420.

marino, D. (1997). *Wild garden: Art, education and the culture of resistance*. Toronto: Between the Lines.

Massey, D. (1998). The spatial construction of youth cultures. In T. Skelton & G. Valentine (Eds.), *Cool places: Geographies of youth cultures* (pp. 121–129).

Mazzarella, S. R. (2005). *Girl wide web: Girls, the internet, and the negotiation of identity*. New York: Peter Lang.

McCarthy, C., Giardina, M. D., Harewood, S. J., & Park, J. (2003, Fall). Contesting culture: Identity and curriculum dilemmas in the age of gobalization, postcolonialism, and multiplicity. *Harvard Educational Review, 73*(3), 449–465.

McKenzie, M. (2009). Pedagogical transgressions. In M. McKenzie, P. Hart, H. Bai, & B. Jickling (Eds.), *Fields of green: Restorying culture, environment, and education* (pp. 211–224). Cresskill, NJ: Hampton Press.

McKenzie, M. (2008). The places of pedagogy: Or, what we can do with culture through intersubjective experience. *Environmental Education Research, 14*(3), 365–377.

McKenzie, M., & Timmerman, N. (2008). The relationality of web-based hypermedia research: A working example in teacher education. In S. Springgay, R. Irwin, C. Leggo, & P. Gouzouasis (Eds.), *Being with Art/o/graphy* (pp. 124–140). Roderdam: Sense Publishers.

Mitchell, C., & Weber, S. (1999). Reel to reel: Popular culture and teacher identity. In C. Mitchell & S. Weber (Eds.), *Reinventing ourselves as teachers: Beyond nostalgia* (pp. 164–188).

Ntonio, A., Astin, H., & Cress, C. (2000). Community service in higher education: A look at the nation's faculty. *Review of Higher Education, 23*(4), 373–398.

Payne, P. (2003). The technics of environmental education. *Environmental Education Research, 9*(4), 525–541.

Pickerill, J. (2006). Radical politics on the net. *Parlimentary Affairs, 59*(2), 266–282.

Pitt, A., & Britzman, D. (2003). Speculations on qualities of difficult knowledge in teaching and learning: An experiment with psychoanalytic research. *Qualitative studies in education, 16*(6), 755–776.

Pollan, M. (2007). *The omnivore's dilemma: A natural history of four meals.* Toronto: Penguin.

Russell, C. L., Sarick, T., & Kennelly, J. (2002). Queering environmental education. *Canadian Journal of Environmental Education, 7*(1), 54–67.

Sarick, T. (2001). *This zine is 100% naturally queer.* Unpublished Major Project, Faculty of Environmental Studies, York University, Toronto, Canada.

Sittirak, S. (1998). *The daughters of development: Women in a changing environment.* London: Zed Books.

Stack, M., & Kelly, D. M. (2006). Introduction to special issue: The popular media, education, and resistance. *Canadian Journal of Education, 29*(1), 1–4.

Weaver, J. A., & Grindall, K. (1998). Surfing and getting wired in a fifth grad classroom: Critical pedagogical methods and techno-culture. In J. L. Kincheloe & S. R. Steinberg (Eds.), *Unauthorized methods: Strategies for critical teaching.* London: Routledge.

Weis, L., & Fine, M. (2003). Extraordinary conversations in public schools. In G. Dimitriadis & D. Carlson (Eds.), *Promises to keep: Cultural studies, democratic education, and public life* (pp. 95–123). New York: RoutledgeFalmer.

Williams, R. (1977). *Marxism and literature.* Oxford: Oxford University Press.

Willis, P. (2003, Fall). Foots soldiers of modernity: The dialectics of cultural consumption and the 21st-century school. *Harvard Educational Review, 73*(3), 390–415.

Wilson, A. (1991). *The culture of nature: North American landscape from Disney to the Exxon Valdez.* Toronto: Between the Lines.

Wilson, B. (2006). Ethnography, the internet, and youth culture: Strategies for examining social resistance and "online-offline" relationships. *Canadian Journal of Education, 29*(1), 307–328.

Zembylas, M. (2002). "Structures of feeling" in curriculum and teaching: Theorizing the emotional rules. *Educational Theory, 52*(2), 187–208.

AFFILIATIONS

Marcia McKenzie,
College of Education,
University of Saskatchewan,
Canada

Constance Russell,
Faculty of Education,
Lakehead University,
Canada

Leesa Fawcett,
Faculty of Environmental Studies,
York University,
Canada

Nora Timmerman,
Faculty of Education,
University of British Columbia,
Canada

LEARNING RESEARCH AND RESEARCH AS LEARNING

JUTTA NIKEL, KELLY TEAMEY, SE-YOUNG HWANG,
BENJAMIN ALBERTO POZOS-HERNANDEZ, WITH ALAN REID
AND PAUL HART

10. UNDERSTANDING OTHERS, UNDERSTANDING OURSELVES: ENGAGING IN CONSTRUCTIVE DIALOGUE ABOUT PROCESS IN DOCTORAL STUDY IN (ENVIRONMENTAL) EDUCATION

OVERVIEW

Discussions of whether the importance of doctoral studies lies principally with the produced *outcomes* as in the doctoral thesis or journal publications, or with the *process*, as in academic progression and professional growth, are familiar to debates and research in higher education more generally, but are rare in the field of environmental education. In this chapter, we aim to stimulate debate about the processes and effects of undertaking a doctoral study and being a doctoral student in this field. The chapter is based on a collaborative thinking and writing process, rooted in a common interest to promote critical and reflexive dialogues amongst doctoral students and their supervisors about understandings and experiences of carrying out doctoral work. Key to our exploration is the importance and opportunity of engaging in a constructive interpretive dialogue *about* process whilst focusing simultaneously on various personal and academic experiences at different stages *during* those selfsame processes.

We start by introducing the debate on academic context and research in doctoral studies in higher education using extracts from the literature [Box 1]. We then offer three heuristics to generate reflections on the multitude and diversity of doctoral research experiences, including our own, within and across personal, institutional, cultural, academic and discursive contexts and boundaries. The heuristics have been developed and revised in the course of reading literature, as well as from reflecting on the commonalities and diversity of themes within our own stories and discussions. We then each share aspects of our stories to illustrate the importance of interrogating/problematising the doctoral process, illuminating and fleshing out complexities of identity, agency, power relations and career progression associated with doctoral research. As members of this particular research community, we recognise that our ongoing engagement with the current discourses and practices of the field of environmental education research and converging fields related to environmental education (for example,

R. Stevenson and J. Dillon (eds.), Engaging Environmental Education: Learning, Culture and Agency, 167–197.

education for sustainable development) have been shaped and continue to be informed by variously mundane, transformative, and often painful learning experiences and encounters associated with our doctoral studies. While the chapter title suggests 'understanding others' and 'understanding ourselves' as important constituents to supervisory discussions and interactions, both are understood as important processes servicing additionally wider goals: those of academic progression, professional growth, progress in the field, and balancing process and product within shared deliberations on these aspects of doctoral studies.

INTRODUCTION

Research studies into higher education have traditionally enquired into the nature of doctorates[1], focusing on desired outcomes and its fundamental pedagogies (i.e., independent, self-directed study and supervision), the nature and provenance of research questions, and student selection (Hockey, 1991; Neumann, 2007). Hockey (1991), in reviewing research outcomes in relation to understandings of the process of social science doctoral studies, identifies tensions in the positions that frame such studies. On the one hand, questions of scholarship emphasise the high intellectual entry abilities of students and the originality of the outcomes alongside the expected contributions to knowledge in a research area. On the other, there is recognition of the incompleteness of understanding and abilities of students in process (and in graduating), and the provision of research training and continuing professional development as complementary, necessary phases. Hockey (1991, p. 320) uses the metaphor of a doctoral student as a "gentleman scholar" to describe the first position (see also Text 1.1 in Box 1 for an example), and that of an "apprentice" to capture the nature of the other (see Text 1.2 and Text 1.3 as examples).

While different theoretically and empirically-based perceptions on the doctoral process can still be recognised in student handbooks, quality assurance documents, supervisory communication or informal talk, in recent years interpretative, feminist, critical and post-structural approaches, as well as others informed by epistemological considerations[2], have both shaped and re-directed interests in understanding and interrogating doctoral processes. Despite their different foundations and goals, such perspectives share a desire to problematise the "status of autonomy or independence as the goal of postgraduate pedagogy" (Johnson et al., 2000, p. 145). This problematising takes place, for example, with a view to the context of the development of mass higher education with respect to issues of gender, ethnicity and race (see Box 1, Text 1.4), and have often served to highlight questions about perceptions and practices related to self-worth, self-efficacy and self esteem with which students enter their studies, be that in relation to the perspectives or lifeworlds of students, supervisors, or other stakeholders, including host communities, family, industry or academia.

Current debates on the nature and objectives of doctoral studies also seek to address the context of the observed and presumed transformations within knowledge-based economies in relation to knowledge production. The process of producing knowledge is increasingly prioritised as being that which is "produced in collaboration" with and by other agencies rather than solely in or through the academy. This emphasis on collaboration foregrounds requirements of high levels of interdisciplinarity and transdisciplinarity on behalf of the researcher and the institution (Gee *et al.,* 1996; Johnson *et al.,* 2000, p. 145; Enders & de Weert, 2004), see Text 1.5, Text 1.6 and Text 1.7).

Box 1: Extracts from the literature

Text 1.1
"Remaining substantially unaltered since the introduction of the degree in Australia after the Second World War, and deriving in large part from the practices developed in England in the 40 years prior to that (Simpson, 1983), the supervision relationship is personalised and frequently protracted. Through the pedagogical technologies of 'supervision' and of 'study', an intelligible academic identity is produced, a licensed scholar, a 'doctor', who, appropriately credentialed, is deemed safe to pursue research unsupervised, autonomously." (Johnson *et al.,* 2000, p. 136)

Text 1.2
"The PhD thesis is a 'masterpiece' of academic work. In saying that, however, it is useful to recall the original sense of 'masterpiece'. That is, a piece of work that confirmed the status of the 'master' craft worker, and the transition from apprenticehood. Too often, the notion of the 'masterpiece' dominates doctoral work in its more romantic sense – the great *chef d'oeuvre.* Many graduate students need to be disabused of the latter notion, and have their sights set on the more realistic and more appropriate kind of aspiration. ... They need to keep before them the appreciation that [the] thesis itself is not the be-all and end-all of the research enterprise, nor of the graduate student's career. The thesis itself is just one of a number of outcomes of the research work. ... If student and supervisor become obsessively focused on making the thesis alone the ultimate goal, then they can both all too easily lose sight of the more general issues of academic progress and achievement." (Delamont, Atkinson & Parry, 2004, p. 110)

Text 1.3
"This study looks at the relationship between these students and supervisors as legitimate peripheral participation. The main feature of this are that novice members are given enough credibility to be considered as 'legitimate' members of their target communities and are given 'less demanding' practices to perform to learn the craft of their 'masters'. It is argued that this concept is a productive tool to understand the nature of learning at the PhD level, it is realized differently in various fields of study." (Hasrati, 2005, p. 557)

Box 1 (Continued)

Text 1.4

"..., the 'traditional' (no matter how recent) personalised and privatised practices of the PhD supervision pedagogy are deeply problematic in the context of the development of a mass higher education system where PhD candidature has become much more frequent. For Yeatman (1998, p. 23) it is simply inadequate to the demands of a situation where many supervisees are barely socialised into the demands and rigours of an academic scholarly and research culture. It is especially inadequate to the needs of many new PhD aspirants who, by historical-cultural positioning, have not been invited to imagine themselves as subjects of genius. These include all those who are marginalised by the dominant academic scholarly culture: women, and men or women who come from the non-dominant class, ethnic or race positions. When PhD candidature was infrequent, the rare one of these could distinguish themselves as an exception to the rule of their particular gender, ethnic or class category, and show that by their highly exceptional qualities, they deserved to be admitted as a disciple." (Johnson *et al.*, 2000, p. 137)

Text 1.5

"[...] New pathways and more hybrid forms are emerging that result in a variety of roles and relationships. Some question whether the conventional PhD thesis is still the only or best way to generate the research needed for the knowledge economy or to train researchers. Others are more reserved and adopt a more pluralistic view, including alternative forms of doctoral education. In such a view the all-embracing life's work of, say, a historian or mathematician could well exist alongside a doctorate obtained in a postmodern training-career trajectory." (Enders & De Weert, 2004, pp. 132–133)

Text 1.6

"... PhD students should be trained and prepared to enter not only the endogenous academic market but also a wider variety of careers. In order to achieve this, students should circulate between different organizations inside and outside academia during or after their PhD, [...] where doctoral students can wend their ways through the types of locations, just as it is to be expected in their later career. This opens new directions for career management away from academic tenure, which as the authors argue is not the only possible option for young academics. This is a challenging view since doctoral students are conceived as the vehicles for the production and dissemination of knowledge. By stressing this function of doctoral education, it seems that the mere training component of doctoral education with a view to producing an independent researcher remains in the background." (Enders & De Weer, 2004, p. 132; in Dany & Mangematin, 2004)

Text 1.7

"Peet (2002) expands on the educative aspect of hegemonic relations through the establishment of an AIM (Academic-Institutional-Media) complex theory to relate power that development discourses exercise within discursive practices. According to the AIM complex (Peet, 2002), discourses are better able to become hegemonic by originating in theories elaborated by academics, often in elite institutions, usually leading universities with vast endowment funds (i.e., Harvard, Yale, Oxford, Cambridge, etc.). These theories are often sought by leading 'knowledge-based' institutions (think-tanks, research corporations) that most often lean in the conservative direction. Movement of personnel and ideas between these knowledge-based institutions, businesses and academic institutions are eventually integrated into government thinking and policy-making, particularly if they fit within the government administration's economic and political agendas. Eventually these theories are translated into languages that can be digested by the informational media – respected newspapers (national and international), popular magazines and news commentary shows on TV and radio." (Teamey, 2007: 30)

In light of the kinds of statements represented in Box 1, it is unsurprising that recent studies and scholarship are questioning the overemphasis on the perceived high level of independence doctoral students have when entering doctoral studies, as well as the goal of becoming an independent autonomous scholar in academe.[3] As we explore below, questions about the role and dynamics of the complexities of identity, agency and power relations are variously implicit and implicated in the doctoral research process, and there are no clear-cut or normative responses to the challenges they bring, to the student and their supervisor(s).

More broadly, in this chapter we aim to open up these debates about the nature and objectives of doctoral studies in relation to the field of environmental education by focusing our attention on the *process* of doctoral studies. We understand the doctoral process as a unique one; not primarily in terms of a high level of independence but as a largely individual project experienced as a 'plunging into the depths' of methodological, epistemological and ontological issues like no other study or later professional experience. Given its standing as a comparably unique 'rite of passage', we also regard the doctoral study as an opportunity and space that invites the doctoral candidate to decide how (best) it might be capitalised upon. For example, a view emphasising the process undertaken during the journey of creating the outcome invites questions of the kind: (i) which different styles and types of learning are engaged and legitimised; (ii) can we unmask additional learning as in 'making visible the invisible' in the traditional ways of narrating and presenting process and outcomes of doctoral studies, at conferences and in journal publications; (iii) (how) do we engage the 'unexpected' or 'unplanned' in the 'doing' of a PhD; (iv) do we address tensions of following and sustaining a passion whilst still conforming to the stringent expectations of the doctoral study degree; and overall, (v) are the holistic aspects of doing a doctoral study mirrored in our stories and accounts, and thereby is space and critical attention given to the experiential aspects of those involved in the study?

In order to address such questions, we argue for *engaging in a constructive interpretive and critical dialogue* that pushes the boundaries for what it means to participate and engage in a doctoral study within the field of environmental education. We understand such a dialogue as a useful tool for bringing about a re-focusing of attention about doctoral studies' outcomes (i.e., the thesis) toward the process undertaken during the journey of creating the outcome. [4]

However, while we argue for considering the implications of doctoral studies for the academic progress and achievement of the doctoral students themselves, we must also consider the *advancement of a research field and the research community* that the student relates to and their ensuing interactions. For example, such a view invites us to consider how we: (i) account for where topics and motivation come from for a doctoral project and how this is shaped by participating in a local research community, and possibly other communities, during the doctoral time-frame; (ii) examine the 'openness' of research and researchers: conceptually, culturally, emotionally, spiritually, psychologically and strategically (i.e., decisions to participate in different events, conferences, related work projects, etc.); (iii) generate a deeper understanding of the current realities of how the field is evolving; and (iv) explore a focus on the individual as contributing to the future of a field, how it is envisioned, and one's later role (e.g., as a 'manager' within or 'leader' of a research field), in contrast to expecting scenarios that promote the thesis as the primary outcome or view the doctorate as largely a matter of being a part of a wider research programme (cf. Reid & Nikel, 2003).

In particular, the last point raises questions about one's perceptions and the realities of career opportunities and structure before, during and after the doctorate, as well as in relation to oneself, the thesis and the community. It invites a looking forward and around and not always backward; or even imagining the doctoral study as a spiraling, reflexive and unpredictable path rather than the 'linear' trajectory suggested by a chronological view.

As we have found (and show below), such challenges also suggest we collectively reflect on how we go about (and what constitutes) nurturing a vision of what one might do in the future, where the field might take the doctoral candidate, and where the student and others might take the field, as well as how we experience or address how other fields might intersect or collide during or after the doctorate. For example, given the issue of overlapping fields, part of the doctoral process lies in recognising the boundaries and relations of one's field and tackling the multiple layers and complexities of a particular field as one progresses in one's understanding about the topic and the nature of research. In terms of environmental education and education for sustainable development (ESD), boundary recognition and conceptual progress is especially challenging owing to the disparate and porous nature of the fields and their boundaries. As doctoral students, we had a strong sense of a lack of familiarity and certainty regarding the existence of a 'canon' or 'corpus' of environmental education research, which we see inflected in the tensions surrounding any attempt to come up with collective conceptual agreements of what environmental education and ESD are and where their boundaries lie. The challenges are particularly brought to a head when students have to negotiate living with and after postmodernism and deconstruction in a globalised research field, particularly when the higher education institution, academic milieu and host national culture are not familiar to or congruent with one's lived experience and expectations.

A further challenge relates to the fact that much of the research occurring within environmental education and ESD is deliberately positioned as aiming to critique and challenge norms and the status quo (as exemplified by Robottom & Hart, 1993). Therefore there is a wide range of conceptual and critical knowledge needed not only within the fields of environmental education and ESD that are in themselves ambiguous, but in other overlapping fields (e.g., related to sociology, political theory, environmental science, educational theory and development studies). Indeed, Gonzalez-Gaudiano (2005, p. 245), in discussing the role and nature of ESD, notes: "it is very important to notice that in this signifying system known as ESD, what we see as a component that might interconnect diverse elements is the fact that they are fields of social intervention which have generated different ways of disagreeing with the status quo...". In both fields, critiquing the process of doing a doctoral study rather than being over-focused on outcome, can help challenge the status quo of discourses about doctoral studies.

INITIATING CONSTRUCTIVE DIALOGUE

The initial idea for our collaboration arose from a shared enthusiasm in our informal networks to present and discuss our doctoral studies at an Ecological and Environmental Education Special Interest Group symposium at the Annual Meeting of the American Educational Research Association (AERA) in April 2006. We felt inclined to pursue a position that emphasised the process and experiences rather than report on research designs and provisional findings.

We already knew each other and the topics we were researching, and we had all enrolled in a PhD programme in Education, which in the UK is primarily empirical rather than taught in nature. For PhD students it is common that there are no compulsory research training elements required, but optional units on master's programmes or within generic skills training programmes are offered. The recommended supervisory time for full-time students is around two hours per month and for part-time students around two hours every two months. Recently, some PhD students have been assigned to more than one supervisor (the more traditional scenario). For a full-time student, the PhD is expected to be completed in three to four years with the submission of a thesis and an oral examination. The oral examination (*Viva Voce*) usually takes the shape of a one-and-a-half hour to three hours non-public examination with an external examiner and an internal one (to the academic department within which the student is enrolled). The supervisor can be present, but does not take an active role.

However, whilst we shared similarities in researching (or having just finished researching) for a higher degree in a UK university, our countries of origin or our study's focus were not those of the UK. In addition, we were not at the same stages in our doctoral studies at the time of preparing the symposium (2006) or writing this chapter (2007–8); Se-young Hwang (Korea) was at the initial stages of her doctoral study, Kelly Teamey (USA) and Benjamin Alberto Pozos-Hernandez (Mexico) were close to examination, and Jutta Nikel (Germany) had recently graduated. A summary of our doctoral research studies can be found in the appendix to the chapter.

In preparation for the AERA 2006 Symposium, we arranged a day's meeting in Bath with the aim of discussing each other's processes and developing ideas about how to 'present' it to an audience in an interactive symposium. Prior to the meeting Alan Reid circulated a variety of articles (Hockey, 1994; Linden, 1999; Caffarella & Barnett, 2000; Johnson *et al.,* 2000; Winter *et al.,* 2000; Pearson & Brew, 2002; Read *et al.,* 2003; McCormack, 2004; Ridley, 2004; Lovitts, 2005, amongst others) on studies investigating doctoral processes in and during higher education. Along with Alan, we discussed the studies in relation to their relevance to our own experiences. In so doing, we became engaged and immersed in each other's stories about the up and downs, milestones, and turning points we had experienced to date in our doctoral journeys in the field of environmental education and ESD. During our participation at the AERA 2006 Symposium each of our presentations discussed our particular doctoral project alongside experiences and reflections on the process. Alan Reid (who was the lead supervisor of Jutta Nikel and Se-young Hwang) and Paul Hart (who, while being based at the University of Regina in Canada, is also a visiting professor at the University of Bath), acted as discussants, and reflected on the presentations as well as their experiences and views as members of the research community, with its diverse interests in and understandings of undertaking and supervising environmental education research.

While dialogue was clearly happening at these early stages, we regard that time now as more about monologuing or conversation rather than constructive and critical dialogue. At first, the ambiguity in the quality of our dialogue through the process of collaboration did not appear important as we were not working with a shared definition or understanding of 'constructive or critical dialogue' in mind. However, it became clearer after AERA that a shared understanding was needed as part of that process, particularly as we sought to engage with elements in which personal experiences are directly related to more abstract accounts of research, community, identity, power relations and ongoing processes of transformation or induction. As a result, we reflected over the course of 2006 and 2007 upon the representation of these aspects in our aural accounts, in the three heuristics we had developed, and in our written stories. The heuristics and our stories were shared with other audiences, and then revised, re-told and rewritten to track the evolution of our own individual and group thinking and experiences.

In this process, we individually and collectively strived to reveal our senses of agency and identity as 'labourers, dwellers and travellers', living through the tensions between the boundaries of the academic 'field' and 'community', as well as the struggles and joys experienced as personal life itself became more situated within a foreign or international culture. However, our involvement and commitment was without doubt also influenced by our own personal and political agendas to become and remain involved in this collaborative thinking and writing. For Benjamin, for example, what stood out was the opportunity for learning about academic writing and styles within this group in his writing up phase, and networking with researchers at the University of Bath (and primarily, at the Centre for Research in Education and the Environment) as a leading group in the field, where he experienced an openness to a variety of methods and approaches and a critical stance he had not experienced beforehand. Se-young, at the beginning of her doctoral study, experienced a peer-driven phase of exploring different perspectives on her research topic and their influence on the investigation object and research questions. For her, reflecting on her experience as a doctoral student early on provided another perspective to that being developed with her supervisors (meta-perspective). The collaborative element literally forced Se-young to write her story, and in so doing, helped her pin down her thoughts and opened up ideas to include this as elements of the writing in her thesis. Jutta, who had recently graduated, was keen to innovate and challenge conventional ways of talking and presenting about doctoral studies (with reference to the AERA 2006 presentations) in the field of environmental education, as well as to network with doctoral students in other UK universities. For Kelly, a key motivational element was to address the lack of a 'culture of sharing' she had experienced in her institution during the process of the PhD and in the wider field. 'Sharing one's journey' could contribute to deeper understandings of the current realities of how the field is developing and offer ways to push boundaries of what people presume about doing a PhD, including for some of us, beginning to address our sense of how we 'work the hyphens' of the activist-researcher-scholar identity complex.

In the next section, we introduce the three heuristics which helped us to engage with each other's stories and which we have used to write about our experiences. It is important to note that the four stories are offered as examples for the reader to illustrate the scope and range of the thinking the dialogue and reflections generated, rather than that they be regarded as final or end products of this collaboration.

THE HEURISTICS

In the course of doing a doctoral study, customary questions we each have to engage include: *Where do your conceptualisations, problems and questions about and for research in education come from? Why might anyone be interested in your research? What sort of question is your question? What would be a different sort of question? What is necessary and sufficient to answer your research question(s)/ solve your research problem(s)? How do you know this?*

In contrast, the following three heuristics are considered as useful tools to shed light on other, less talked about aspects of the process of a doctoral study.

The first heuristic (Figure 1) titled *'context'*, highlights important aspects of being a research student in the social sciences.[5] Drawing on the categories found in (Deem and Brehony 2000, p. 150) (shaded circles in Figure 1), the heuristic extends the list with categories derived from our own experiences and discussions (non-shaded circles). We added: transition identity and one's background; the added

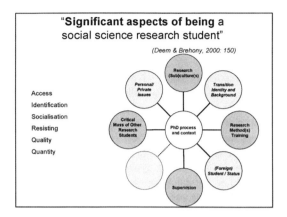

Figure 1. Aspects of being a social science research student

challenges of being a foreign student in contrast to those arising from being a domestic; and personal and private issues that happen along the way. Issues of access and equal access addressed by Deem and Brehony (2000) are broached through considerations along the lines of those processes taking place, such as identification, socialisation, resisting, quality and quantity.

In addition, there is an empty circle to emphasise that the aforementioned are likely to be influential factors but are not all encompassing. One might consider adding 'funding' or 'natural ability' or 'talent' as further significant aspects, depending on one's context or viewpoint. The following questions might be of use for exploring Figure 1: *How influential do you consider these aspects as being or having been significant to being a research student? How influential do you perceive these to the research students you have supervised or advised? In what ways have you considered their totality and interaction as being significant for you? How would you fill the empty circle?*

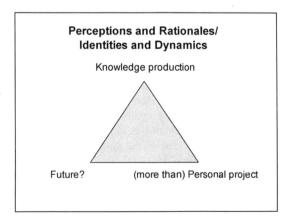

Figure 2. Perceptions and Rationales / Identities and Dynamics.

The <u>second heuristic</u> (Figure 2) focuses on *'perceptions and rationales, identities and dynamics'*. This heuristic develops an understanding of doing research at the doctoral level as an intentional project: i.e., working towards a goal or an objective. Three common responses are arranged as corners of a triangle: 'I am producing new (explanatory) knowledge'; 'It is a personal challenge'; and 'It is important to achieve for what I want to do afterwards' (e.g., to have access to a certain position or to be(come) part of a scholarly community).

A slightly different way of looking at this heuristic is by starting with the questions: *What do you see yourself doing? What other commitments are you 'caught up in'? What are the circumstances influencing these commitments?* And, *What are the reasons or drives for your commitment in the research?* Of course, the heuristic is not meant to be static but should be considered dynamically, taking account of both intentional and coincidental events (such as in recognition of random encounters and moments in the field, but also at different stages of the doctoral study). Alternatively, one can explore this heuristic by focusing on external as well as internal perspectives. For example, *How is what you are doing in a doctoral study perceived within the institution and organisation you work within?* Or, *What are your supervisor's perceptions for you being a doctoral student and doing a doctoral study and herself/himself being a supervisor in this process?* Or, leading to questions of location and dynamics: *Where would you locate yourself? Has it changed? What has changed it? Have you made the most of all three possibilities? Who or what else do you want to represent with your work?*

The <u>third heuristic</u> (Figure 3), is headed by a contested statement: *'Doctoral study is the primary road into the scholarly community'*. Immediately one can question whether it is a pre-determined and maintained 'road' or more that of trail-blazing or a flexible 'route' in the direction? Moreover, whether it is and really should be *the* primary road?

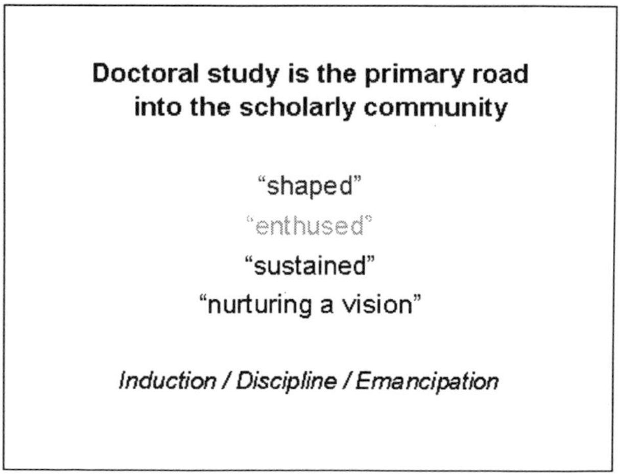

**Doctoral study is the primary road
into the scholarly community**

"shaped"

"enthused"

"sustained"

"nurturing a vision"

Induction / Discipline / Emancipation

Figure 3. Doctoral study is the primary road into the scholarly community.

Leaving these questions aside for the moment, the heuristic helped us shed light on the processes associated with being a doctoral researcher and doing doctoral research that can define or make us understand and/or realise how we relate to a wider scholarly community or a 'field' during the research study, but more importantly, afterwards. In relation to being 'shaped', 'enthused', 'sustained' and 'nurturing a vision', many interpretations are possible. A few that we found useful for discussion were: being shaped as being challenged; being enthused in terms of to 'stay' in or 'leave' academia; be(com)ing sustained by being a part of (and apart from) a scholarly community; nurturing one's vision of what I want in the future; and, where the field might take me but also where I might want to take the field. Thus, we ask(ed): *How have you experienced these processes? How were they played out and in what contexts? What opportunities were there to initiate conversations and actions related to these processes? How do you see their individual importance in a doctoral study in general and in your case?*

In all this, we do recognise that how doctoral study processes are initiated and transpire varies, as nuances of induction, discipline or emancipation play out differently in diverse institutional, organisational, personal and situative contexts. Consequently, understandings of identity, agency and power are experienced and communicated very differently, as we show below.

DOCTORAL STUDENTS' STORIES OF LIVED EXPERIENCES

The stories that follow in the next section were crafted and re-written several times, thus tensions between our lived experiences and choices to write particular stories had to be acknowledged, shared, and discussed through the reading and writing of each other's stories and reflecting upon different aspects of the heuristics presented above. The struggles we faced here largely reflected two aspects to our 'hesitations': on the one hand, a shared sense of uncertainty about what one presumes to be worth telling and the points one wants to make, and on the other, the experience of and a preference for remaining tentative about what meanings this may evoke in others and after their interpretations. Writing in such ways has meant critically re-engaging with memory work throughout which meanings have been negotiated and (re)constructed, alone and in dialogue.

Se-young's Story - Telling My Story as Part of Research Process

I came to the UK to undertake a PhD in 2004. Three years on, I am at the stage of intensive writing up of a doctoral thesis. What shall I tell about my experiences as a doctoral student? The complexity of the processes seems overwhelming. There are still indescribable qualities of experience that hinder my own effort to make sense of it; however, I believe telling about what I now know is still worthwhile. Central to this struggle is a growing awareness of the tensions among my multiple identities (be that as a person or as doctoral student) that have shaped my journey during the doctoral study. I chose to study at the University of Bath with an expectation that my academic professionalism could be nurtured well among a supportive research community, through cultural and academic learning experiences of the 'environmental education field'. Understanding why people come to be engaged with environmental education was an initial central question I sought answers to through my doctoral study. The decision to inquire into the phenomena of school environmental education in Korea through teachers' stories of their own experiences was practical and straightforward, considering my cultural background and orientation to qualitative research. My first year at Bath was devoted to deepening understandings related to research on teachers' thinking and practice, different perspectives on qualitative inquiry, and the broad field of environmental discourse. I recall this period as coloured by feelings of 'getting lost', both in striving to find my own space and position as a 'foreigner' in new living conditions and in academic culture. Like other international students, a lack of confidence in English was also one of my key concerns, and it was painful to find hard attempts ending in vain. The question of "Why am I here?" was thus pursued in both an existential and a scholastic sense. In fact, they were so intertwined that I began to realise that my cultural identity shaped the ways and contexts of my research project, and vice versa, throughout the research process.

My fieldwork experience in Korea the following year offered me an unexpected opportunity to take a fresh look at my research project through conversation with teachers and colleagues. When we spoke about the research topic and design, I was often asked concerning, "Why are you researching about Korea while studying in the UK?" In reply to my request for advice on my research project, one Korean professor made a similar point. It seemed to me that there was a taken-for-granted assumption in Korean higher education that an overseas degree meant gaining 'newer' or 'advanced' ideas and knowledge, and making these applicable to a Korean context. This well represents a deeply ingrained expectation of the role of academics in our culture. Thus, in rethinking the question of 'why' I was engaged in doing research as being more than something emerging out of my personal motivation, I began to reflect on prevailing cultural narratives. Indeed, by and large, Koreans tend to ascribe the rapid economic and social progress to an attitude of '"keeping up with' the global, Western standard" and support a national ethos of 'zeal' that is so ingrained within our culture of education, as recognised in the popular term, 'educational fever'. I grasped that this was 'ideological', in the ways that it shaped normative thought and practice in defining what good research practice is, and I thought I wanted to resist the idea of my role as a 'trend-setter'. Yet there seemed to be no straightforward ways for doing research differently.

It was mainly the sharing of ideas and perspectives of environmental education with teachers during interviews that engaged me in further reflections on the role of a researcher. I felt there was a strong need for teachers to develop curriculum approaches that can radically cha(lle)nge the current knowledge-based, narrowly defined version of environmental education found in Korea. I could also recognise their passion and creativity obstructed by conventional thinking and doing education. During a second round of interviews in 2005, Korea faced a dramatic situation when the internationally recognised stem cell research by a Korean scientist team became embroiled in scandal. This drove the whole nation into turbulence and shock. Unsurprisingly, some of the science teachers participating in my study did not hesitate in taking up this issue in expressing their clear advocacy for a critical approach to the value-laden nature of science. For my research, witnessing this dramatic event and how teachers coped with it in their own ways provided me with an invaluable spur to further examine teachers' stories in terms of the cultural and social discourses that impinge on teachers' everyday life context and schooling context, and how these are constituted, negotiated and narrated.

In so doing, I began to see more ambivalent and vulnerable qualities in teacher identities, and to develop narrative inquiry in ways that sought to illuminate the realities of educational practice from cultural perspectives. To expand the analysis of teacher narratives, I cautiously started to reconstruct narrative texts through moving between teachers' own voices (*emic*) and my analytic frame (*etic*). In drawing on discussions with my supervisors, Korean undergraduate students at the University of Bath and fellow research students about their own ways of reading the stories as part of data analysis, I attempted to engage in a constant critical reading of the teachers' and my own stories. In this process of interweaving of research phenomena and data, theoretical perspectives, teachers' voices, and my own and others' interpretations, a distinct narrative genre of the thesis emerged.

As I came close to completion of my doctorate, I was encouraged to present my research project to a wider international audience, in order to enhance reflections on research from other academic and cultural perspectives. For me this meant struggle and frustration as well as excitement and inspiration. In spite of intellectual exchange and learning opportunities, sometimes I ended up dissatisfied without knowing why. For example, at the 8th Invitation Seminar on Environmental and Health Education in Switzerland, I set an ambitious target: one of the presentations I prepared was concerned with the question of 'researching environmental education as if culture mattered' (Hwang & Reid, 2007). Based on my own doctoral research experience and a critical dialogue with my lead supervisor, I aimed to invite scholarly attention and discussion to the notion of seeing research endeavour in terms of its 'culture', in that culture can offer a temporal coherence in a social space, but this is always of contested significance (Barker, 2000). For engaging in self-reflections on one's own research practice and academic identities, we proposed consideration of three key dynamic components: a 'research field', 'international community', and the (local) 'identity' of the researcher. While the participants showed great interest in this issue, I still found it puzzling to discover that the issue was reduced or confined to matters of political correctness in terms of naively advocating the 'inclusiveness' of 'minorities' during the discussion. I realised that in spite of assumed open-mindedness, participating in an intercultural dialogue does not automatically or readily ensure better understanding of each other.

This story can only begin to relay tiny aspects of my own thinking, experiences and perspectives on the doctoral research experience. Everybody has their own personal, cultural, and academic backgrounds and histories, and therefore, we are bound to be strangers or newcomers to one another. I am still not convinced where I belong exactly in this research field. My experience so far teaches me not to be terrified of being exposed to foreign situations or being a stranger, however, how hard it is!

Benjamin's Story – 'A Long and Winding Road'

My interest is in developing tools that support classroom learning. I ask myself, how do I prove that these tools can support effective learning? Which criteria of effectiveness do I use to make my point? Do we (Mexicans) really need such learning tools? If so, how do I implement my ideas about these learning tools?

I decided to undertake a PhD in which I evaluated the effectiveness of my self-developed board game ('Mexico City: an environmental tour') for use in environmental education learning, with a parallel aspiration, to become an adviser to educational decision-makers in Mexico, or a director of an educational organisation (operating nationally or internationally).

Initially, I wanted to tell my story by following the second heuristic (Figure 2); however, after discussions with the others (co-authors) I decided to tell my story by following the first (Figure 1) as this heuristic better matches how I experienced my PhD journey. As outlined in Figure 1, the PhD process can be understood in terms of being shaped/influenced by seven circles, which I see as "spheres". In my case all seven were significant and interrelated. In what follows, the seven will be highlighted with italics, and I start my story by considering the sphere related to transition identity and background, as from this sphere three issues emerged.

Firstly, the transition of identity from *being a biologist to becoming an educational researcher*. This transition is related to the sphere of research culture. From my three years prior experience doing research in ecology I could recognise the differences between doing research in biological science and in educational research (i.e., methodology), as exemplified in the following quotations: 'Research, particularly for students in arts, humanities and social sciences, is conceived as an independent, solitary activity...' (McCormack, 2004). In contrast, 'the research process is fundamentally different in disciplines where the student engages in empirical study in a laboratory group'; moreover, 'scientific research requires the study of purportedly objective phenomena, which can be seen as being outside the individual' (Wright & Cochrane, 2000).

Secondly, as a graduate student, I found the transition of identity from *dependent to independent learner* very problematical because in 'educational terms, individual autonomy and independence can only be achieved through submission to pedagogic norms' (Donald, 1992; in Johnson *et al.*, 2000). As noted above, I felt I needed more supervision because my background in biology and work experiences did not help me understand educational jargon easily or the types of skills necessary to conduct social science research.

Thirdly, the transition of identity from *being single to being married*. Near the beginning of my PhD I got married. In my case, marriage and doctoral studies were totally incompatible. My marriage demanded a lot of time. Given the incompatibility, one year and a half into my doctorate, just after collecting data from my fieldwork in Mexico City, I interrupted my doctoral studies for nearly five years. I moved to Athens in 1999 and went back to my university in the UK (Cambridge) at the end of 2003, when I got divorced. In the period of 2003–2005 my conditions were overwhelming. First, I was broke economically, and with no scholarship I had to work part-time, which really limited my possibilities to catch up.

Second, I was psychologically down. Third, in terms of supervision, I had a different supervisor who was not directly involved in environmental education because my original supervisor retired.

From the three transitions mentioned above, the third (being married) most deeply affected my PhD learning process. In other words, the consequences of the interruption were that I had three fundamental flaws in relation to the research method training sphere. One flaw is in terms of methodology, another is in terms of the status and priority of literature review, and the other in terms of scholarly writing.

With reference to methodology, in Cambridge, the first year of doctoral studies includes taught courses in several topics related to educational research. I remember that during the first year of my doctoral studies the value of educational research was highly questioned (see Hargreaves, 1996). The issue of methodology was at the heart of the first year of my PhD. It was very frustrating that I could only be a listener in one lecture when two professors had a discussion on educational research (mainly related to methodology); they invited us to participate, I simply was unable to. Also, I couldn't understand lectures about the philosophy of research in education. My point is that if you are coming from sciences and you start graduate studies in education then, philosophy is both one of the most useful subjects for conducting high quality educational research and also it is one of the most challenging to deal with. If I would supervise someone with similar cases like mine, I would strongly recommend efforts be placed in understanding the general ideas of Plato and Descartes in relation to dualism, followed by a synthesis of the critics (of dualism), for example, Kant, Dewey, Wittgenstein and Heidegger. Then, understanding notions associated with postmodernism (as an "umbrella" term), to reflect on the ideas from the later Martin Heidegger (after *Being and Time*). Then, studying ideas from Heidegger's French "acolytes" - Lyotard, Foucault, and Derrida, among others. With this background, a PhD apprentice should be able to understand the points of key texts commenting on methodology in environmental education (e.g., Hart, 2000) and from there they would be well equipped to develop sound research proposals.

Another fundamental flaw that I had was my partial understanding of doing a decent literature review, i.e., comprehensive and relevant. In this case a scholar from the University of Bath advised me to read the paper of Boote and Beile (2005) which argues for the centrality of literature reviewing, and of being 'scholars before researchers'. Another flaw was the lack of opportunities to develop skills for scholarly writing (Caffarella & Barnett, 2000). This was an issue related to the quality of my supervisions, and my lack of opportunities (I was working part-time) to share more time with other graduate students, because the Faculty of Education at Cambridge really encourages the sharing of academic work with peers. The first version of my thesis was very long (140,000 words) and I had to reduce it to less than 80,000 words. This process required prioritising and setting boundaries (Glaze, 2002). Relatedly, the foreign student sphere was relevant because English is my second language, and as an overseas student, there were issues particularly in getting a visa.

In relation to having a critical mass, when I started my PhD at Cambridge there were at least five academics involved in environmental education; when I came back, there was one and he was in the process of changing institution. So, I developed the second part of my PhD when environmental education was not a supported research area for the Faculty of Education in Cambridge.

Consequently, the interruption of several years affected my transition process to becoming an effective, independent graduate scholar. All these limitations became apparent when I submitted my dissertation, for the first time. Thanks to the comments, advice and recommendations of my examiners, my thesis is approaching the required level for the successful completion of the doctorate. Lovitts (2005) makes the point that if universities take the successful completion of the dissertation as the event that marks the changeover from student to independent scholar, then this is the 'critical transition'. For me, it has been a very critical transition, better characterised as 'a long and winding road'.

Kelly's Story - Induction / Discipline / Emancipation: Being and doing the PhD

Reflecting upon my PhD experience, I am struck by how much could be written. After all, I have chosen to dedicate several years of my life to a single endeavour that has been fraught with intense highs and lows: emotionally, socially and intellectually. Such a journey of be(com)ing a doctoral researcher and doing doctoral research has entailed induction into several new communities of practice at different times, discipline to learn and understand, and fleeting moments of emancipation once I have been able to comprehend the language within that community. None of these have been static.

Pearson and Brew (2002) attempt to capture such experiences and perceptions by setting out four different perspectives on what a research process might entail: *a domino effect* (synthesising separate elements), *layering* (discovering, uncovering or creating underlying meanings), *trading* (marketplace exchange of knowledge products), and *taking a journey* (discovery and transformation). While it is difficult to categorise my experience into just one of these, they each express something of the process, at different stages.

To start with, the continued 'domino' effect of 'layering' together experiences of deeper engagement into a range of relevant literature, conferences, discussions and field work often led me to a place of identity instability that questioned the very purpose for which I was 'doing' a PhD. Referring to the second heuristic (Figure 2), the intention of doing the PhD drifted through layers of intense emotion, intellectual challenges and stimulation that simultaneously addressed the intention of producing new knowledge, engaging in a personal project or learning 'journey', and setting forth into a future that I felt passionate about. The 'doing' of a PhD acted in some ways as the solution to a more idealised future, but then I gradually began asking more serious questions that related to: *What have I got myself caught up in exactly? Why am I doing this, and for what and whose purposes?* Several times, I moved toward a feeling of the need to engage in acts of resistance (i.e., by 'walking out' of my PhD and committing to a social movement that was more directly active on what I was trying to understand rather than observing from a more privileged 'research' position) as I felt that which is needed to access what it is to do a PhD has countered aspects of why I decided to embark upon a PhD journey. The rules and norms guiding the process and production of doing a PhD were contradictory to the alternativeness and alterity I was seeking in and through my research. Resistance occurred in terms of theorising, methods I used in acquiring data, and addressing institutional obstacles encountered in my PhD programme.

The journey of my doctoral research study then has entailed choice and chance, induction and discipline, emancipation and struggle. I have undertaken this journey as a full-time student, part-time working student, and interrupted student, as well as going to work 'in the field' for two semesters. Along the journey, my research aims, objectives and questions went through significant changes to accord with what I was learning and experiencing. The shifts and changes that occurred during the process can be described as accidental but also as a reaction to being open to the intellectual and subsequent emotional transformations I felt were occurring.

When I enrolled in the MPhil/PhD course in Education at King's College London in September 2000, my original research proposal focused upon the impacts of virtual (ICT-based) environmental education experiences on students' environmental dispositions. By the end of the first academic year (September 2001), my research focus altered dramatically, to examining the links between environmental education and poverty reduction in Pakistan. At the end of my fourth year, my focus continued to evolve, shifting the environmental component of 'environmental education' from the centre to the periphery and the notion of 'power' taking its place. The context of Pakistan remained.

The initial alteration of my research focus resulted from my involvement in research contracted by the UK Department for International Development (DFID) to King's College London and the University of Bath in June 2000. As an academic team, the research focused on the most appropriate ways DFID could mainstream environmental education in developing countries alongside the overarching objectives of pursuing and delivering poverty reduction. At King's, the research involved undertaking 28 interviews with a range of development organisations (donor agencies, non-government organisations (NGOs), academics and government officials) in Karachi, Islamabad and Gilgit.

The aggregation of research findings and research experiences in Pakistan and through working with a donor organisation, DFID, struck a chord of passionate interest from which I felt overpowered; I could not *not* continue to engage with these issues. Referring to heuristic two and three, the road I was taking was being shaped into a 'web of fascination and intrigue' that delved into the depths of what knowledge production, my future and a personal project meant for me, particularly as I felt my worldview being continually challenged and re-formed through emotional and intellectual reverberations. My research was re-directed toward deeper questions emerging from the issues that arose through the DFID research such as: *How are development policies being interpreted and how is this affecting what is being done in practice?* And, *How do the power struggles between different development agencies contribute to differences of understandings?*

I discovered that my view of reality most closely aligned with that expressed in critical theory as a 'field of possibilities, the task being to define and assess the level of variation that exists beyond what is empirically given' (de Sousa-Santos, 1999, p. 29). In particular, I was interested in learning more about critical discourse analysis (CDA) as a theory and a method (Chouliaraki & Fairclough, 1999). I was drawn to the tenets of CDA being unified in their explicit focus on examining power relations at play within social relations, particularly those that create instances of social injustice.

To further explore these hints of power relations, I delved into literature on critical theory, post-structuralism, discourse analysis, and post-development (e.g., Escobar, 1995; Sachs, 1997; Rahnema & Bawtree, 1997). These theoretical explorations were greatly inspired through several conversations I had with a fellow PhD student, Ana Maria Duque-Aristizébal, who had started a few years ahead of me and was focusing upon discourses of environmental education in her home country of Colombia (Duque-Aristizábal, 2002). I felt a connection with her insights and experiences that resonated with these underlying issues of power and language. Reading about discourse and power and gaining further understandings of development theories, I saw the marginalisation of environmental education practices as being a response to mainstream development not identifying environmental education as a priority within its agenda of a prescribed solution to eliminating poverty and an inability to view things holistically.

I was finally able to return to Pakistan to carry out ethnographic interviews in July and August 2003. I decided to return again to Pakistan three months later (December 2003) and speak at a conference in Islamabad. I saw this opportunity as being valuable for gathering feedback about my research from people living and working in Pakistan. The final interview during this visit to Pakistan was with a semi-autonomous education NGO in Karachi (January 2004). During the interview, the managing director enquired into my research as I enquired into their work. He was particularly interested in my use of work by Foucault and Escobar and my own criticisms of assumptions within mainstream development practices, especially as I was an American. Toward the end of the interview, he interjected that I should come and work with them immediately for six months. He was trying to restructure all of the different programmes and explained that it would be an opportune knowledge exchange for both of us. The offer came unexpectedly and immediately captured my interest; so much so that it went beyond a topic of consideration to something that I felt I had to do. I felt a sense of obligation to plug gaps in my cultural knowledge of Pakistan that I hadn't gained from texts and the limited time I had spent in Pakistan during previous research visits. I wanted to understand how tangible some of these theories were in reality. Furthermore, I felt that discourse analysis (irregardless of being 'critical') was inadequate to really locate and pinpoint the power-related complexities that I aimed to grasp a better understanding of.

Living and working in Karachi those six months was a profound learning experience, so much so that I felt it would have been possible to re-focus the topic of my entire research study toward micro-power relations within the organisation. However, as I did not go there to 'do' explicit ethnographic research, ethical issues impeded this as a possibility. In addition, the interview data I had previously gathered from other organisations were more than adequate to pursue my research questions. In the end I decided to use some of the experiential data I had gathered during my work experience in Karachi in a focused case study that employed ethnographic tools. My research questions changed again through data analysis as well as my experiences living and working in Pakistan for a longer period of time. I therefore sidelined the focus on 'environment' and centred on the notion of power and hegemony within my research questions, such as: *How can we use de-centred conceptual understandings of power and hegemony to better understand the complexities of power relations that constitute the development field?* And, *How might development and education be re-conceptualised within the context of Pakistan according to the discursive practices that already exist within the field?*

Experiences of working in Karachi left me with feelings of extreme frustration at my inability to be more 'active' against the injustices I witnessed first-hand because of the competing responsibility of finishing this research study. Delamont (2002, p. 166) describes rich field experiences acting as a 'permanent hangover' to a researcher's ability to readjust back to ordinary life. Fine (1994, p. 15) argues that researchers 'who represent themselves as detached only camouflage their deepest, most privileged interests'. My research is explicitly critical of positivistic knowledge that dominates development decision-making through policy measurement techniques, particularly in the emphasis given to an explicit focus of being political. I aspired to create and be involved in a space that has the capacity to lead to new questioning with subsequent new practices that are more just. I found that the academic space for deep critical questioning of development practices is accessible, although it seems to often fall short of moving into the realm of activism. The sharp divides that can exist between academia and activism are ones that I feel can be bridged, although the structure for that to happen is not always readily in place, particularly with the defined requirements that coincide with completing a doctorate in academia.

This description of my research journey then is one that reflects the necessity of being *inducted* into a variety of communities; academic and cultural. Academically, I have sought to engage with the field of education research and environmental education research, language and literacy research, development theory and political theory. Culturally, induction has been an ongoing process in the UK as I am a foreigner and London is such an international city. In Pakistan, cultural contrasts were most striking being white, non-Muslim, female, non-Urdu speaking, tall and American. *Discipline* came in many forms as well: the constant quest for funding, locating adequate knowledge to address my queries (from textual sources, PhD supervisors, key informants and experiences), handling supervisor-student conflicts, acquiring an academic literacy sufficient to finish a PhD dissertation, conditioning myself to be able to live comfortably in Pakistan, addressing anti-Americanism in Pakistan, using critical theory that cannot quite capture the realities of what I experienced and witnessed, and so forth.

Has *emancipation* occurred? Sure, in moments. However, once a sense of emancipation occurs, there is always the next quest, the next step in the journey... and any quest brings with it moments of induction, discipline, emancipation and struggle; simultaneously and separately. The overwhelming and underlying challenge seems to be about allowing for an 'openness' of the learning journey that is the essence of both 'being' and 'doing' a PhD.

Jutta's Story –From Doctoral Student to Postdoctoral Researcher: Continuity and Transformation

I had just graduated from my doctoral studies when we initiated this collaborative thinking and writing process. At this point, I was at a position to reflect on my PhD experiences largely from the perspective of closure. In other words, I could now see single experiences, processes and encounters in the light of their overall influence and importance. While such a reflective process provided interesting insights, I also strongly felt that I wanted to look ahead and move to other areas and challenges. For me reflecting on, and in so doing, understanding the doctoral research process, helped me to start to position myself and to define the next phase in the progression of my research and professional life.

In relation to the three heuristics, the triangle (Figure 2) best illustrates how my understanding of the process of doing a doctoral study expanded. It shifted from understanding the notion of contributing to the body of knowledge as the main outcome, towards my own professional development and my role and responsibilities as member of a research community and research fields.

There are two events that I consider as turning points for changing my understanding. The first occurred around two-thirds of the way into my PhD research, when as a result of my advanced analysis I started to question the relevance of my initial research questions. My study investigated student teachers' understandings of sustainable development, education and ESD in three European countries. With cohorts of research participants in three different cultural contexts, part of the investigation focused on the impact of culture, particularly national culture, as a factor influencing understandings and meaning making. During the data analysis however, it appeared that there was more commonality across the three cohorts than within them. A difficult decision to make here then was whether to continue with the comparison in terms of the three cohorts emphasising national differences, or to leave this aside and focus on the categories developed by different perspectives on how they ascribe responsibility to oneself and others (see Nikel, 2007). While this decision is easily worked into the thesis narrative, the actual process was difficult to come to terms with. It raised issues about the role and flexibility of initial research questions, the process of initially setting them up, the nature of qualitative research (being naturalistic and emergent, for example) and moreover, the expectations of people reading the work as a cross-national study.

The second event took place during the last months of my PhD study. It took place at the interface between finalising the analysis, framing the findings, and being able to discuss the research process for the final oral examination. It was a crucial period for gaining a more in-depth understanding of what I had been engaged with in the previous years and its relevance, particularly in terms of for whom and for what? In lengthy conversations with my lead supervisor, we discussed the minutiae of the processes and principles underlying analysis, writing up and the *viva voce*, with the expressed intention of clarifying my understandings of the purposes of each, in order to use this as an overall guiding frame for discussing and accounting for my work. In essence, I came to see the researcher as simultaneously a learner, knowledge producer and story writer. I understood data analysis and interpretation as processes concerned with focussing what the researcher might contribute to a body of knowledge. In the writing up, this was to be taken further: an activity that is about finding an effective way to write about the real process ('journey') while telling a convincing story supporting the argument(s) ('destination' or outcome). Finally, I came to understand the process of a *viva voce* as the place where there is discussion about this path (the 'journey' and 'destination'), and moreover, the qualities and skills that were being developed along that path, of becoming and in being a researcher.

Reflections from a Postdoctoral Researcher

In the time following the completion of my doctoral study I was offered a postdoctoral fellowship in which I was asked to continue working in the area I had researched before. Thus I faced the question about making choices about 'What to do with your doctoral research project' after completion in the context of environmental education/ESD and research on teacher thinking as research fields.

The majority of doctoral students complete a research project and write a doctoral thesis based on this, which is then followed by efforts to disseminate methodological innovations and/or findings in one to three academic journal articles. After graduation, many students move on to new places and projects, often to work on rather unrelated, but larger research areas, than environmental education (as in my case). Even in working in postdoctoral positions within the same university rather than in new institutional settings, most graduates find themselves confronted with their own and others' questions about how the doctoral study might be taken 'further' and made more 'relevant' to their research field and community. The outcome is likely to be influenced by one's own and shared considerations about development of the research field, career plans, and interpretations of the doctoral and postdoctoral study and training. It is not difficult to see that both, 'taking your doctoral study work further' and 'making it more relevant' can be interpreted in different ways. Contextual and individual considerations can, for example, focus on extended dissemination, follow-up studies using existing and new data and established research networks, and research reviews.

The crucial question in my view is, what are the implications (the benefits and missed opportunities) of choices available to an individual, but also for the research field, in particular for a small research field like environmental education? I view this as a version of the second heuristic. In order to free myself in choosing an obvious area or one very close to the research centre's programme (in my case, at CREE), I spent time finding out about general trends in social science research as well as the latest understandings of the future of research at universities and the skill profile expected of a modern researcher. In doing so I reflected on my own options within several dimensions: my own research community; gaps identified in research field reviews; my interests; career management advice; characteristics of a modern researcher in a postmodern university (Rip, 2004); suggested professional skill development patterns emphasising 'getting better at doing' research (Dall'Alba & Sandberg, 2006); and academic research trends mapped between international and national oriented research agendas and administration and market forces driven funding options (Vincent-Lancrin, 2006).

While I felt empowered by the ideas and arguments in these studies to make a more conscious choice and to feel part of or opposed to something 'bigger', I found it difficult to talk with people about this. In conversations with peers I got a sense that what I was doing in making choices was perceived as being very systematic and thorough but had little in common with how others made or make their choices for future research topics. It made me question whether talking of contributing to/leading/advancing one's research communities or research fields is actually an integral part of the way people frame their research and involvement in research programmes, or rather rhetorical in nature?

MAKING SENSE OF THE STORIES

The four stories briefly presented in this chapter illuminate and flesh out some of the complexities represented in the three heuristics presented earlier, particularly as they relate to matters of identity, agency, power relations and career progression implicated in the doctorate and doctoral research process. They each represent different stages and versions of the process, raising particular issues faced in different phases of the doctoral study and weaving together various concepts articulated in each heuristic that we each felt were most relevant to further structure and elaborate upon our own journeys.

An obvious place to start is with the process of selecting initial research questions that endures through the course of the doctoral study, which can be both onerous and tenuous. It can be onerous given the lack of confidence that is often experienced at the beginning in trying to understand and find a position from which to understand, question and examine; and tenuous in that research questions may shift slightly (as in Jutta's case) or significantly (as with Kelly). Although each of us experienced a sense of instability and 'getting lost' at the onset of the PhD, Se-young's story focuses most heavily on this issue. This is most likely due to the phase in which she wrote her story, in that this was closer to the beginning of her journey. Benjamin's story also adds to this, highlighting the challenges of moving from a natural science to a social science background, with the differences in philosophical positioning(s) and research methods expected in a social science doctorate.

Of course, we all encountered varying degree of *'cultural'* issues, being 'outsiders' not only more generally in the environmental education academic field (as beginners), but in a higher education programme in the UK as international students (as foreigners). The experience of entering and being accepted into an academic 'community of practice', in this case that of the environmental education field, led to episodes of angst, frustration and difficulties but also excitement for each of us. In addition, we have each faced cultural tensions within our fieldwork either through researching in country contexts that are not our own (Kelly and Jutta) or within our own country contexts as 'insiders' whilst having to explain why it is that we decided to undertake research as 'outsiders' through a foreign university in spite of the fieldwork being 'at home' (Se-young and Benjamin). Se-young has emphasised some of the cultural challenges she faced in terms of pre-conceived notions and values of receiving a 'Western' doctorate, while for both Jutta and Kelly, we must also recognise that even as a 'Western' doctorate one undertaken in the UK can widely differ from the expectations of doctoral studies in Germany and the USA. The challenges of having British English as a second language were most present in the stories of Se-young, Benjamin and Jutta.

Aside from cultural issues encountered in different ways during the PhD process, several other themes have been highlighted in the four stories: *economic hardships, personal relationships, supervisor challenges* and a general *sense of identity crisis* (most of which are expressed in relation to Figure 1). Benjamin and Kelly each wrote of the stark reality of constant economic hardships and challenges that served as a distraction and source of worry over the course of the PhD process. Kelly was forced to locate constant employment over the course of her PhD studies, hindering the time she could allocate to her studies. Although she gained valuable work experience through various employment contracts, it meant that the PhD itself took two extra years. Benjamin and Kelly also hinted at dramatic personal relationship shifts that they endured through different phases of their research. For both, the commitment and passion they held to their research served as barriers to the development of their closest relationships, which consequently resulted in their termination. Benjamin (and Kelly) also highlighted the identity, guidance and support challenges that having to change supervisors can invoke. In particular, Benjamin's story emphasises the arduous difficulties faced when there is a lack of a supportive research community within the institution through which one is pursuing a PhD, leading to feelings of loneliness and isolation. Jutta and Se-young, on the other hand, experienced supportive and stable guidance from their supervisors (both were co-supervised by William Scott) and a vibrant research community at the University of Bath over the course of their PhD processes.

Finally, we all pursued a PhD with some sort of vision of a future professional career or social change type of objectives (or a combination) and/or deeper questions that we felt compelled to explore. Although each of us addressed these issues to some extent in our stories, Jutta's story emphasised these issues most strongly, largely because she had completed her PhD at the time of writing. Jutta notes that it was at the end of her PhD writing process that she began to engage larger questions of what it means to be a researcher in terms of being a learner, a knowledge producer and a story writer; and it is as a post-doctoral fellow she has been able to engage the sense of responsibility she feels about what to do with doctoral research after it has been completed, how research questions can be made relevant to the everyday world, and how it all fits in with the nature of qualitative research generally and the field of environmental education more specifically. The touchstone for all four of us can be found near here: being united through the common pursuit of expanding and pushing environmental education into new, more innovative and progressive directions through our research objectives, theoretical positionings, methods and/or analyses.

CONCLUDING REMARKS

With a move toward closing this chapter, we do have to engage the 'So what?' question in terms of why this is important. Why should we consider that the process of the 'during' of the PhD is as important as its outcomes? Does it really matter what goes on 'behind the scenes'? From our collective point of view we argue that the process of the PhD is as important as its outcomes, for doctoral studies more generally and within the environmental education field specifically. We contend that the many other psychological, emotional, spiritual, economic, social, cultural and intellectual elements contributing to the sedimentation represented through the woven layers of the thesis ought to be not just recognised, but legitimised as essential points of reflection and consideration. As Paul Hart stated during the 2006 AERA Symposium: "The doctoral experience is in need of conscious thoughtful and reflexive accounting within the bounds of skepticism and humility".

As stated earlier, we understand the PhD process as a unique one; not just because of the high level of independence granted the student but in terms of it being an individual project 'plunging into the depths' of methodological, epistemological and ontological issues like no other study or most likely, later professional experience. Earlier in the chapter, we argued for the need to acknowledge and legitimise different styles and types of learning during the process, and to unmask additional learning as in 'making visible the invisible'. As we have shown here, this involves sharing and accounting for the 'unexpected' in the 'doing' of a PhD – the journey of learning that one experiences, to address the tension of following a passion whilst still conforming to the stringent expectations of the doctoral study degree, and to mirror the holistic nature of doing a PhD, thereby recognising and addressing experiential aspects.

Clearly the experience of devoting several years of one's life in pursuit of one's research can be challenging and complex, intellectually and emotionally. The four stories shared in this chapter have shed light on this and might be seen as *testimonio* of four active doctoral students and postdoctoral candidates at various stages in their programmes, framed by three heuristics which were generated through discussions that focused on tensions experienced in 'performing' the doctoral student role (i.e., assuming that positionality). Working together in our attempt to understand what was going on in this process entailed engaging in critical reflection beyond substance and method, whether this was between fellow students or student and supervisor(s). Thus we argue for bringing the lived experience of doctoral study into sharper relief by engaging a participatory, critically reflexive process of learning if increasing the quality and value of the experience is the goal.

The fields of environmental education and ESD coalesce around shared aims of challenging and critiquing social norms and the status quo, often from a critical and/or holistic perspective. Arguably, part of this should also involve critiquing and challenging the 'normal' process of doing a PhD that in some instances can be over-focused on a behaviouristic (i.e., positivistic) linear outcome model, and which contradicts the holistic nature of the PhD process. We are *not* contending that an indicator be developed to include these varied elements with the emphasis being on using this as evidence of designing and having being able to execute a 'good PhD'. Indicators such as these would slide us back into a positivistic model, focusing us on the letter rather than the spirit of this discussion. Rather, we have argued that individual experiences be critically valued, reflected upon and addressed in a manner that reflects the innovative movements of social science research more generally and environmental education and ESD specifically, particularly given the holistic and critical possibilities of environmental education and ESD, but also to continue working the hyphens of the activist-researcher-scholar complex to create research cultures marked by sharing and openness.[6]

NOTES

[1] For example, in terms of doctoral studies in education, there are at least two possible routes in the UK at the moment; the PhD route and the professional doctorate, EdD. We focus on the PhD route in discussing doctoral studies, unless indicated otherwise.

[2] An example of the later is the influence of the widely cited work of Gibbons *et al.* (1994) who differentiate between "objective knowledge that is generated by researchers about practice" (Mode 1) and "knowledge which is created and used by practitioners in the context of their practice" (Mode 2).

[3] Without doubt, postgraduate and doctoral supervision are heavily researched areas within studies of Higher Education (Linden, 1999; Pearson & Brew, 2002; Petersen, 2007; Li & Seale, 2007; Hasrati, 2005; Ives & Rowley, 2005). The influence of, more recently, postmodern perspectives haves also shaped how the doctoral student-supervisor relationship and interaction may be understood, and have received much attention. For example, for Petersen (2007), the postgraduate research supervision process can be interpreted as "category boundary work". In this view, "postgraduate supervision entails a relationship in which the boundaries around what constitutes culturally intelligible academic performativity, 'academicity', are negotiated, maintained, challenged and reconstructed" (p. 475). Category boundary work is performed by both supervisor and student – and, we would add, examiners. Petersen makes a strong case for understanding how academic cultures, research cultures and subjectivities are produced and reproduced as part of the process of doing a doctoral study and being a doctoral student.

[4] Others might suggest to make use of autobiographical writing or diaries as other possibilities to unlock potential that makes the doctoral work more relevant to the candidate. For example, in search of constructive dialogues about 'principles' in educational research, Pamela A. Moss (2005) draws on a range of philosophers of science and social theory, such as Bernstein (1992), Hoy & McCarthy (1994) and Bourdieu (1998), to help in addressing problems of understanding the other and in learning more about ourselves through interpretive encounters.

[5] Deem and Brehony (2000) state in their paper, provocatively titled "Doctoral Students' access to Research Cultures – are some more unequal than others?" that research cultures, research

methodology training, supervision, and the critical mass of research students, have come to be seen as significant aspects of being a social science research student. The authors conclude from their data (26 interviews with home and international students in the UK) that "international students and part time students have the most difficulty in accessing peer cultures and academic cultures," but further argue that international students are much more "favourably disposed towards research training cultures than other students" (p. 149).

[6] A proof of this particular pudding is arguably how we then develop, negotiate and reflect on our own approaches to supervision and examination.

REFERENCES

Barker, C. (2000). *Cultural studies: Theory and practice*. London: Sage.

Bernstein, R. J. (1992). *The new constellation: The ethical-political horizons of modernity/postmodernity*. Cambridge, MA: The MIT Press.

Boote, D. N., & Beile, P. (2005). Scholars before researchers: On the centrality of the dissertation literature review in research preparation. *Educational Researcher, 34*(6), 3–15.

Bourdieu, P. (1998). *Practical reason: On the theory of action*. Cambridge: Polity Press.

Cafarella, R. S., & Barnett, B. G. (2000). Teaching doctoral students to become scholarly writers: The importance of giving and receiving critiques. *Studies in Higher Education, 25*(1), 39–51.

Chouliaraki, L., & Fairclough, N. (1999). *Discourse in late modernity: Rethinking critical discourse analysis*. Edinburgh: Edinburgh University Press.

Dall'Alba, G., & Sandberg, J. (2006). Unveiling professional development: A critical review of stage models. *Review of Educational Research, 76*(3), 383–412.

Dany, F., & Mangematin, V. (2004). Beyond the Dualism between lifelong employment and job insecurity: Some new career promises for young scientists. *Higher Education Policy, 17*(2), 201–219.

Deem, R., & Brehony, K. J. (2000). Doctoral students' access to research cultures-are some more unequal than others? *Studies in Higher Education, 25*(2), 149–165.

Delamont, S. (2002). *Fieldwork in educational settings: Methods, pitfalls and perspectives* (2nd ed.). London: Routledge.

Delamont, S., Atkinson, P., & Parry, O. (2004). *Supervising the doctorate: A guide to success* (2nd ed.). Maidenhead: SRHE/OUP.

Donald, J. (1992). *Sentimental education. Schooling popular culture and the regulation of liberty*. London: Verso.

Duque-Aristizabal, A. (2002). *Environmental education discourses in Colombia: A study of values, politics and power*. Unpublished doctoral thesis. London: King's College.

Enders, J., & de Weert, E. (2004). Editorial science, training and career. *Higher Education Policy, 17*(2), 129–133.

Escobar, A. (1995). *Encountering development: The making and unmaking of the third world*. Princeton, NJ: Princeton University Press.

Fine, M. (1994). Negotiations of power inside feminist research. In A. Gitlin (Ed.), *Power and method: Political activism and educational research*. London: Routledge.

Foucault, M. (1980). Power/knowledge. In C. Gordon (Ed.), *Selected interviews and other writings 1972–1977*. Brighton: Harvester Press.

Gee, J., Hull, G., & Lankshear, C. (1996). *The new work order: Behind the language of the new capitalism*. London: Allen & Unwin.

Gibbons, M., Limoges, C., Nowotny, H., Schwartzman, S., Scott, P., & Trow, M. (1994). *The new production of knowledge. The dynamic of science and research in contemporary societies*. London: Sage.

Glaze, J. (2002). PhD study and the use of a reflective diary: A dialogue with self. *Reflective Practice, 3*(2), 153–166.

Gonzalez-Guadiano, E. (2005). Education for sustainable development: Configuration and meaning. *Policy Futures in Education, 3*(3), 243–250.

Hargreaves, D. A. (1996). *Teaching as a research-based profession: Possibilities and prospects.* Cambridge: Teacher Training Agency Annual Lecture.

Hart, P. (2000). Requisite variety: The problem with generic guidelines for diverse genres of inquiry. *Environmental Education Research, 6*(1), 37–46.

Hasrati, M. (2005). Legitimate peripheral participation and supervising PhD students. *Studies in Higher Education, 30*(5), 557–570.

Hockey, J. (1991). The social science PhD: A literature review. *Studies in Higher Education, 16*(3), 319–332.

Hockey, J. (1994). New territory: Problems of adjusting to the first year of a social science PhD. *Studies in Higher Education, 19*(2), 177–190.

Hoy, D. C., & McCarthy, T. (1994). *Critical theory.* Oxford, UK: Blackwell.

Hwang, S., & Reid, A. (2007, March 25–30). *Researching environmental education as if culture mattered: Review and observation.* Invitational Seminar on International Environmental and Health Education, Monte Verità, Switzerland.

Ives, G., & Rowley, G. (2005). Supervisor selection or allocation and continuity of supervision: Ph.D. students' progress and outcomes. *Studies in Higher Education, 30*(5), 535–555.

Johnson, L., Lee, A., & Green, B. (2000). The PhD and the Autonomous Self: gender, rationality and postgraduate pedagogy. *Studies in Higher Education, 25*(2), 135–147.

Li, S., & Seale, C. (2007). Managing criticism in PhD supervision: A qualitative case study. *Studies in Higher Education, 32*(4), 511–526.

Linden, J. (1999). The contribution of narrative to the process of supervising PhD students. *Studies in Higher Education, 24*(3), 351–365.

Lovitts, B. E. (2005). Being a good course-taker is not enough: A theoretical perspective on the transition to independent research. *Studies in Higher Education, 30*(2), 137–154.

McCormack, C. (2004). Tensions between student and institutional conceptions of postgraduate research. *Studies in Higher Education, 29*(3), 319–334.

Moss, P. A. (2005). Toward "Epistemic reflexivity" in educational research: A response to scientific research in education. *Teachers College Record, 107*(1), 19–29.

Neumann, R. (2007). Policy and practice in doctoral education. *Studies in Higher Education, 32*(4), 459–473.

Nikel, J. (2007). Making sense of education 'responsibly': Findings from a study of student teachers' understanding(s) of education, sustainable development, and education for sustainable development. *Environmental Education Research, 13*(5), 545–564.

Pearson, M., & Brew, A. (2002). Research training and supervision development. *Studies in Higher Education, 27*(2), 135–150.

Peet, R. (2002). Ideology, discourse, and the geography of hegemony: From socialist to neoliberal development in postapartheid South Africa. *Antipode, 34*(1), 54–84.

Petersen, E. B. (2007). Negotiating academicity: Postgraduate research supervision as category boundary work. *Studies in Higher Education, 32*(4), 475–487.

Rahnema, M., & Bawtree, V. (1997). *The post-development reader.* London: Zed.

Read, B., Archer, L., & Leathwood, C. (2003). Challenging cultures? Student conceptions of 'belonging' and 'isolation' at Post-1992 university. *Studies in Higher Education, 28*(3), 261–277.

Reid, A., & Nikel, J. (2003). Reading a critical review of evidence: Notes and queries on research programmes in environmental education. *Environmental Education Research, 9*(2), 149–164.

Ridley, D. (2004). Puzzling experiences in high education: Critical moments for conversation. *Studies in Higher Education, 29*(1), 91–107.

Rip, A. (2004). Strategic research, post-modern universities and research training. *Higher Education Policy, 17*(2), 153–166.

Robottom, I., & Hart, P. (1993). *Research in environmental education: Engaging the debate.* Geelong: Deakin University.

Sachs, W. (1992). *The development dictionary: A guide to knowledge as power.* London: Zed Books.

Simpson, R. (1983). *How the PhD came to Britain: A century of struggle for postgraduate education.* Guildford: Research into Higher Education Monographs.

De Sousa Santos, B. (1999). On oppositional postmodernism. In R. Munck & D. O'Hearn (Eds.), *Critical development theory: Contributions to a New Paradigm.* London and New York: Zed Books.

Teamey, K. (2007). *An exploratory study of the orders of discourse between policies and discursive practices in the development field: A case study of education in Pakistan.* Unpublished PhD Dissertation, London: King's College.

Vincent-Lancrin, S. (2006). What is changing in academic research? *European Journal of Education,* *41*(2), 169–202.

Winter, R., Griffiths, M., & Green, K. (2000). The 'academic' qualities of practice: What are the criteria for a practice-based PhD? *Studies in Higher Education,* *25*(1), 25–37.

Wright, T., & Cochrane, R. (2000). Factors influencing successful submission of PhD theses. *Studies in Higher Education,* *25*(2), 181–195.

Yeatman, A. (1998). Making research relationships accountable: Graduate student logs. In A. Lee & B. Green (Eds.), *Postgraduate studies: Postgraduate pedagogy.* Sydney: University of Technology Sydney.

Corresponding author:
Jutta Nikel
University of Education Freiburg,
Germany (Jutta.Nikel@ ph-freiburg.de)

Kelly Teamey
Department of Education,
University of Bath, UK

Se-Young Hwang
Department of Anthropology,
University of Sussex, UK

Benjamin Alberto Pozos-Hernandez
Cambridge University, UK

Alan Reid
Department of Education,
University of Bath, UK

Paul Hart
Faculty of Education,
University of Regina, Canada

APPENDIX

Se-young Hwang

Se-young's thesis investigates the phenomena of school environmental education in Korea by developing teachers' stories as a main focus of inquiry and data form. Based on interviews with secondary school teachers, narrative inquiry resulted in a unique framework of three narrative forms: formative, argumentative, and repertoire.

In formative narratives, five teachers' short narratives are presented through a frame of plot ("vision"), and ways of representing teacher narratives in the way that they matter to teachers themselves are discussed. Argumentative narratives illuminate the paradoxical discursive practice in the school institutional context, and ways in which the idea of 'environmental education teacher' is contested by individual teachers' personal or collective strategies that enable them to create cracks in culturally more pervasive narratives of 'hero' teachers. Finally, the idea of repertoire is used to show that through participating in environmental education, teachers develop or expand their personal curriculum topics and methods. This suggests that encouraging diversity in teachers' curriculum repertoires is important for professional development.

In conclusion, the study's narrative inquiry contributes to ways of valuing teachers' personal narratives as a useful tool for understanding teachers' way of thinking and knowing and positioning environmental education as creating cracks and ruptures in school education. The thesis was completed in August 2008.

Benjamin Alberto Pozos-Hernandez

My research study is about evaluating the effectiveness of a board simulation-game known as 'Mexico City: an environmental tour.' To evaluate its effectiveness I focus on two aspects which are (i) a quasi-experiment to assess short- and long-term effects with view to changes in students' pro-environmental attitudes, and (ii) the student voice and their written description of their learning experiences.

A convenient sample of 757 students (15–17 years old) from 7 high schools in Mexico City participated in this study. Two 5-Likert-type questionnaires were used to collect attitudinal data and analysed by using one-way ANOVA. Follow-up data were collected to assess whether these changes in attitudes persisted after six months indicating long-term learning effects. Results consistently showed that the simulation-game was effective when it was used as follows: students played it once and then engaged in a role-play. Students then played the simulation-game for a second time. Long term effects were observed with changes that were seen to persist six months later. Students' opinions were analysed in the light of eight categories that had been identified from the literature. The students' opinions helped me towards greater understanding about why they engaged so positively with the simulation-game, raising further research questions.

Kelly Teamey

Kelly's thesis addresses complex power relations within discursive practices of the development field in Pakistan (using education as a case study) through a conceptual apparatus comprising a Foucauldian notion of power and discourse and Laclauan view of hegemony that is situated within a critique of post-development theory. The research uses a critically reflexive positioning that incorporates an ethnographic perspective toward a range of interviews with development organisations in Pakistan; textual analyses of international and national development and education policies; and participant observation data from work experiences at an educational quasi-governmental organisation in Karachi.

Theoretical and methodological implications emerging from the research study demonstrate the value of applying a more rigorous use of power and hegemony within a post-development framework; employing a non-essentialising view of hegemony to map complexity and locate discourses struggling within a given terrain to better understand power relations and their effects; and combining orders of discourse and field theory. Practical considerations include the importance of 'practicing what you preach' for those pursuing radical and alternative approaches; the journey of an exploratory PhD; and the applicability of using hegemonic concepts to engage with complexity, identify moments of fragmentation and critically scrutinise assumptions embedded within mainstream development and education practices.

Jutta Nikel

My doctoral research is a tri-country study of trainee teachers' understandings of the purposes of education, their conceptions of sustainable development and the task of education for sustainable development (ESD). At the centre are case studies of 30 student teachers from initial teacher education programmes from three European countries, England, Denmark and Germany (10 from each country). While they are diverse in their personal, professional and subject disciplinary backgrounds, and they work in a variety of school subject areas, all the students share the objective of becoming members of the teaching profession in the primary or lower secondary schools of their countries, and thus each one currently faces the additional challenge of understanding and responding to national, cross-cutting policy initiatives on sustainable development and ESD.

The findings highlight the widespread importance of 'taking responsibility' and 'having responsibility' as key notions in interpreting their professional role and student learning in relation to ESD. A developed explorative framework suggests that in making sense of ESD, student teachers are draw to one or more of at least four identifiable rationalities for ascribing responsibility to oneself or others, where each rationality articulates a different set of responses to questions about the prioritized locus of agency and the nature of the decision-making process. For further information see Nikel (2007).

ROB O'DONOGHUE AND HEILA LOTZ-SISITKA

11. NEW POSSIBILITIES FOR MEDIATION IN SOCIETY: HOW IS ENVIRONMENTAL EDUCATION RESEARCH RESPONDING?

A BROAD HISTORICAL VANTAGE POINT

..to understand political struggles, economic difficulties and intellectual debates, we must be able to define the historical situation in which they develop (Touraine, 2001, p. 8)

African universities have, since their inception in the colonial era, been governed by a colonial framing of research agendas and modernist trajectories. Keeley and Scoones (2003), for example, explain how agronomy in the French colonies in Africa was shaped by the 'particular form of science' that arrived in Mali as the French set about expanding the production of cotton. French scientific research, at the time (in the post World War 1 period) emphasized the economic development of the colonies, which introduced scientific ways of improving the particular production of cash crops, dealing with pests and improving varieties, locating early university-based research in patterns of bureaucratic and state formation. Expatriate researchers from universities in France, England and Belgium were brought to the colonies to set the agenda for research, as most of the colonial universities offered research and teaching programmes that were accredited by universities in the 'mother country'. While the number of expatriate researchers working in African universities may have declined in recent years, with the emphasis now on short-term consultancies (from the 'donor country'), funding and technical inputs from mother and donor countries continues to shape research. What is of note here is how research agendas are coupled with particular research conventions and processes of administrative and social organization[1] that are seldom explicit.

During the colonial era, there were only a handful of universities in Africa, and the university in Africa emerged as a post-independence phenomenon, introduced by new nation states[2] as a key aspect of the formation of the nation state (Mamdani, 1996). A number of anomalies exist in the post-independent university system in Africa, notably the ongoing institutional dependencies that existed after independence (particularly with regards to curriculum and research); the inability of the newly forming nation states to adequately fund and resource universities due to debt-servicing and structural adjustment programmes of the IMF and the World Bank which reduced spending on education, health and social

R. Stevenson and J. Dillon (eds.), Engaging Environmental Education: Learning, Culture and Agency, 199–215.

services; and the influence of the development aid industry, which has skewed the emergence of African research trajectories to reflect 'donor priorities and interests'. Locally initiated research 'for the public good' in African universities is therefore in its infancy, and a robust and original research trajectory that responds to the complex socio-cultural, economic and ecological histories in Africa is yet to emerge.

Mamdani (1996) argues that African society has reached an intellectual 'impasse', which is expressed in a tension between rights and culture discourses. These discourses are essentially encompassed in axes of tension across rights, individualization and modernization discourses (currently propelled by neo-liberal economic frameworks and globalization discourse) and culture talk (a return to Africanism, and the traditional 'cultural fabric' and indigenous knowledges that exist in African societies). He argues that a new synthesis is needed and that recourse to 'either-or' perspective will not address this intellectual impasse. His thesis, developed in great depth in his book *Citizen and Subject* is that this dialectic is a remnant of colonial intrusion. Post-colonial research, he argues, has been limited to a de-racialising of society, and has not yet addressed one of the fundamental aspects of the colonial legacy, namely the nature of the institution and its social *habitus*. In many ways, he is arguing for new forms of mediation in African societies that are currently somewhat hamstrung within the complexities of this intellectual impasse.

Research approaches, and research methodologies form part of the universities' institutional social *habitus*, and it is this that we address in this paper, arguing that a re-orientation of research in environmental education is part of a larger project of re-orienting the African university in the context of its recent mandate to seek greater situatedness and relevance in the sustainable development of African society (WSSD, 2002, African Union, 2006).

Southern Africa, like other sub-regions in Africa, is situated within a broader global(ising) environment dominated by neo-liberal political economy. This political economy is driving diverse social-ecological transformations as indicated in the recently emerging discourses surrounding sustainable development (Lotz-Sisitka, 2004). A recent concern associated with the neo-liberal political economy of the sustainable development agenda arose through an earlier review of development and educational practices in southern Africa that revealed an anomaly of deepening poverty against an economic empowerment rhetoric accompanying post-colonial development (ibid). In probing the emergence of research for 'the public good' in an African context, this paper seeks to inform an environmental education research agenda that opens forms of mediation that are less blind to some of the sustainability challenges in African contexts of poverty, vulnerability and risk.

African histories, and the history of research in African universities, is intimately intertwined with global developments, as witnessed by the recent global inscription of sustainable development as a salvation narrative for society at the turn of the 21st century (with education around the globe being re-oriented within this increasingly ambiguous narrative). This is notable in recent education for sustainable development (ESD) discourses generated in the institutional halls of

UNESCO, the International Union for the Conservation of Nature (IUCN) and other global organizations and how these processes are influenced by and influencing research priorities and trajectories on a global scale.

Touraine (1997, 2001) argues slightly differently for social research for the public good. He does not adopt a 'salvation narrative' discourse as reflected in the recent tradition of ESD. He argues that the contemporary challenge for society is to overcome the division of politics into the dual worlds of pure subjectivity and identity on the one side (as seen in increased individualisation), and on the other, the release of an "...unfettered instrumentalism[3] driven by market and technological imperatives" (Delanty, 1999, p. 182). Delanty (ibid.) presents a thesis in which he argues that the challenge of overcoming this apparently irreconcilable dualism[4] "... must be seen as one of articulating new possibilities for mediation". He argues further that there seems to be a 'new convergence' in social theory that recognizes the need to theorise new forms of mediation between agency and structure, culture and power, life-world and system, experience and rationalization. In this context, social theorists appear to be responding to the changed circumstances of the present with theories of reflexive or high modernity which, in different ways, are characterized by discourses of creativity, reflexivity and discursivity (ibid). It is difficult to reconcile these with the intermeshing of individual and technical rationality in global salvation narratives. This chapter follows the influence of discursivity (associated with the linguistic turn in research) and reflexivity (associated with a cultural turn in research) as well as briefly touching on creative dimensions of generative change within and across these.

Research questions guiding our inquiry are:
- In what way/s is environmental education research engaging with '*new forms of mediation*' amidst agency and structure, culture and power, life-world and system, experience and rationalization?
- What critical insights can this analysis provide to inform education for sustainable development[5] in a southern African context, and how do these insights relate to environmental education research for 'the public good'?

We begin this inquiry against the broader social history briefly sketched above, with a brief historical overview of developing environmental education research trajectories in southern Africa.

The changing research practices explored in this study suggest that historical processes of institutional mediation need reorientation as societies and the challenges facing humanity have changed. Conventional processes of research and social mediation in Africa arose in an interplay of science and education that shaped a structural functionalist[6] mediation of colonial modernization. A widening emergence of democracy, accompanied by a participatory turn, is reflecting a 'new interest' in forms of collaborative mediation that are more socially and culturally situated for reflexive learning and change in relation to environmental issues and risk. A cluster of environmental education research initiatives, undertaken in post-colonial social environments and examined below, appear to be exhibiting features of what mediating processes of environmental education research for the public good might look like. Some of the cases examined below are beginning to engage with themes such as power, reflexivity, historicity, risk, culture, situated learning, pluralist ways of knowing, ethics, participation, agency and socio-ecological justice. The characterizing features of these emerging research initiatives may hold particular significance for a post-colonial research agenda.

First, we discuss research and education in social mediation as brought to and developed in African society by modernist institutions of education and research.

Research and Education as Structural Functionalist Mediation

Early environmental education pedagogy and research reflects an interplay amongst scientific research that narrated environment concerns and established education research conventions centred on objective measures of awareness, attitudes and behaviour. The interplay of environmental research and education is now largely taken for granted in processes of institutional structural functionalist mediation where problems are determined by science and solutions are realized through interventions designed to bring the necessary changes into effect.

Amidst a sustained institutional interplay of environmental science and education imperatives, patterns of conservation and later, environmental education research emerged. Here a tightening of early survey research (info/opinion poles after Gallup) gave rise to instrumental measures of awareness and attitude for the rational mediation of society through education. Education research instruments were commonly applied in:
– Pre-tests to benchmark prior states before;
– Interventions to give effect to the desired change in behaviour and;
– Post-test measures to determine impact/changed state.

An early dominance of empirical analytical instrumentalism reflected in objective measures of awareness and attitude softened under critical review and came under increasing scrutiny and doubt with the emergence of participatory perspectives.

A Developing Participatory/Reflexive Turn

The transition to democratic governance in South Africa brought a closer coupling of research and education as pedagogy for social transformation notably in processes of participatory action research. Democratic change was also accompanied by processes that reflect a reclaiming of African identity and cultural heritage, most notable in African Renaissance imperatives. It is important to note how emerging socially critical/liberation perspectives reflect:
– A close coupling of liberation ideals and democracy in a communicative rationality of deliberative change;
– A developing pedagogical coupling of research and education within situated learning actions for mitigating risk in developing socio-ecological context.

Within the latter trajectory, environmental education research in post-colonial southern Africa has, for a number of years, been shaped by the intent of enabling social transformation. Early on the influence of the Frankfurt School critical theorizing, amalgamated with the political ideology of Paolo Freire's liberation politics, best expressed in his *Pedagogy of the Oppressed*, led to the emergence of numerous studies influenced by an emancipatory genre of critical theory. It took many years for researchers to work through some of the implications of research imperatives developed within a 'philosophy of consciousness' (Popkewitz & Brennan, 1998) for empowering and emancipating The Other. Janse van Rensburg (1995), Lotz (1996), and O'Donoghue (1999) raised concerns about participatory action research processes of co-optive emancipatory engineering that was unlikely to achieve these ends. The debates on participatory research have been raging ever since, with the most recent analysis describing a pre-inscription of idealized perspectives for change to be mediated into effect through educational activities (Lotz-Sisitka & O'Donoghue 2006).

Through these deliberations a more careful and broader analysis and synthesis of developing participatory orientations in environmental education research has emerged. Fifteen years ago, Janse van Rensburg (1995) argued powerfully for environmental education research to be seen as a process of social transformation. This research emphasized reflexivity as an appropriate response to socio-ecological degradation and risk. O'Donoghue's (1997) research on long-term social history illustrated processes of social transformation in colonial eastern southern Africa and drew attention to the relationship between environmental education processes and social change in African contexts through emphasizing historicity and culture as important dimensions in environmental education as a research process. Other work on environmental education research and social transformation include engagements with reflexive socially critical processes of empowerment[7]. These studies all show concern for social situatedness, concerns for working with others in research enterprises and the establishment of discursive relationships with co-engaged participants in environmental education research.

DELIBERATIVE RE-SEARCH IN SOCIO-HISTORICAL CONTEXTS OF RISK

We turn now to a review of four clusters of environmental education research projects that provide a deeper analysis of trends in environmental education research[8]. In particular, we seek to examine features of these projects that might be seen as new processes of mediation on a developing landscape of environmental education research.

1. Participatory Action Research in Community Contexts

A post-colonial leveling of power gradients gave rise to a plethora of participatory initiatives. Early ideologies of emancipation/liberation were short-lived against a more pragmatic co-engagement within the limited resources available. The realities of social contexts provided researchers working in these contexts with motivations for their research work which reached beyond simplistic ideologies of emancipation/liberation, as they sought methodologies and approaches (within their participatory intent) that could contribute meaningfully to social change in

O'DONOGHUE AND LOTZ-SISITKA

context and in tangible/material ways. In this way a collaborative engagement within situated culture developed as a reflexive process of mediation where deepening poverty, vulnerability and risk constrained the capability of local actors working with the researchers (Lupele, 2002; Babikwa, 2003).

Case 1 (Babikwa, 2003)

In his research with farmers and NGOs in Uganda, Daniel Babikwa (2003) explains the many tensions, contradictions and inconsistencies that arise in community-based environmental education programmes which only become visible when working with these groups in socio-historical contexts. Working with NGO representatives and farmers, Babikwa explains how educators in these contexts, setting out with educational theories and intentions meant to empower 'the other', often fail due to the defective way in which educational ideas are put into practice in local contexts. He explains how educators working in this context failed to work responsively with socio-economic, political and cultural factors such as income and land distribution, the different dimensions of poverty, gender and specific individual and group interests that influenced access to, and management of key resources, even though these issues were identified in a 'baseline study' undertaken in the context (p. 64). He argues that this process led to inappropriate identifications of factors impeding the agricultural programmes. He also pointed to the erroneous assumptions in critical pedagogies which assume that learners 'know' what they need to learn, noting that in trying to overcome 'top-down' forms of educational mediation facilitators err on the other extreme where they rely too heavily on learners' prior experiences (p. 71). His engagements in a local context also revealed more complex dynamics associated with power relations and note that he found it difficult to categorise any group of individuals as entirely oppressed, powerless or powerful. Poor as most the farmers were, this did not imply that they were necessarily oppressed or powerless, e.g., they exhibited the power to reject or undermine the NGO's efforts.

Case 2 (Lupele, 2003)

In his research to develop learning support materials with communities in Zambia, Justin Lupele explains the complex dynamics of action research processes in contexts of risk and vulnerability. Through contextual profiling he identified a range of socio-ecological factors that provided capital for engagements within two community contexts: Chiawa and Nalusanga. Both communities are located in game management areas which form a 'buffer zone' outside the national parks and are faced with numerous issues and risks associated with poverty. Through action research processes, Lupele generated new insights into local environmental issues and through this process community members were able to more explicitly express their perspectives on local issues. Community members participated in the development of a series of posters which are now used by members of the community in clinics, schools and even in taverns to discuss environmental issues

204

and possible responses. Deliberations with communities centred on how issues were represented and also encompassed cultural questions such as how language should be used and represented in the posters. Power relations also emerged as an important dynamic in engaging with environmental issues in a local context. Without close attention to local dynamics, and processes of working with people in context to re-search and explain their experiences, the research could have been ill-conceived and inappropriate. Small, but significant details noted, for example, are the way in which the communities were related to and 'ruled' by their matrilineal chieftainess. This factor proved to be significant in shaping the educational interactions.

2. Learning Support Materials in Resource Poor Environments

Mediating curriculum change through policy and teacher professional development in post-apartheid South Africa has proved to be a complex process that has been shaped by cultural histories in schools and the nature and status of 'Bantu Education' which left teachers without the necessary curriculum development skills and experience (in the previous regime they were simply required to implement a syllabus with pre-defined textbooks, and had little or no say in the curriculum of how it should/could be implemented). A radical shift to constructivist and outcomes-based approaches to curriculum left many teachers confused and unable to work with the new curriculum. Harley and Parker (1999, drawing on Durkheim) explained the problem as too radical a shift from a context of mechanical solidarity (with strong boundaries and low levels of independence) to a context of organic solidarity (with weak boundaries and more independence). In this context, new forms of mediation were needed to enable teachers to make the transition into a more open, democratically framed curriculum. Strategies centered on the provision and use of tangible learning support materials were used to provide practical tools for mediating learning, particularly in resource-poor environments (Mbanjwa, 2003; Russo, 2004;).

Case 1 (Mbanjwa, 2002)

In his research with teachers in the Foundation Phase (Grades 1–3) of the formal education system, Sibonelo Mbanjwa used action research strategies in working with teachers in classrooms to improve their use of learning and teaching support materials. He worked with teachers and community members in the Makana District to plan and develop a set of materials and then spent time in classrooms with teachers working on ways of using the teaching and learning support materials. His study provided useful insights into the contexts of teaching and learning, and found that, for example, teachers needed materials to strengthen their own knowledge of the subject (in this case waste management) and also that successful use of learning support materials was closely associated with the way in which language use is supported in classrooms (most learners in South Africa learn in a language that is not their home language). His study supported teachers to develop skills for selecting and using materials more successfully in multi-lingual and under-resourced classrooms, and highlighted the crucial role of learning support materials in building a more open-ended, democratic culture of teaching and learning in South African classrooms. Again the close attention to working with teachers in the socio-cultural context characterized this research. Early contextual profiling was significant in preparing the researcher and teacher for working together successfully on the co-engaging research initiative.

Case 2 (Russo, 2003)

Vladimir Russo looked at a similar concern from the vantage point of a professional development course. Here resource-based-learning was part of a course with participants being tasked to work with resource packs on workplace-based assignments. The course process was developed as a process of mediation for educators to clarify and take up better ways of working with the curriculum and learners in their classroom contexts. Here a resource-based action research process was used to scaffold and mediate better classroom practice. The teacher was also the researcher as he worked alongside learner groups and reported on what was done and what happened. In his research design Vladimir worked with the course coordinators to help clarify and refine the course design as well as interviewing the participants and reviewing assignments to gather evidence on how the process was playing out.

3. Intergenerational Community Knowledge and Curriculum Propositions

Indigenous knowledge has recently been seen to reflect world-views that in some way oppose Western science, a knowledge system that came to displace and overshadow indigenous ways of knowing within modernist trajectories during the colonial intrusion into Africa. With hindsight, these social processes reveal an appropriation of local knowledges into formal academic fields, a social process that was experienced as a marginalizing oppression of the indigenous peoples in Africa and their knowledge systems. The indigenous knowledge research that follows found few opposing ideas in need of mediation; instead pointing to how knowledge practices and ways of knowing come to be mediated within learning actions in the socio-ecological realities of the world today (Asafo-Adjei, 2004; Hanisi, 2006; Kota, 2006).

Case 1 (Asafo-Adjei, 2003)

In a rural school in the Eastern Cape, Robert Asafo-Adjei (2004) worked with learners and community members to re-orient aspects of the agricultural science curriculum. The agricultural science curriculum was previously determined by the apartheid state's vision for black children to become farm labourers and was largely irrelevant in contemporary rural society where farm labouring jobs are increasingly scarce. Robert sought to develop a module for the agricultural curriculum that was based on local culture and context, and through re-searching indigenous ways of knowing and doing that were relevant to three species of wild food plant (imifino) in the local context. He and his learners together with older members of the community were able to pilot a module on *from imifino to umfuno* for the agricultural curriculum. In this research, learners talked to members of the community, they tried out the 'looking after' of wild food plants in the school vegetable garden (turning *imifino* into *umfuno*) and Robert himself talked to various community members about the socio-cultural practices associated with the wild food plants. Juxtaposing local knowledge of the wild vegetables with more traditional 'agricultural science' knowledge, Robert and his learners were able to provide a new approach to curriculum in his school.

Case 2 (Kota, 2006)

Lutho Kota is a teacher working at Nosizwe High School in Pakamisa township near King Williams Town. As a young African professional, Lutho feels driven to uncover and recover much of the wisdom in indigenous ways of knowing that enabled the Xhosa to thrive as a pre-colonial democratic order prior to the imperial occupation and conquest of the region. She has a passionate interest in health and nutrition with so many community members being affected by poverty and infected with HIV-AIDS. In her research she found a widening use of *amaRewu* in the care of people suffering from HIV-AIDS. *AmaRewu* was found to stabalise their digestive system and they commented about its use in the old days to give energy for work in the fields. Her initial research pointed to how the making of *amaRewu* was now seen as a practice of the poor and for the sick, with most of the people of King Williams Town/Bisho now not drinking it at all or preferring to buy it in cartons from the supermarket. Lutho chose to work with women in the local community to provide learners with the opportunity to uncover their indigenous heritage and to research changing patterns of production and consumption in modern times. Learners researched the food preferences of the local people, noting whether they made and consumed homemade or preferred to buy commercial *amaRewu* that is now available in differing fruit flavours in the local shops. The learners found that people still valued the home-made over the commercial. Notable here was how the participants brought diverse experiences and plural perspectives into their engagement with indigenous and commercial foods. Contrary to the expectation of significant differences between indigenous (local cultural know-how) and scientific propositions (curriculum concepts) the cases were notable for how these corresponded and were complementary in developing learning interactions.

Case 3 (Hanisi, 2006)

Nosipho Hanisi, a science teacher in Grahamstown, noted that many members of the community associated with the high school at which she teaches science had lost knowledge associated with indigenous fermented foods, notably *umqombothi* (*sorghum* beer). Nosipho thus set out to engage community members in her lessons by inviting them in to give a demonstration of the making and cultural significance of *umqombothi*. She supported the learners to share all they knew about *umqombothi* and alcoholic fermentation. The students then took on the role of researchers when attending a demonstration conducted by parents. Nosipho mediated the learning process by conducting focus group discussions with all involved. She noted that the students struggled to apply and make sense of the concept of alcoholic fermentation but had developed a good grasp of the making of *umqombothi* and its cultural significance. Being responsible for teaching the concepts of science she developed activities to support learners to link the two. Alcoholic fermentation as a practice of Xhosa cultural significance was picked up by the learners and contrasted with alcohol abuse in the school and local community context. How colonial interpretations of Nguni culture and the religious beliefs of Christians had served to marginalise and foster a widening urban rejection of isiXhosa cultural practices related to fermented foods was also deliberated by the learners. In their learning and discussion they developed new insights and respect for Xhosa fermentation practices that bring out the food value and nutrition in the grain.

Indigenous knowledge research is bringing forward new ways of theorizing the relationship between culture and power, experience and rationalization (see for example Masuku & Neluvhalani, 2004).

4. Hands-on Sense-making and Auditing Re-search

Early 'sensory awareness' activities in natural settings served to popularize learning interactions that involved hands-on experiences in nature. Here the proximity of the encounter experiences shaped moral imperatives that have served to extend ethical considerations to encompass the natural world. The worm in the apple of these processes is how an idealizing inculcation of strong feelings for nature does not always provide adequate exposure to some of the harsher realities of the natural world. The mediated sensory encounter of the wonders of nature alone is proving to be a poor way of mediating a human sense of natural processes without tangible measures that more closely model the world in sense-making interactions. The three case studies that follow open up some of the dimensions of mediating encounters in nature through audit research activities and within the place-based experiences in everyday life.

Case 1 (Kohly, 2005)

Nikki Kohly was contracted to coordinate the review and simplification of a hands-on water test kit. Concepts of and information on biodiversity and water issues had been challenging for learners to work with. Chemistry concepts and test results were complex to interpret and the kit cumbersome to work with. Simplifying the tests was a relatively easy task but exploratory work revealed a serious conceptual hurdle. A concern for hands-on encounter experiences of the wonders of water life was not providing the necessary sense-making for learners to read and understand scientific information on biodiversity. Working with story, after de Young and Monroe (1996), provided ways of enhancing sense-making but the breakthrough came in work with a Social Realist ontology after Archer (1995). This work led to a re-ordering of the enquiry activities so that real stories of what others had done and a sense-making sensory experience activity preceded experiential meaning-making encounters in the local river. This work brought the sacred ideal of sensory mediation in nature into question and pointed to the need for both the proximity of encounter experiences and interpretative meaning-making to ensure that environmental learning is sustained as experiential induction into an unquestioned idealizing doctrine of mediating learning in the wonders of nature. Elaborating sensory experiences with sense-making and work with a heuristic to open up an image of a balanced interplay between an ethic of proximity and story-sharing reason circumvented a potential ideological conflict at nature centres.

Case 2 (Hoffmann, 2006)

Pat Hoffmann examined how teachers on a professional development course undertook environmental audits. The research design did not include any mediation beyond the case study convention of member checking but the outcomes of this study provide useful insights on mediation. Evidence of contrasting audit processes (measurement and validating impression) and careful work with theory, suggests that much of the audit work in schools plays out as a process of affirming solidarity that something must be done about a problem. Here the conventional wisdom is affirmed but there is little grasp of the realities of the problem. It appears that these are best provided by measures that represent the concerns in ways that provide a tangible grasp to inform responses to mitigate the concern. The most interesting outcome was a better sense of how auditing processes in which a close engagement with reality, coupled with a measure of detachment, can lead to the construction of a more reality-congruent account and a more realistic assessment of the environmental issue in focus. This approach is proving useful for designing research to factor in local participants as researchers noting that there is a need for both the prevailing conventional wisdom (cultural capital) and a tangible grasp of the matters at hand for the outcomes of the research to inform actions to mitigate the problem under review.

Case 3 (Farrington, 2006)

Katie Farrington worked with 13 young adults for 15 months during which time the group undertook a series of place-based activities using cameras to take photographs and to write stories about their lived environments. This process enabled participants to represent and voice their sense of place and the environment concerns of their community that arose within this. The evidence suggests that knowledge of context, place-based activities, education processes and situated social capital form the basis of meaningful pedagogical engagement with environment concerns. The study points to how the historical interplay of scientific knowledge about environmental issues and the institutional imperative to communicate this through education tend to exclude the experiential knowledge/cultural capital that we now recognise as necessary for mediating a meaningful grasp of local environment concerns.

CO-ENGAGING RESEARCH DESIGNS THAT FACTOR IN LOCAL PARTICIPANTS AS RESEARCHERS

The four clusters of case evidence on the mediation of society reflect a de-centering shift from the education researcher simply interpreting the data to a co-engagement process involving local researchers in ongoing interpretative deliberations. A design shift to add this co-engaged dimension to a conventional research process does not constitute a radical shift and the death of rigorous academic research. Nor does a design shift such as this imply the adoption of the ideals and increasingly systematised plan/act/reflect conventions of participatory action research. Far from this being a break from or an abandonment of conventional research rigor[9] for the prospect of greater educational impact/adoption, these processes appear to reflect an enhanced rigor for engaging the socio-cultural and ecological contingencies of developing contexts.

Most of the cases examined were constituted in quite different disciplinary areas drawing on diverse case study research conventions and all reflect or provide insights into new forms of mediation in society for the public good. The processes of research examined have thus not involved an abandonment of rigor or method but simply reflect an added dimension of contextual co-engagement in the questions at hand.

A characterizing features of this *oeuvre* is a greater concern for processes of research/education as situated learning actions involving:
– Deliberative co-engagement with and within socio-cultural contexts of vulnerability and risk (Re-search to clarify history, context and concerns)
– Reflexive learning actions of engaged re-orientation within these developing contexts (Educative/learning imperatives/innovations for more just and sustainable human life-style choices).

In the case of Babikwa, Lupele, Mbanjwa, Asafo-Adjei, Kota, Hanisi and Farrington, and to a lesser extent in Hoffmann and Kohly, we see patterns of deliberative co-engagement with and within socio-cultural contexts of vulnerability and risk. In all cases issues of language and culture were foregrounded as being significant in the co-researching processes. Power relations were also featured in these co-engagements and in all cases research design decisions placed researchers within and/or alongside a community of practice that acknowledged their role as a participant in the learning process. Clarification of history and context were also strong features of all of these research projects with Babikwa seeking insight into the roots of traditional approaches to education that were used in the contexts in question while Lupele sought linguistic history, educational history and political history as well as insights into environmental histories. Mbanjwa's study focused on curriculum history and the history of educational change experiences in classrooms while Russo probed histories of professional development for insights into how a resource-based course design came to be viewed as a way of engaging participants in workplace innovation. Asafo-Adjei, Kota and Hanisi sought insights into community history and cultural history, noting the influence of modernization processes on community members' perceptions of eating fermented foods and imifino (wild vegetables). In the case of Kohly and Hoffman, history and context were foregrounded in context-specific applications of auditing processes to inform co-engaging ways of working on the contingencies of local environmental concerns.

It is apparent that the scope and focus of each research process was broader than a conventional 'research project'. The research was also an educative experience for the communities of practice in which the researchers were working. Babikwa's research story tells of how the extension workers, the NGOs and the farmers themselves became more aware of how they could better respond to questions of sustainable development. Lupele's story tells of how community members in Chiawa were able to work with the posters they helped to produce to generate further community deliberations, discussions and actions in response to the issues and risks they had identified (after he had left the research process and site) and Farrington opens up engaging ways of working with the environment concerns of local youth, so that youth could narrate and share new expressions of their sense of place that would not normally have been part of curriculum activities in the school. Mbanjwa's story tells of how teachers were more able to select and work with learning and teaching support materials following their engagement in the research process, and Kota and Hanisi's stories tell of how learners, teachers and parents probed local culture and history in relation to local health and nutrition concerns, leading to a new respect for cultural heritage and closer links between school and community. In Russo's research we see work with a course to scaffold the engaging use of materials that involved a variety of local community-based assessments of environmental issues and Hoffman clarifies some of the implications of the way processes such as this play out in capacities to engage environment concerns in practical ways.

Situated Learning Actions and the Politics of the Subject

The research projects discussed above all provide insight into emerging processes of mediation that are arising as research in environmental education in southern Africa. They seem to reflect a move away from earlier 'structural functionalist' and 'facilitative engineering' modes of educational research towards a genre of research which reflects a 'researching engagement with local re-searchers'. This process appears to be giving expression to pedagogical dimensions in environmental education research as a contextually engaging genre of re-search for mediating environment-human relational interactions in developing contexts of vulnerability and risk. Here re-searching with communities, in communities of practice, seems to be a pedagogical process where the rigor of the researching process informs the situated learning taking place. The re-searching process allows for deeper engagements with history and context thus situating the learning processes as co-engaging and reflexive processes of deliberation (debate/negotiation and reflection) and innovation, all aimed at strengthening capability and local contributions to change. Touraine explains this more eloquently as a process of democracy, involving the agency of the subject (in social context):

> ....struggle for political freedom, battles for social rights, the recognition of the cultural rights of all and an awareness of our responsibilities to the past and the future, to our environment and to our physical and psychological integrity, are all so many figures of democracy, That is why democracy is synonymous with the politics of the Subject, of a Subject that is always involved in collective emancipatory actions. (Touraine, 2000, p. 246)

Some Research Tools for Mediating Contextual Co-Engagement for the Public Good

From the analysis, and in the 'genre' of more co-engaging research designs that factor in local participants as researchers we have identified an emergent collection of sensitising constructs from the literature and simple heuristic devises that have been effectively worked within local socio-ecological contexts of risk and vulnerability:
- Socio-cultural heuristics of environment and bioregional contexts (contextual profiling of intermeshing of historical, social, cultural, political, economic and biophysical processes)
- An open-ended triad of socio-ecological controls (power relations/axes of tension between self, society and nature)
- Social realist onto-epistemology for sense-making and practical reason (seeking ontological depth insights into capability and agency)
- An open process framework for active learning in school curriculum contexts (scoping learning interactions in curriculum processes)
- An open-ended heuristic on deliberative ethics (imperatives of proximity/ reason)

These are opening up vantage points and orientations (sensitizing constructs) for research that allows a working with people and data generated in and about contexts of practice, a co-engaged and contextual extension of conventions that are centred on theory/hypotheses and abstracting representations of context. A follow up to this chapter, would require a depth probing of the role of these sensitizing constructs in shaping and framing an 'emerging genre' of research practice as tentatively discussed here.

Could this picture, documenting the emergence of new forms of mediation in society through co-engaging research-as-pedagogy (a potential new 'genre' of research?), provide a new vantage point on research for the 'public good'? In African contexts where the social *habitus* of institutions (universities and their research programmes) are coming under scrutiny in post-colonial contexts could this provide a vantage point for beginning to examine environmental education research responses to increasing vulnerability and risk? Is it possible, out of this historical picture, to generate new research agendas on 'sustainable development' that are not captivated by colonial intrusions, undemocratic formations and globalizing discourse? More importantly, can this emerging 'genre' of research contribute to democracy, capability and the agency of the Subject, in a context where adequate responses to risk and vulnerability in African communities (research for the 'public good') are often matters of life and death.

NOTES

[1] The social justice challenge here appears to be making implicit processes of social control and management explicit, particularly for research in relation to the livelihood practices of those already marginalized within the modernist, post-colonial order.

[2] This was most often done with donor funding as the colonial powers gave over state administrative power for the mediating hand of research to inform development processes, policy and state practices.

[3] This unfettered instrumentalism is leading to ethical poverty (Shiva, 2003) increases in socio-ecological risk and environmental degradation (UNEP, 2002), increased inequality and higher levels of poverty and vulnerability (UNDP, 2003). Sustainable development discourse is increasingly being appropriated by the market (Bond & Guiliwe, 2003), with the result that a sustainability discourse of ecological modernisation is emerging as a dominant narrative that is falling far short of addressing the growing socio-ecological crisis, and is not addressing socio-ecological justice questions, or ecological sustainability questions adequately, both of which are central to enabling and sustaining 'a public good'.

[4] A legacy of Western and colonial intellectual practice where complex socio-cultural and historical issues are reduced to binaries in research discourse.

[5] It should be noted that, in southern Africa, issues of sustainability were synonymous with conservation and environmental education as these engaged environment and sustainability concerns in the region. As the global salvation discourse of ESD was set against what came before it, the assumption was that sustainability concerns were not being engaged and there was the need for something new to give effect to the desired global change.

[6] Institutional structural functionalism is notable in the theory of social action after Talcott Parsons, the works of Ralph W. Tyler and an instructional program as a functioning instrument of education.

[7] For example: Lotz, 1996; Mokuku, 1999; Lupele, 2003; Babikwa, 2004; Price, 2004; Raven, 2005; Burt et al., 2005 and others.

[8] The cases selected are broadly representative rather than comprehensive.

[9] Clearly a foregrounding of 'black box' conventions of empirical analytical and statistical verification as rigor in research is being questioned and displaced by a co-engaged rigor of historico-empirical re-search in developing context as a mediating process of reflexive social reorientation in the face of increasing socio-ecological risk.

REFERENCES

African Union (AU). (2005). *Revitalising higher education in Africa. A synthesis report. African Union.* Department of Human Resources, Science and Technology.

Archer, M. (1995). *Realist social theory: The morphogenetic approach.* Cambridge: Cambridge University Press.

Asafo-Adjei, R. (2003). *From Imifino to Umfuno: A case study foregrounding indigenous knowledge in school-based curriculum development.* Unpublished Med Thesis, Rhodes University, Grahamstown, South Africa.

Babikwa, D. (2004). Tensions, contradictions and inconsistencies in community-based environmental education programmes: The role of defective educational theories. *Southern African Journal of Environmental Education, 21*, 61–80.

Burt, J., *et al.* (2004). *Critical review of participatory practice.* Unpublished working documents. Grahamstown: Rhodes University Environmental Education and Sustainability Unit..

Bond, P., & Guliwe, T. (2003). Contesting sustainable development: South African civil society critiques and advocacy. In G. Mhone & O. Edigheji (Eds.), *Governance in the New South Africa. The challenges of globalisation* (pp. 313–345). Cape Town: University of Cape Town Press.

Delanty, G. (1999). *Social theory in a changing world. Conceptions of modernity.* Cambridge: Polity Press.

De Young, R., & Monroe, M. (1996). Some fundamentals of engaging stories. *Environmental Education Research, 2*(2), 171–187.

Farrington, K. (2006). *Engaging sense of place in an environment of change: Youth, identity and place-based learning activities in environmental education.* Unpublished MEd Thesis, Rhodes University, Grahamstown, South Africa.

Hanisi, N. (2006). *Nguni fermented foods: Working with indigenous knowledge in the life sciences.* Unpublished Med Thesis, Rhodes University, Grahamstown, South Africa.

Hoffmann, P. (2006). *Reviewing the use of environmental audits for learning in school contexts: A case study of environmental auditing processes within a professional development course.* Unpublished Med Thesis, Rhodes University, Grahamstown, South Africa.

Irwin, P. (2005). *Directory of environmental education research in Southern Africa.* Rhodes University, Grahamstown, South Africa.

Janse van Rensburg, E. (1995). *Environmental education and research in southern Africa: A landscape of shifting priorities.* PhD Thesis, Rhodes University, Grahamstown, South Africa.

Keely, J., & Scoones, I. (2003). *Understanding environmental policy processes: Cases from Africa.* London: Earthscan.

Kohly, N. (2005). *Water quality testing materials for situated environmental learning. Research Report.* Grahamstown: Rhodes University Environmental Education and Sustainability Unit.

Kota, L. (2006). *Local food choices and nutrition: A case study of Ama-Rewu in the FET consumer studies curriculum.* Unpublished Med Thesis, Rhodes University, Grahamstown, South Africa.

Le Grange, L. (2004). Embodiment, social praxis and environmental education: some thoughts. *Environmental Education Research, 10*(3), 387–400.

Lotz, H. (1996). *The development of environmental education resource materials for Junior Primary Education through teacher participation: The case of the We Care Primary Project.* Unpublished D.Ed Thesis, University of Stellenbosch, Stellenbosch.

Lotz-Sisitka, H. (2004). *Positioning southern African environmental education in a changing context.* Howick: SADC REEP/Share-Net.

Lotz-Sisitka, H., & O'Donoghue, R. (2006). *Participation, situated culture and practical reason.* In M. Rickinson, C. Lundholm, & N. Hopwood (Eds.), *Environmental learning: Insights from research into the student experience (pp. 111—127).* Dortrecht: Springer.

Lupele, J. (2003). *Action research case studies of participatory materials development in two community contexts in Zambia.* Unpublished Med Thesis, Rhodes University, Grahamstown, South Africa.

Mamdani, M. (1996). *Citizen and subject. Contemporary Africa and the legacy of late colonialism.* Kampala: Fountain Publishers.

Masuku, L. (1999). *The role of indigenous knowledge in/for environmental education: The case of an Nguni story in the schools water action project.* Unpublished med thesis, Rhodes University, Grahamstown, South Africa.

Masuku, L., & Neluvhalani, E. (2004). Indigenous knowledge in environmental education processes: Perspectives on a growing research arena. *Environmental Education Research, 10*(3), 353–370.

Mbanjwa, S. (2002). *The use of environmental education learning support materials in OBE: The case study of the creative solution to waste project.* Unpublished MEd thesis, Rhodes University, Grahamstown, South Africa.

Mokuku, T. (1999). *Education for environmental literacy: Participatory action research in the science curriculum in Lesotho*. Unpublished PhD Thesis, Rhodes University, Grahamstown, South Africa.

O'Donoghue, R. (1997). *Detached harmonies: A study in/on developing processes of environmental education*. Unpublished PhD Thesis, Rhodes University, Grahamstown, South Africa.

O'Donoghue, R., & Janse van Rensburg, E. (1999, January). Indigenous myth, story and knowledge in/as environmental education processes. In *Indigenous knowledge in/as environmental education processes*. Environmental Education Association of Southern Africa, Monograph no. 3, EEASA, Howick.

O'Donoghue, R., & Neluvhalani, E. (2002). Indigenous knowledge and the school curriculum: A review of developing methods and methodological perspectives. In E. Janse van Rensburg, J. Hattingh, H. Lotz-Sisitka, & R. O'Donoghue (Eds.), *EEASA Monograph: Environmental education, ethics and action in Southern Africa* (pp. 121–134). Pretoria: EEASA / HSRC.

Popkewitz, T., & Brennan, M. (Eds.) (1998). *Foucault's challenge: Knowledge and power in education*. New York: Teachers' College Press.

Price, L. (2004). Participatory curriculum development: Lessons drawn from teaching environmental education to industry in Zimbabwe. *Environmental Education Research, 10*(3), 401–408.

Raven, G. (2005). *Course processes that enable the development of reflexive competence: A case study of an environmental education professional development course*. Unpublished PhD, thesis Rhodes University, Grahamstown, South Africa.

Russo, V. (2003). *A resource-based learning approach to professional development: The case study of the ACEE* (Rhodes University Advanced Certificate in Environmental Education). Unpublished MEd thesis, Rhodes University, Grahamstown, South Africa.

Shiva, V. (2003). Environment and sustainability. In W. Fisher & T. Ponniah (Eds.), *Another world is possible: Popular alternatives to globalisation at the world social forum*. Cape Town: David Phillips. Novia Scotia: Fernwood Publishing Ltd, London: Zed Books.

Touraine, A. (1997). *What is democracy?* Boulder, CO: Westview Press.

Touraine, A. (2001). *Beyond neoliberalism*. Cambridge: Polity Press.

Touraine, A. (2000). *Can we live together? Equality and difference*. Cambridge: Polity Press.

UNEP (United Nations Environment Programme). (2002). *Africa environment outlook: Policy and action recommendations for a sustainable future*. Nairobi: UNEP.

UNDP. (2003, Summary). *Human development report 2003*. New York: Oxford University Press.

Rob O'Donoghue and Heila Lotz-Sisitka
Environmental Education & Sustainability Unit,
Rhodes University, South Africa

CONCLUSION

ROBERT B. STEVENSON WITH CAROLYN STIRLING

12. ENVIRONMENTAL LEARNING AND AGENCY IN DIVERSE EDUCATIONAL AND CULTURAL CONTEXTS

Environmental education is concerned with engaging learners in examining the relationship between humans and nature, or stated another way, between society and its social systems, on the one hand, and the biophysical or non-human natural environment and its ecological systems, on the other. And as Scott and Gough (2003) argue:

> learning is central to the relationship between society and nature. People learn, organizations learn and, in a sense, the environment learns as nature responds to the results of human learning and activity. (p. 8)

These authors further characterize environmental learning as "learning that accrues from an engagement with the environment or environmental ideas" (p. 14). Furthermore, with the emergence over the last 20 years of the language of sustainable development and sustainability in international policy, they argue that sustainable development itself is a learning process through which we need to learn to build our capacity to live more sustainably (Scott & Gough, 2003). Thus, learning is viewed as central to creating a more environmentally sustainable, and, I would add, more socially just, future. In other words, learning is involved in improving both the condition of the planet and the human condition.

The previous chapters in this book examine environmental learning in a full range of educational settings in diverse international contexts, including Canada, Denmark, the Netherlands, South Africa, Sweden, the United Kingdom and the United States. The case studies from these different educational and cultural contexts illuminate the challenges of engaging children and adults in meaningful learning regarding the complexity of environmental issues, as well as document and offer insights into the promising possibilities of such engagement.

The first contributors to this volume, Rickinson and Lundholm, begin by emphasizing the complexity of learning within more formal environmental educational activities and the need for improved research-based understandings of the environmental learning process. A lack of empirical research on learning processes in environmental education, as well as efforts to conceptualize how such processes might be understood to occur, has been recently noted (Rickinson, 2006). The chapters in this volume help address this situation and contribute to deeper understandings of this complexity through their empirically-based case studies of

R. Stevenson and J. Dillon (eds.), Engaging Environmental Education: Learning, Culture and Agency, 219–237.

the learning process in action in school, community and workplace or other settings and the conceptual analyzes of environmental learning in media culture and in research. In order to illuminate the significance of their contributions and to highlight commonalities and differences across the cases, this concluding chapter begins by drawing on analytic frameworks from the literature on learning theories and then relates them to the challenges of environmental learning.

CONCEPTIONS OF LEARNING

Several of the authors in this volume point out the well-documented limitations of a transmission model of learning and teaching (Kelsey & Dillon, Laessoe & Carlsson) that has dominated most environmental education and interpretation programs and activities for decades (Stevenson, 1987, 2007; Kelsey & Dillon, this volume). In such a model, learning is essentially defined as the passive acquisition of facts, concepts and skills. It involves acquiring a new piece of information or skill which, when internalized, can become a useful resource if the learner sees a purpose and use for it (Scott & Gough, 2003). If the information to be acquired or task to be learned is complex, then this behaviourist view of learning involves breaking down the information or task into component parts that can be transmitted separately. The learning process is then assumed to involve the accumulation and association of the relevant components of information or skills in the individual's head. In this limited model, learning is separated from the social context other than serving as the source of motivation to learn through providing positive and/or negative reinforcement.

Cognitive perspectives on learning treat the learner as a more active agent, although to different degrees. According to information processing models, the mind can be viewed as a computer in actively processing information or input and producing responses or output (Marshall, 1992). In contrast to this input-output focus, cognitive constructivists (such as Piaget and Perry) emphasize what is taking place within the individual's mind which they view as actively constructing knowledge, rather than passively receiving information or focusing on inputs and outputs. From a constructivist learning perspective, individuals construct knowledge or understanding in responding not to external stimuli but to their interpretations of those stimuli by extracting meaning from information and connecting it to previous constructions of meaning. Thus, "according to constructivists, learning consists of building on what the learner brings to the situation and restructuring initial knowledge in widening and intersecting spirals of increasingly complex understanding" (Marshall, 1992, p. 11). From a cognitive perspective, the learner must be intrinsically motivated to engage in this approach to learning.

Social constructivists, beginning with Vygotsky, believe cognitive constructivists neglect the social or collaborative nature of learning. They emphasize "the role of social interactions through which contexts, knowledge, and meanings in everyday life are constructed and reconstructed" with "learning and thinking situated in social contexts rather than occurring solely in an individual's mind" (Marshall, 1992, p. 11). So in social learning theory, "interactions between people are viewed as possibilities or opportunities for meaningful learning" (Wals & Noorduyn, this volume, p. 73) from the communication and dialogue that takes place. Social learning theorists also note that the potential and quality of learning is dependent in part on the presence of diverse perspectives, so that participants are exposed to other ways of thinking, and at the same time there is social cohesion among the people involved, so that these different perspectives are treated seriously as a contribution to advancing everyone's understanding.

An extension of the social constructivist perspective is offered by sociocultural theorists who argue that the former approach does not illuminate the sources that learners use or draw upon to form their understanding from social interactions with others (Ogawa *et al.*, 2009). Not only is learning viewed as situated in social practices that occur in everyday communities of practice (Lave & Wenger, 1991), but cultural tools and practices - most notably language, for Vygotsky (1978) and many others – used in these communities enable individuals to make culturally defined sense and meaning of the world. These interactions take place in communities and engagement in learning stems from participation in communities where learning is valued (Greeno *et al.*, 1996).

Sociocultural (or situative) approaches have increasingly been used to understand learning and development (of all students) in a way that takes culture as a core concern .... These frameworks assume that social and cultural processes are central to learning and argue for the importance of local activity settings in children's learning. From this perspective, understanding learning requires a focus on how individuals participate in particular activities, and how they draw on artifacts, tools, and social others to solve local problems (Nasir & Hand, 2006, p. 450).

Cultural processes are viewed as mediators of human activity and learning, including in ways that can both facilitate and constrain learning (Lee, 2008). For example, the work of Medin and Bang suggests that

ecological reasoning among the Menominee can be traced, in part, to intergenerational practices involving fishing. Although nearby European Americans also routinely fish, the two communities give very different cultural meanings to the practice. And Menominee who live in Chicago, for example, still maintain ecological beliefs about the natural world, largely through social ties and traditional belief systems (cited in Lee, 2008, p. 274).

Cultural historical activity theory (CHAT), as part of the family of sociocultural theories, focuses on activities or cultural practices as sites where meaning is negotiated and communities are formed, while emphasizing the role of social, historical and cultural factors in understanding how social structures shape activity and influence learning. CHAT is seen by its advocates as representing a response to the struggle to conceptualize and study the relationship between learning and the social context in which it occurs by foregrounding "the many contextual layers that surround human activity, thus illuminating how a person engaged in an activity is linked in a complex network that is both social and historical" (Ogawa *et al.,* 2009, p. 85). Thus, it offers a "powerful framework for understanding how learning occurs" (Ogawa *et al.,* 2009, p. 84) and meaning develops over time from participation in multiple social interactions and networks in particular contexts. In other words, there is a belief that "learning and knowledge are situated within a context, culture and activity in which they develop" (Nasir & Hand, 2006, p. 460). So learning is mediated by activity which in turn is mediated by social, historical and cultural factors that shape the context in which activity and learning occur.

In sum, CHAT treats learning as "the process by which people master and appropriate cultural tools and meanings while engaged in activity" (Ogawa *et al.,* 2009, pp. 84–5) or an activity system. Activity systems have been framed as comprising six interrelated and mutually constituted elements: object (the purpose behind the activity), subject (the individual or group working toward the object), mediating artifacts (signs and tools), community (within which the relationship occurs), rules (shared within the community), and division of labour (positioning of community members) (Cole & Engestrom, 1993). Analytically, the study of an activity system "becomes a collective, multivoiced construction of its past, present, and future zones of proximal development" (Engestrom, 1999, p. 9).

To summarize these perspectives on learning in somewhat parsimonious fashion, behaviorist perspectives focus on learning as the passive acquisition of information and skills; cognitive constructivists emphasize the active construction of knowledge or understanding through an individual's interpretation of information; social constructivists are concerned with constructing knowledge or understanding through collaboration and dialogue; sociocultural or situated theory views learning as situated in social practices of specific communities, and finally cultural-historical activity theory locates learning as the outcome of activity in specific communities (Vare, 2008). As others have pointed out (for example, Greeno *et al.,* 1996; Reid & Nikel, 2008), not only are there some similarities across these different conceptions of learning, such as the dynamic nature of learning, but there are also complementary characteristics for different kinds of learning. For example, although there are continuing arguments in cognitive science about the respective roles and relative significance of neurological forces in the brain as compared to the active construction of meaning and understanding by the learner (Frawley, 1997), there seems little dispute that both processes are at work in learning (Starratt, 2003). This means that learning demands active engagement and intentional effort on the part of individuals and is shaped by the learner's prior knowledge and personal and cultural experiences. In addition, much (if not all) learning is situated or tied to particular contexts, that is, it is influenced by the context and activity in which it is embedded (Brown, Collins & Duguid, 1989), and occurs through social interaction (that is, it is largely a social activity). The implications of these perspectives for, first, the processes and then the substance of environment-related learning are next examined.

LEARNING PROCESSES IN ENVIRONMENTAL/SUSTAINABILITY EDUCATION

Critical Inquiry

Since the promulgation of influential reports emerging from international conferences in the 1970s, the goals of environmental education have been widely identified as developing not only awareness and knowledge of human-environment relationships and problems, but also the skills and motivation for investigating and working toward the resolution of environmental issues (Tbilisi Declaration, 1978). In other words, besides developing knowledge of and sensitivity to environmental concerns, education is seen as providing opportunities for individuals to thoughtfully and critically appraise environmental situations, to make informed decisions about such situations and to develop the capacity and commitment to act in ways that sustain and enhance the environment. Education for sustainable development (ESD) or sustainability (EfS) has been similarly conceptualized, at least by socially critical scholars, as a process of critical inquiry in which learners are encouraged "to explore the complexity and implications of sustainability as well as the economic, political, social, cultural, technological and environmental forces that foster or impede sustainable development" (Fien & Tilbury, 2002, p. 10). So the goals of EE and ESD or EfS have a similar focus on learning as a process of critical inquiry into environmental issues and concerns.

   Critical inquiry, argued Sirotnik (1991), is "dialectical, dialogical and deliberate." Sirotnik described the dialectical as a knowledge-building process, which we engage in almost daily, of continually questioning and re-questioning, constructing and re-constructing knowledge. The dialogical involves competent communication between and among communities of practice. Deliberate is the third characteristic because critical inquiry is not "something that happens serendipitously or casually" but must be "worked at with rigor and continuity" (p. 247).

The Dialectical

Cognitive learning theorists argue that knowledge building begins with what the learner brings to the situation, including their experiences, interests, skills and values. Young people's "reasoning about the natural world is predicated on their experiences with the natural world rather than on a universal pattern" (Medin & Bang cited in Lee, p. 274), and so the decline in children's opportunities to interact with the natural world (Blanchet-Cohen, this volume) is an important factor shaping their environmental learning that must be taken into account. Their interpretations of human-nature relationships are made in the light of these (in)experiences. In addition, as Rickinson and Lundlom's (this volume) studies reveal, students not only interpret (and reconstruct) an activity or task from their own framework of understanding, but also their "difficulties with environmental learning activities can be as much due to issues of emotions and values as to challenges of knowledge and understanding" (Rickinson & Lundholm, this volume, p. 26). On the other hand, while children and youth's direct experiences with nature are declining, their engagement with popular media has been increasing. And potentially, as McKenzie and colleagues (this volume) argue, some of these experiences can evoke emotionally powerful responses (such as empathy, discomfort, and sense of belonging) that enable sensory, as well as cognitive, learning in relation to socio-ecological issues.

Issues concerning human-environment relationships are inherently complex, normative, dynamic, shaped by specific local contexts, uncertain, and filled with tensions, especially in the context of the current globalized post-industrial era that itself is characterized by complexity, uncertainty and risk (Hargreaves, 2003). Yet Blanchet-Cohen (this volume) observes that the way the children she studied positioned themselves in relation to environmental problems suggests they are ready and open to engage in the complexity of environmental issues. Thus, she argues that teachers should embrace rather than avoid complexity. In doing so, teachers need to recognize that constructing knowledge about these issues and relationships is neither exclusively nor primarily a matter of passive assimilation of discrete facts or information about the environment. Constructivist learning theorists emphasize that it requires making sense or meaning of information as learners actively interpret, construct and re-construct information and ideas that are tentative and subject to revision. This kind of learning also involves analyzing multiple interrelated factors, understanding multiple viewpoints, and responding to rapidly and constantly shifting scenarios.

The Dialogical

Social learning theorists emphasize that social "interactions between people are viewed as possibilities or opportunities for meaningful learning" (Wals & Noorduyn, this volume, p. 73). Learning can be "enriched when it involves more than one learner because the insights and perspectives of others can fill out the limitations, partiality, and tentativeness of the individual's knowledge" and so within a community of learners there is "a better chance of arriving at richer, more complex interpretations" (Starratt, 2003, p. 36–7). This two-way process of communication is particularly important when dealing with complex or contested information or ideas that require engaging the learner in discussing and negotiating the meaning – and/or determining the usefulness (Scott & Gough, 2003) – of these ideas. It enables learners to see how their personal meanings relate to the personal meanings of others (Starratt, 2003).

Wals and Noorduyn (this volume) emphasize that any process seeking to "address sustainable living will inevitably involve diverging norms, values and constructions of reality" (p. 73) and these differences need to be explicated and examined as a way to enhance the dialogue and identify strategies for using these conflicts as a learning process. This perspective requires space to be created for dialogue rather than the transmission or exchange of viewpoints. However, as Kelsey and Dillon (this volume) reported in examining efforts to foster conversational learning between visitors and volunteer guides at a major U.S. aquarium, a transition from authoritative communication to dialogic communication can be difficult. They attributed the reasons for this difficulty to the guides' own educational experiences of an information transmission model of teaching and learning, the more challenging and less predictable nature of dialogue, the need for a stronger command of the information, and the power of structures such as the volunteer guide training programs, and an institutional "identity as a purveyor of science authority" (p. 107).

A study of the collaborative efforts of a neighbourhood to design a community garden revealed the importance of and conditions for high quality communication in which procedures, choices and results are shared formally and informally with all those involved (Wals & Noorduyn, this volume). Not only, the researchers reported, is such communication crucial to avoid marginalizing any stakeholders, but it should also include openness, trust, access, and transparency. They noted that an outside facilitator can monitor and stimulate these characteristics, as well as deal with conflicts, maintain focus, demonstrate progress, and help create a positive atmosphere. In addition, they recommend that all those involved should be informed of the uncertainty and risks involved in participating in an interactive process of civic engagement in sustainability.

The Deliberate

A deliberate and rigorous process of disciplined inquiry in schools has been delineated as engaging students in using prior knowledge (facts, concepts, and theories) that other inquirers have provided; striving for in-depth understanding of problems; and expressing ideas and conclusions through elaborated communication (Newmann, Secada & Wehlage, 1995). In-depth understanding goes beyond passing familiarity and "occurs as one looks for, tests and creates relationships among pieces of knowledge that can illuminate a particular problem or issue" (Wehlage, Newmann & Secada, 1996, p. 25). In constructing knowledge through disciplined inquiry students organize, interpret, synthesize, analyze, and evaluate information. The expression or representation of this knowledge can involve oral or written discourse, products or performances. The production of various kinds of media is one example that can provide students (or adults) with the opportunity to tell a story of their understanding and interpretation (McKenzie *et al.,* this volume).

Deliberate inquiry has been described as a way of life rather than a task or an event that comes to an end (Sirotnik, 1991). It has parallels to Dewey's notion of reflective inquiry (and action) which he defined as involving "active, persistent and careful consideration of any belief or practice in light of reasons that support it" (Zeichner & Liston, 1996, p. 9). Reflection, according to Dewey, is more than a logical and rational inquiry and problem solving process – it is a holistic way of consistently thinking about and responding to problems: in other words, a way of being. This distinction is represented in one of four profiles identified by Blanchet-Cohen (this volume) of the means by which early adolescents from many diverse cultures were involved in environmental activities. One group viewed environmental involvement as a way of life, rather than a specific initiative or project. From a sociocultural learning theory perspective, for these students, environmental learning was not manifested or mediated in a single activity or just in an educational setting, but in the context and activities of their daily lives.

Deep Reflection

As just foregrounded, these three elements of critical inquiry – the dialectic, the dialogical, and the deliberate - also demand the capacity to reflect deeply and critically on one's experiences, assumptions, beliefs and values and those of others, as well as on the contextual factors that shape ideas, values and practices, concerning human-environment relationships. Meanings, interpretations and judgments can be examined through reflection in two realms: the private and the public, or in Prawat's (1991) terms, in "conversations with self" and "conversations with others." Thus, reflection can be viewed as both a meta-cognitive mechanism or activity and a social or dialogical practice (Hoffman-Kipp *et al.,* 2003).

Self-reflective individuals selectively choose which particular events, artefacts and symbols are subjects for reflection and so limit the multiplicity of meanings that can be constructed (Cinnamond & Zimpher, 1990). Therefore, social interactions are important for expanding the understandings and interpretations that are constructed from reflection. However, these interactions can also be limiting for reflection if the discourse communities in which they occur do not comprise individuals who bring diverse sets of knowledge, histories and cultural perspectives. In addition, reflection, which along with inquiry can be a normative ideal of the discourse community, can be viewed as not only a social endeavor but also as situated in particular activities. For example, students engaged in a group environmental project or community members working on a neighbourhood committee to develop policies (such as on domestic cats, as described by Clark, this volume) can be understood as using artefacts (e.g., arguments, statistics, stories) for reflection as they interact and exchange ideas with others in goal-directed activities (Hoffman-Kipp *et al.,* 2003). From a CHAT perspective, reflection and learning as human activities are culturally mediated as they involve the use of language, symbols and concepts, all of which have histories of meanings and use (Hoffman-Kipp *et al.,* 2003). Language and concepts are both constraining and enabling forces as they are required to express and question assumptions, beliefs, and values, as well as alternative possibilities, while other artefacts used for reflection can similarly be limiting or enhancing. Therefore, it is important to be sensitive to – to reflect on – how these cultural systems, as well as one's own culture and history, shape one's inquiry and learning.

Simply put, reflection is a tool for learning – that involves, according to constructivists, self-examination of emerging understandings of self and the issue(s) that are the subject of inquiry, or unfolds, according to sociocultural or situated learning theorists, in the social practices of discourse communities, or according to cultural-historical activity theorists, in activity systems that are culturally and historically determined. A deliberate and systematic process of dialectical knowledge building should involve treating one's emerging knowledge as tentative and subject to revision based on on-going critical self and collaborative inquiry. This inquiry and reflection also should be directed to the process and activities through which knowledge was constructed, including mediating socio-cultural norms and systems and political-economic structures that define roles and relationships in human communities and their activities.

THE SUBSTANCE OF LEARNING IN ENVIRONMENTAL/ SUSTAINABILITY EDUCATION

Authentic Issues

Since learning demands active engagement and intentional effort on the part of the learner, one of the core challenges of environmental education, as in education in general, is fostering deeper and sustained levels of learner engagement (Reid & Nikel, 2008) in critical inquiry. A lack of an emotional or meaningful connection to a topic or issue results in students merely "going through the motions or appearing to do what was expected without really doing it' (Rickinson & Lundholm, this volume, p. 8). One way this challenge might be addressed, as I have argued elsewhere (Stevenson, 1997), is by focusing learning on authentic activity, such as in-depth inquiries into a specific environmental issue which has been defined as "a socially or ecologically significant problem, somehow related to the environment, about which there are different human beliefs and values" (Ramsey, Hungerford & Volk, 1989, p. 26). Investigating a real issue, rather than merely studying a topic, is likely to be more engaging to students or other individuals provided the selected issue is meaningful and important to them. An intensive in-depth inquiry is also much more likely to result in deep, complex and enduring understandings of an environmental issue and to cultivate habits of environmental thoughtfulness (Stevenson, 1997).

The importance of engagement and authenticity is underlined by sociocultural learning theorists who argue that learning is influenced by the context and activity in which it is embedded. Blanchet-Cohen points out that young people's "participation becomes meaningful as they engage in critical thinking, imagination, and action" (this volume, p. 50) and, therefore, is critical to their development and learning. This process, however, is not linear, straightforward or generalizable but is shaped by the social and cultural context, the opportunities that arise, and the child's efforts to give significance to his/her context and opportunities.

Unfortunately, mass media reporting of environmental issues does not usually encourage such engagement. Storksdieck and Stylinski (this volume) note that reporters must translate complex concepts, policy issues and debates into human interest stories "with clear compelling visuals" and are expected to provide journalistic balance. The results are that science is reconstructed without detailed exploration of underlying issues and equal weight is often given "to competing perspectives even if one side lacks merit or is a minority position" (Storksdieck & Stylinski, this volume, p. 135) – a situation evident in the reporting on climate change. The selected reporting narrative - which often focuses on conflict and controversy - shapes the public's understanding of the nature of an environmental issue and influences the public discourse. In particular, it usually reduces the complexity of issues to simplistic dichotomous positions.

In addition to a process of critical inquiry, there must be substantive and authentic issues to inquire about. An environmental policy issue can be treated as usually involving three broad types of questions: questions of fact and explanation, questions of definition, and moral or value questions (Oliver & Newmann, 1970). For example, the question of why ecological sustainability is important and needs to be addressed involves facts establishing that many current practices, such as levels of use of natural resources, are unsustainable and explanations of what will happen if no changes are made. Definitional questions include the concept of sustainability or sustainable development itself which has been recognized as ambiguous, contested and subject to multiple interpretations (Fien & Tilbury, 2002). Finally, developing strategies for responding to sustainability concerns involves choices that invoke questions of values. Critical inquiry into environmental issues demands examining these three kinds of questions.

As Kelsey and Dillon (this volume) point out, environmental issues are not confined to problems that can be solved by science alone, but involve socio-cultural values and political and economic factors. Thus, there is a normative dimension and a need for both understanding the values of others, as well as moral deliberation on one's own values. To be critical, inquiry must question, based on normative considerations, the interests and ideologies underlying any position or stance on an environmental policy issue (Sirotnik, 1991). Specific socio-ecological values are represented in two sets of interdependent principles espoused in a "world ethic of sustainability" in the Caring for the Earth Charter, namely a responsibility to care for nature and a responsibility to care for each other. Principles related to the first, ecological sustainability, are interdependence, biodiversity, living lightly on the earth, and interspecies equity; while social justice principles are basic human needs, inter-generational equity, human rights, and participation (IUCN, UNEP, WWF, 1991).

However, the difficulty of harmonizing or establishing compatibility of values is revealed by Clark's (this volume) case study in which an "apparent homogeneity of environmentalism among community members was shown to belie a heterogeneous reality of how individual's environmental ethic would implement" (p. 93) actions relating to a policy on whether or not to allow domestic cats to roam freely outdoors (where they can prey on native wildlife). The case studies reported by Wals and Noorstyn, and Laessoe and Carlsson in this volume illustrate the challenges of negotiating a shared understanding and ethical stance and a commitment to live by that stance.

Imaginative Thinking

Authentic critical inquiry and reflection must go beyond understanding and critique of current unsustainable social practices, habits, and systems to generating possibilities for transforming them. Creating ecologically and socially sustainable communities and societies demands the production of new knowledge and creative solutions or resolutions to vexing problems and dilemmas. The reframing of issues and questions, the re-forming of ways of thinking, the repositioning of relationships, and the re-imagining of ways of working and living are all required in order to generate new ideas, as well as to revive or regenerate old promising practices that are more sustainable than current dominant practices.

"Environmental concerns require the reframing of issues thought to be previously understood (and settled) by other meaning frames" (Starratt, 2003, p. 35). For example, Starratt (2003) argues that "a reformation of the meanings associated with market economies" is needed owing to the global scarcity of non-renewable resources and environmental degradation. He points to the example that "traditional cultural meanings" have been challenged by critical and feminist theorists who framed important new questions about power and gender relationships. The treatment and re-use of brown waste water for human consumption is an example of rethinking the cultural meaning of such waste. These kinds of reformations also may require individuals and communities to reposition themselves in relation to both nature and their social and political practices.

The search for new ways of working and living and the rejuvenation of more sustainable old ones calls for both creativity and hybridization in our thinking (Wals, personal communication). In a globalized and post-modern world characterized by complexity, constant and virtually instantaneous flows of information, and rapid change, there has been a move from the differentiation of cultural categories and identities and the segmentation of social scientific knowledge to increasing cultural and scientific hybridization and knowledge integration across different disciplinary fields. Given the complexity, uncertainty, and interconnections of environmental issues with social-cultural and political economic ones, there is a need for multifaceted perspectives and integrative approaches that lead to learning and knowledge construction through weaving different modes of thinking from multiple disciplines to create new integrative concepts, principles, and systems (Blake, Sterling & Kagawa, 2009). This process includes exploring and reinterpreting our experiences from alternative perspectives and re-imagining new applications of traditional understandings to different problems (Starratt, 2003).

Imagining such new ways of thinking and acting and new positioning in relation to the environment and others can be facilitated and expressed through engaging learners in the production of diverse forms of media. Studies have indicated that youth are not passive recipients but actively create personally relevant texts from popular media (Weis & Dimitriadis, 2008), such as magazines and music, to negotiate their sense of self and community. In other words, multi-media communication technologies can be used productively to engage students in creative and imaginative thinking about new possibilities for more sustainable lifestyles and livelihoods. On the other hand, while children and youth's direct experiences with nature are declining, their engagement with popular media has been increasing. And potentially, as McKenzie and colleagues (this volume) argue, some of these experiences can evoke emotionally powerful responses (such as empathy, discomfort, and sense of belonging) that enable sensory, as well as cognitive, learning in relation to socio-ecological issues.

McKenzie (2009) draws on Rizvi's arguments that first, engaging the imagination in this way is usually seen and practiced as developing an individual capacity as distinct from social and cultural imagination. And second, as an individual pursuit and one mediated by one's cultural and political world, the boundaries of imagination are limited. She adds that, on the other hand, Appadurai's and others' idea of social imaginaries "offers possibilities for how people can collaboratively invent and administer more sustaining and sustainable social and cultural systems" (McKenzie, 2009, p. 223).

LEARNER AGENCY

Dominant practices in environmental education that focus on transmitting information tend to treat learners as consumers "instead of acknowledging them as actors in a transformative process" and thereby reproduce existing power relations (Rathzel & Uzzell, 2009, p. 16). Rickinson and Lundholm (this volume) conclude that the major implication of their two empirical studies is the need to treat learners as active agents, rather than passive recipients, of environmental learning. Blanchet-Cohen cites Mayall's (2000) argument that even children are not only social actors who hold, express and act on perspectives on their lives, but also are agents who influence relationships, decisions and events. Paying attention to children's agency demands attention to their "powers, or lack of powers, to influence or organize events [and] to engage with the structures that shape their lives" (Mayall, 2000, p. 3, cited by Blanchet-Cohen in this volume). Questioning the assumption that children are passively shaped by social structures and processes, Blanchet-Cohen argues for the power of children to shape social change while acknowledging that such change is a result of mediation between internal and external factors and part of a process of "learning about the environment, themselves or finding their place in the world" (p. 52). Creating opportunities for students to participate in real-world problem solving is intended to help them develop "a sense of their own agency and collective capacity to alter their neighborhoods or communities for the better" (Smith, 2007, p. 192).

The concept of agency has evolved from a focus on individual action to recognizing the importance of mutual responsibility in and for action. Edwards (2005) points out that: "Earlier Taylor had described agency as a capacity to identify the goals at which one is directing one's action and to evaluate whether one had been successful (Taylor, 1977)" (p. 169). She notes that more recently, Taylor has cautioned against neglecting responsibility for and to others, thereby gesturing toward the notion of mutual or collective responsibility. Others have avoided the individual versus collective issue by defining agency simply as "the exercise of will and conscious action" (White & Wyn, 1998, p. 315). This issue foregrounds the importance of examining different kinds of agency, rather than treating agency as a unitary concept. Of particular relevance to environmental learning are the concepts of reflexive, relational and transformative agency.

Reflexive agency, according to Bourdieu, refers to "the capacities of socially and culturally situated agents to reflect upon their social conditions, criticize them, and articulate new interpretations of them" (Bohman, 1999, p. 145). In addition, reflection also might be extended to visioning alternative possibilities of social conditions. As Bohman (1999) points out, since Bourdieu argued that "cultural constraints on power and dispositions" are part of these conditions, the place of cultural pluralism becomes significant. When a diversity of cultures are represented in dialogue and collective reflection, then cultural constraints are more likely to be revealed and more space is created for a wider range of alternative interpretations and possibilities. On the other hand, deeper conflicts are likely to emerge (Bohman, 1999). In contexts where

"inequalities related to participation in public deliberation will play a greater role in reproducing relations of power and domination," ...[reflexive agency] requires not only changing beliefs and desires, but also the social conditions under which agents reflect, deliberate and cooperate with each other to widen their universes of discourse. By doing so, they may also change their existing relations of power" (Bohman, 1999, p. 147).

Thus, issues and relations of power intersect with culture, learning and agency. Laessoe and Carlsson (this volume) describe a number of conflicts that illuminate the persistent role of power even in participatory processes; for example, between management's efforts to develop a traditional community in the workplace while also demanding flexibility and a willingness to accept changes that undermine employees' sense of acceptance and stability, and offering opportunities to young employees to influence their workplace which also serve to exercise control through socialization by senior employees. Finally, a contrast is drawn between technical and management approaches to change focusing on top-down transmission of technical information, on the one hand, and socio-cultural and pedagogical approaches, on the other hand, which involve employees in improving their action competences. These approaches, the authors argue, can be complementary or conflicting. The choice of approaches and the possibilities for sustainable development are closely related to the workplace culture. For example, the use of a pedagogical approach within a management culture was found to create "a tension between participation as a matter of individual learning and as a matter of collective influence" (Laessoe & Carlsson, this volume, p. 125).

Besides a vision of change, there is also a need for the capacity to work toward change which is addressed by the concepts of relational and transformative agency. Relational agency has been introduced as a conceptual tool to address the nature of purposeful joint action in a changing system and the role of mediation in such action as a result of joint interpretations of the purpose or object of change (Edwards, 2005). Relational agency has been described as "a capacity to offer support and to ask for support from others" (Edwards, 2005, p. 168) or "a capacity to align one's thoughts and actions with those of others in order to interpret problems of practice and to respond to those interpretations" (Edwards, 2005, pp.169–70). First, however, is the recognition that another individual may be a resource but that there is a need to work at eliciting, identifying and negotiating the use of that resource in order to align oneself in joint action. Therefore, according to Edwards, it represents "an enhanced version of personal agency"

(p. 172) and a shift in focus from "individual action to action with others as a step towards recognizing and being able to examine a capacity for working with others" (p. 169).

Finally, transformative agency assumes collective responsibility for transforming social practices and conditions and involves both reflection on and transformation of such practices. It speaks to the power of coalition building and organizing and collective action. Working collectively, at least effectively, also depends on developing the capacity of relational agency. However, educational institutions traditionally have focused far more on the development of individual competence and agency than on fostering collective agency, such as an understanding of the role of social movements and the politics of change and the development of collaborative skills and dispositions (Stevenson, 2006). Participatory learning to achieve *Gestaltungkompetenz* or citizen competence (Reid & Nikel, 2004; de Haan, 2006) in Germany and the Danish action competence in EE (Jensen & Schnack, 1997), as well as the ENSI project in Europe which engaged students in action research on their investigation of environmental issues, are examples of conceptual and empirical studies in the environmental education literature that are concerned with the development of individual and collective student agency.

Blanchet-Cohen's study (in this volume) reveals that there are multiple ways in which children engage with the environment and multiple forms in which they express their environmental agency. Their agency was captured in four profiles of environmental involvement identified by the author: (1) taking the lead in initiating and establishing an environmental project; (2) expressing involvement through the use of art, writing or speech; (3) practicing activism in a group; and (4) viewing environmental involvement as a way of life. The children studied by Blanchet-Cohen were insightfully aware of their own strengths and limitations in enacting positive environmental or social change which was seen "as emerging from the interaction between context and the individual child's strategic manuevering, whether it be through critical thinking, imagination, or action" (p. 52). Thus, their positioning of themselves in relation to environmental issues suggests that the development of elements of reflective, relational and transformative agency was evident among these children.

Learning "can be viewed as a change process resulting from a critical analysis of one's own norms, values and constructions of reality (deconstruction), exposure to alternative ones and the construction of new ones (reconstruction)" (Wals & Noorstyn, this volume, p. 74). This need highlights the importance of and need to strengthen human agency as individuals and communities search for information and ideas, across disciplinary boundaries, and work with others to respond to environmental concerns.

RESEARCH AS LEARNING AND LEARNING TO RESEARCH (Carolyn Stirling)

Engaging in environmental education is a lifelong process as learners constantly seek information and meaningful understanding. Opportunities to learn and understand about that which was previously unknown are provided by research which "is about satisfying a need to know, and a need to extend the boundaries of existing knowledge through a process of systematic inquiry" (Smith, 1999, p. 170). Through participating in and conducting research, learners are able, for example, to test ideas and theories, compare and contrast different approaches, develop new insights, generate new explanations and theories, identify new questions and further areas for investigation, and suggest applications for policy and practice. Learning to research therefore is a key part of engaging with environmental education, whether for developing deeper understandings of issues of learning and pedagogy or seeking creative and imaginative solutions to current theoretical, policy or practice concerns.

Environmental education is transdisciplinary and draws from a wide range of fields. Being able to negotiate disciplines from the (natural and social) sciences and the arts requires an understanding of the role of different epistemologies in making knowledge claims. Through engaging in different kinds of research processes, learners can actively construct knowledge from multiple perspectives about the world at personal, local, regional and global levels that can inform transformative policies and practices for creating healthier and more sustainable lifestyles and communities.

As Nikel, Teamey, Hwang, Pozos-Hernandez, Reid and Hart (this volume) show, the production of knowledge through research is more than a personal project. Knowledge production can be a ritual of progression through academic institutions, but this does not exclude it from being a process of personal enrichment, identity development, community engagement, collaborative effort or transdisciplinary inquiry. Descriptions of student experiences and discussions about the objective of study in Nikel et al. (this volume) illustrate that process and outcome are critical components of the research process. While Nikel et al. support their argument in the context of doctoral studies in environmental education, the wider implication of this argument for environmental education is a need to emphasize method in conjunction with the results or conclusions of research. As students conduct research as part of the learning process, regardless of the level, they learn how to research. For example, Teamey (in Nikely et al., this volume) in her doctoral research negotiates not only complex and challenging cultural contexts but strives to maintain personal integrity as she struggles to 'practice what you preach', all the while reflecting on theoretical and methodological implications in a post-development framework. While teachers and students remain constantly cognizant of the process they are employing as they undertake research and encounter a wide range of personal and academic experiences, they are also conscious of the production of research as they work towards personal and professional goals. Understanding that within any learning process research is both a verb that describes a series of critical reflection and action processes, and a noun that describes the product or outcome of such a process is integral in understanding the dynamic and multifaceted pursuit of knowledge production.

The production of knowledge has a long history in the Western research tradition. As O'Donoghue and Lotz-Sisitka (this volume) document, the history of Western models of research and the ways in which Western philosophies about research and development were implemented in Africa have indelibly marked epistemology and methodology in South African institutions. This institutional social *habitus* is addressed by these authors as they explore the complexities of re-orientating the African university towards sustainable development for African societies amid the legacy of colonization, post-colonial discourse and "a broader global(ising) environment dominated by neo-liberal political economy (p. 200)". Research is not static and is constantly evolving as new ideas and contexts compel researchers to reflect on the way they conduct research. The vast fields of environmental education and sustainable development require all learners to mediate traditional research practices and the historical context of their research with pedagogical processes that are collaborative, engage with communities as participants, seek social transformation and democratic change, and generate research agendas for the public good. This pedagogical, epistemological and methodological process requires deeper engagement with history, culture and context as rigorous "researching process informs the situated learning taking place (O'Donoghue & Lotz-Sisitka, this volume, p. 211)". Thus, research and learning are in constant dialogue as learners seek ameliorative ways to learn about the world, construct knowledge and address current environmental concerns.

Engaging environmental education requires captivating learning that interacts with current theories, knowledge and concerns about the environment and our interactions with it. Research plays a key role in learning and knowledge creation as learners use research as a tool to learn more about their world and use learning as a tool to research more about their world. Within this dialogue between research and learning, the intersections of learning, culture and agency create transformative spaces for innovative thinking, meaningful learning and transformative action on environmental issues. Understanding others and understanding ourselves through and in diverse cultural contexts is integral to environmental education as we seek goals that will transform our interactions with and relationship with the environment.

CONCLUSION

As both the discourse of EE/ESD/EfS and the case studies in this book reveal, environment-related learning is highly complex, imprecise, broad in scope, and both ambitious and ambiguous in aspirations and expected outcomes (Stevenson, 2007). Therefore, it is not surprising that it is pedagogically challenging to structure and facilitate such learning. Contemporary learning theories offer some broad guidance on how teachers and facilitators might proceed. For example, constructivist learning theorists argue that learning is a highly interactive and social process of constructing (and reconstructing) personal meaning and that to achieve meaningful understanding, especially of conceptually difficult or complex knowledge, learning through deep inquiry into authentic tasks is required. Rather than supporting the common practice of teaching for acquisition of knowledge and skills first and then for meaning and transfer later, cognitive research indicates that knowledge and skills can be addressed, and better retained, in the context of learning and making meaning of key concepts and applying skills to meaningful and authentic problems or tasks.

Learning in environmental and sustainability education therefore can be viewed as a process of participation in critical inquiry into authentic environmental issues (of policy and practice), in actions to address environmental or sustainability concerns, and in on-going deep individual and collective reflection on the processes and outcomes of inquiry and action. Authentic critical inquiry and reflection, however, must go beyond understanding and critique to generating possibilities for transforming current unsustainable social practices, habits, and systems. Creating opportunities to participate in real-world inquiry and problem solving also helps youth and adults develop a sense of their own individual and collective agency and capacity to improve the quality of life of their neighborhoods or communities (Smith, 2007). As Blanchet-Cohen found, young people's "participation becomes meaningful as they engage in critical thinking, imagination, and action" (this volume, p. 51).

Yet these broad principles also raise many questions. For example, how can inquiry processes be structured to enable learners to investigate their own theories or perspectives on socio-ecological issues and sustainability and to confront any inconsistencies or discrepancies in these theories? Given that knowledge related to environmental and sustainability issues can be full of uncertainties, contradictions and paradoxes, and that there are limitations to which humans can tolerate ambiguities, how do we support learners to engage in continuous learning? How can we become sensitive to and able to take into account how our own culture and history shapes our approach to environmental inquiry and learning? What are appropriate concepts, analytic frameworks and imaginaries (e.g., stories, metaphors) that might guide a search for alternative practices and futures that are more sustainable?

Environmental education scholars, policymakers and practitioners should be both cognizant of advances in theories of learning that might continue to inform their research or practice concerning learning and learners, while at the same time using their own experiences and inquiries to question and advance these same theories, especially as they relate to the particular processes, substance, contexts and challenges of environment-related learning. As more attention is devoted to the increasing socio-ecological challenges facing the planet – challenges that are characterized by complex problems requiring multifaceted and interdisciplinary approaches - traditional boundaries of inquiry should continue to be crossed with the potential to offer new insights and new ways of thinking about learning, culture and agency in environmental education.

REFERENCES

Blake, J., Sterling, S., & Kagawa, F. (2009). *Getting it together: Interdisciplinarity and sustainability in the higher education institution.* (Occasional Paper 3). Plymouth, England: Centre for Sustainable Futures, University of Plymouth.

Bohman, J. (1999). Practical reason and cultural constraint: Agency in Bourdieu's theory of practice. In R. Shusterman (Ed.), *Bourdieu: A critical reader* (pp. 129–152). Oxford: Blackwell.

Brown, J., Collins, A., & Duguid, P. (1989). Situated cognition and the culture of learning. *Educational Researcher, 18*(1), 32–42.

Cinnamond, J., & Zimpher, N. (1990). Reflectivity as a function of community. In R. Clift, R. Houston, & M. Pugach (Eds.), *Encouraging reflective practice in education* (pp. 57–72). New York: Teachers College Press.

Cole, M., & Engestrom, Y. (1993). A cultural-historical approach to distributed cognition. In G. Salomon (Ed.), *Distributed cognitions: Psychological and educational considerations* (pp. 1–46). New York: Cambridge University Press.

de Haan, G. (2006). The BLK '21' programme in Germany: A 'Gestaltungskompetenz'-based model for education for sustainable development. *Environmental Education Research, 12*(1), 19–32.

Edwards. (2005). Relational agency: Learning to be a resourceful practitioner. *International Journal of Educational Research, 43*, 168–182.

Engestrom, Y. (1999). Activity theory and individual and social transformation. In Y. Engestrom, R. Miettinen, & R. Punamaki (Eds.), *Perspectives on activity theory* (pp. 19–38). New York: Cambridge University Press.

Fien, J., & Tilbury, D. (2002). The global challenge of sustainability. In D. Tilbury, R. Stevenson, J. Fein, & D. Schreuder (Eds.), *Education and sustainability: Responding to the global challenge* (pp. 1–12). Gland, Switzerland: IUCN.

Frawley, W. (1997). *Vygotsky and cognitive science: Language and the unification of the social and computational mind*. Cambridge, MA: Harvard University Press.

Greeno, J., Collins, A., & Resnick, L. (1996). Cognition and learning. In D. Berliner & R. Calfree (Eds.), *Handbook of educational psychology* (pp. 15–46). New York: Macmillan.

Hargreaves, A. (2003). *Teaching in the knowledge society: Education in the age of insecurity*. New York: Teachers College Press.

Hoffman-Kipp, P., Artiles, A., & Lopez-Torres, L. (2003). Beyond reflection: Teacher learning as praxis. *Theory into Practice, 42*(3), 248–254.

IUCN, UNEP, WWF. (1991). *Caring for the earth: A strategy for sustainable living*. Gland, Switzerland: IUCN, UNEP, WWF.

Jensen, B., & Schnack, K. (1997). The action competence approach in environmental education. *Environmental Education Research, 3*(2), 163–178.

Lave, J., & Wenger, E. (1991). *Situated learning: Legitimate peripheral participation*. New York: Cambridge University Press.

Lee, C. (2008). The centrality of culture to the scientific study of learning and development: How an ecological framework in education research facilitates civic responsibility. *Educational Researcher, 37*(5), 267–279.

Louv, R. (2005). *Last child in the woods: Saving our children from nature-deficit disorder*. Chapel Hill, NC: Alongquin Books of Chapel Hill.

Marshall, H. (1992). Seeing, redefining, and supporting student learning. In H. Marshall (Ed.), *Redefining student learning: Roots of educational change* (pp. 1–32). Norwood, NJ: Ablex Publishing.

Nasir, N. S., & Hand, V. (2006). Exploring sociocultural perspectives on race, culture and learning. *Review of Educational Research, 76*(4), 449–475.

Newmann, F., Secada, W., & Wehlage, G. (1995). *A guide to authentic instruction and assessment: Vision, standards and scoring*. Madison, WI: Wisconsin Center for Education Research.

Ogawa, R., Crain, R., Loomis, M., & Ball, T. (2009). CHAT-IT: Toward conceptualizing learning in the context of formal organizations. *Educational Researcher, 37*(2), 83–95.

Oliver, D., & Newmann, F. (1970). *Clarifying public controversy: An approach to teaching social studies*. Boston: Little Brown.

Prawatt, R. (1991). Conversations with self and settings: A framework for thinking about teacher empowerment. *American Educational Research Journal, 28*(2), 737–757.

Ramsey, Hungerford, H., & Volk, T. (1989). A technique for analyzing environmental issues. *Journal of Environmental Education, 21*(1), 26–30.

Rathzel, N., & Uzzell, D. (2009). Transformative environmental education: A collective rehearsal for reality. *Environmental Education Research, 15*(3), 263–277.

Reid, A., & Nikel, J. (2008). Differntiating and evaluating conceptions and examples of participation in environment-related learning. In A. Reid, B. Jensen, J. Nikel, & V. Simovska (Eds.), *Participation* and learning: Perspectives on education and the environment, health and sustainability. The Netherlands: Springer.

Rickinson, M. (2006). Researching and understanding environmental learning: Hopes for the next ten years. *Environmental Education Research, 12*(3–4), 445–457.

Rizvi, F. (2006). Imagination and globalization of educational policy research. *Globalisation, Societies and Education, 4*(2), 193–205.

Scott, W., & Gough, S. (2003). *Sustainable development and learning: Framing the issues.* London: RoutledgeFalmer.

Sirotnik, K. (1991). Critical inquiry: A paradigm for praxis. In E. Short (Ed.), *Forms of curriculum inquiry* (pp. 243–258). Albany, NY: SUNY Press.

Smith, G. (2007). Place-based education: Breaking through the constraining regularities of public school. *Environmental Education Research, 13*(2), 189–207.

Smith, L. T. (1999). *Decolonising methodologies: Research and indigenous peoples.* London: Zed Books.

Starratt, R. (2003). *Centering educational administration: Cultivating meaning, community, responsibility.* Mahwah, NJ: Lawrence Erlbaum Associates.

Stevenson, R. (2007). Schooling and environmental/sustainability education: From discourses of policy and practice to discourses of professional learning. *Environmental Education Research, 13*(2), 265–285.

Stevenson, R. (2006). Tensions and transitions in policy discourse: Recontextualizing a decontextualized EE/ESD debate. *Environmental Education Research, 12*(3–4), 277–290.

Stevenson, R. (1997). Developing habits of environmental thoughtfulness through the in-depth study of select environmental issues. *Canadian Journal of Environmental Education, 2*, 183–201.

Stevenson, R. (1987). Schooling and environmental education: Contradictions in purpose and practice. In I. Robottom (Ed.), *Environmental education: Practice and possibility.* Geelong, Victoria: Deakin University Press.

Tbilisi Declaration. (1978). *Toward an action plan: A report on the Tbilisi intergovernmental conference on environmental education.* Washington, DC: U.S. Government Printing Office.

Vare, P. (2008). From practice to theory: Participation as learning in the context of sustainable development projects. In A. Reid, B. Jensen, J. Nikel, & V. Simovska (Eds.), *Participation and learning: Perspectives on education and the environment, health and sustainability.* The Netherlands: Springer.

Vare, P., & Scott, W. (2007). Learning for a change: Exploring the relationship between education and sustainable development. *Journal of Education for Sustainable Development, 1*(2), 197–?

Vygotsky, L. (1978). *Mind in society: The development of higher psychological process.* Cambridge, MA: Harvard University Press.

Wehlage, G., Newmann, F., & Secada, W. (1996). Standards for authentic achievement and pedagogy. In F. Newmann & Associates (Eds.), *Authentic achievement: Restructuring schools for intellectual quality* (pp. 21–48). San Francisco: Jossey-Bass.

Weis, L., & Dimitriadis, G. (2008). Dueling banjos: Shifting economic and cultural contexts in the lives of youth. *Teachers College Record, 110*(10), 2290–2316.

White, R., & Winn, J. (1998). Youth agency and social context. *Journal of Sociology, 34*(3), 314–327.

Zeichner, K., & Liston, D. (1996). *Reflective teaching: An introduction.* Mahwah, NJ: Lawrence Erlbaum Associates.

Robert B. Stevenson
James Cook University, Australia

Carolyn Stirling
Department of Educational Leadership & Policy,
University at Buffalo, USA

BIOGRAPHIES

Editor Biographies

Justin Dillon is Professor of Science and Environmental Education and Head of the Science and Technology Education Group at King's College London. After teaching in London schools for 10 years, he joined the staff at King's to work on the National Environmental Database project, in 1989. Justin has researched and published widely in both science and environmental education and he recently directed the "Border Crossings" research project. Justin was elected President of the European Science Education Research Association (ESERA) in 2007. He is a trustee of Sustainability and Environmental Education and has been Chair of both the London Wildlife Trust and the London Environmental Education Forum and is currently Secretary of the Bankside Open Spaces Trust. As well as being an editor of the *International Journal of Science Education*, he is on the editorial board of *Environmental Education Research*, the *Journal of Environmental Education* and several other science and environmental education journals.

Robert (Bob) Stevenson is Research Professor in the School of Education and the Cairns Institute at James Cook University in Queensland, Australia. He was previously on the faculty (and a former Chair) of the Department of Educational Leadership and Policy at the University at Buffalo, USA. Before moving to the United States in 1983, he was a K-12 environmental education curriculum specialist in the Queensland Department of Education, and was involved in co-founding the Australian Association of Environmental Education and the *Australian Journal of Environmental Education* (AJEE). He is a co-executive editor of the Journal of Environmental Education and serves on the editorial boards of AJEE, the *Canadian Journal of Environmental Education*, and *Environmental Education Research*. Among his co-edited books is *Education and Sustainability: Responding to the global challenge* (IUCN, 2002). In addition to environmental education, his research interests focus on educational action research, and teacher and school administrators' use of research.

Contributing Author Biographies

Natasha Blanchet-Cohen is an assistant professor in the Department of Applied Human Sciences in community development at Concordia University in Montreal, Canada. Her research spans a wide range of community and social topics in Canada and abroad, including issues around children's rights and sustainability, child agency, the creation of child-youth friendly cities, engagement of Indigenous youth in health, opportunities for social inclusion, the practice and promotion of environmental education, bridge-building across cultures and practices, and developmental approaches to monitoring and evaluation.

Monica Carlsson is a an associate professor at the Department of Curriculum Research and a member of the Research Programme for Environmental and Health Education - both at the Danish School of Education (DUE), University of Aarhus. She co-ordinates and teaches on DUE's MEd programme in Health Promotion and Education, and teaches educational evaluation on several other Master programmes at DUE. Her research interests focus on curriculum analysis and evaluation of educational approaches within health education and environmental education, based on the concepts of action-competence, pupil participation and school-community collaboration.

Charlotte Clark is a Visiting Assistant Professor in the Nicholas School of the Environment at Duke University, North Carolina, U.S.A. She earned a Bachelor of Science in biology in 1979, a Masters of Environmental Management in 1983, and a PhD in environmental management in 2007, all from Duke. Her primary area of interest is environmental education, specifically in the area of decision-making by the general public on issues of environmentally-related behavior. She studies how informal learning processes engage with behavior change for individuals and communities around environmental issues. Her professional experience also includes directing Duke's Center for Environmental Education and conducting air pollution regulatory work under contract to the U.S. Environmental Protection Agency.

Leesa Fawcett is an Associate Professor in the Faculty of Environmental Studies, York University and Coordinator of the graduate Diploma in Environmental and Sustainability Education. Her research and teaching interests include feminist environmental education, animal studies, and environmental philosophy. She loves learning and teaching with students in the intersections between nature, technology and popular culture. She has co-authored two books and numerous articles.

Paul Hart is a Professor of Science and Environmental Education at the University of Regina, Canada where he teaches both undergraduate and graduate students. He has published widely in the areas of science and environmental education. He is an Executive Editor of the *Journal of Environmental Education* and a Consulting Editor for other journals including *Environmental Education Research* and the *Canadian Journal of Environmental Education*. His research interests include the genealogical roots of teacher's thinking, children's ideas about the environment, and connections between environmental education and social learning.

Seyoung Hwang is postdoctoral scholar at University of Sussex, UK. She completed her Ph.D. at University of Bath in 2008 (Thesis Title: Teachers' stories of environmental education: blurred boundaries of professionalism, identity and curriculum; available at: www.bath.ac.uk/cree/Seyoung.htm). She is currently working on a two year research project concerning stem cell research and bioethics. Her research interest includes teaching and learning in the context of socially controversial scientific issues, narrative inquiry and environmental identity.

Elin Kelsey is an adjunct professor of Environmental Education and Communications at Royal Roads University in Canada. Her research interests focus on public engagement in environmental and conservation/sustainability initiatives and the roles of informal learning organizations. She currently serves as a member of the International Consultative Group of Experts on Biological Diversity Education and Public Awareness for the UN Convention on Biological Diversity. She is the award-winning author of ten books and works with a range of international, national and local organizations to communicate and evaluate environment and sustainability projects. *The Science Case* she wrote for the Pew Environment Group's Global Ocean Legacy Program was instrumental in the 2009 establishment of the world's largest marine reserve in the Pacific Ocean.

Jeppe Læssøe is a professor affiliated with the Research Programme for Environmental and Health Education at Danish School of Ecucation, University of Aarhus. He has an MA in psychology and a PhD in communication studies. He has been involved in a range of interdisciplinary research projects and evaluations, including: a) the history, knowledge interests and strategies of the environmental movement, b) participatory and action oriented adult education related to risk issues and local sustainable development, and c) the socio-cultural dynamics behind changes in modern everyday life and material consumption. His research focus during recent years has been on the strategies, roles and competences of professional mediators.

Cecilia Lundholm is a researcher in the Department of Education, where she is a member of the Conceptual Development research group (ped.su.se/rcd), and at the Stockholm Resilience Centre, Stockholm University. Lundholm's research interests concerns communication and learning about environmental and sustainability issues. Projects on students' learning are being carried out in Sweden and China, addressing learning of natural as well as societal phenomena (as in economics). As part of the new national Graduate School in Education for Sustainable Development a project is under way focusing the teaching and learning of interdisciplinary environmental education in upper secondary school.

Marcia McKenzie is an Assistant Professor in Social Justice and Education in the Department of Educational Foundations, College of Education with a joint appointment in the interdisciplinary School of Environment and Sustainability at the University of Saskatchewan in Saskatoon, Canada. Her research interests centre on education and socio-cultural practice, youth agency and activism, and the politics of social science research. Marcia's current research includes a collaborative project entitled, Discursive Approaches to Teaching and Learning about Social and Ecological Issues, and she is co-editor of the book *Fields of Green: Restorying Culture, Environment, and Education* (Hampton, 2009).

Jutta Nikel is a research fellow in Education at the University of Education in Freiburg, Germany. She currently working on a three year research project on the processes of influence of transnational organisations' agendas on national education systems and coordinating a doctoral research programme on "Developing skills for experimentation in school science and mathematics. Her research interests include conceptual frameworks for sustainable development, quality in education and ascribing responsibility in diverse contexts such as Europe and Sub-Saharan Africa. Jutta finished her Ph.D. at the University of Bath, UK, in 2005.

Leonore Noorduyn is a Dutch journalist with a passion for capturing the essence of what goes on in people's minds in a way that touches the reader. Since 1998 she has her own company 'De Schrijfster' (www.deschrijfster.nl). Her company also organizes trainings and workshops for those who wish to become journalists themselves.

Benjamin A. Pozos-Hernandez has obtained a biology degree and a master in science degree in environmental resources. He has not obtained a Ph.D. degree, yet. He has 9 years experience working as environmental consultant (ISO 14001, environmental impact assessment and environmental planning). He also worked for the Natural History Museum in Mexico City, where he discovered his passion for education and environmental education (EE). He developed EE projects in urban solid waste management and for a natural reserve in the West coast of Mexico. He developed and evaluated learning tools (e.g., simulation-games), as well as EE courses and workshops for teachers and lecturers.

Alan Reid is a senior lecturer in education and member of the Centre for Research in Education and the Environment, University of Bath. He is the editor of *Environmental Education Research*, and coordinates doctoral programmes in research methods in education and management, and teaches on Masters programmes in environmental education, technologies and learning, and qualitative research approaches. His research interests focus on teachers' thinking and practice in environmental education, and policy-related and philosophical issues in environmental education theory, research and practice. Recent publications include, with Jensen, Nikel and Simovska (eds) (2008) *Participation and Learning: Perspectives on Education and the environment, health and sustainability* (Springer), and with Scott (eds) (2008) *Researching education and the environment: retrospect and prospect* (Taylor & Francis).

Mark Rickinson is an independent educational research consultant, who specialises in research and evaluation, research reviews and research training (www.markrickinson.co.uk). He has recently completed a book with Cecilia Lundholm and Nick Hopwood on *Environmental Learning: Insights from research into the student experience* (2009, Springer Press). Mark is also a Visiting Research Fellow at Oxford University Department of Education and the Policy Studies Institute, London.

Constance Russell is an Associate Professor and Chair of Graduate Studies and Research in Education in the Faculty of Education at Lakehead University in Thunder Bay, Canada where she teaches outdoor education, critical pedagogy and research methods. Broadly speaking, her research focuses on critical environmental education, human/animal relations, and interdisciplinary and academic/activist collaboration. She is co-editor of the *Canadian Journal of Environmental Education* and co-editor of a forthcoming book, *Companion to Research in Education* (Sage).

Carolyn Stirling is a Pākehā scholar from Aotearoa/New Zealand. She is a PhD candidate at the University at Buffalo, USA where her dissertation research, "The Politics of Decolonizing Education in Settler Societies," is examining the ways non-Indigenous and Indigenous peoples are using decolonization to resist colonization. Her research interests center on the politics of settlement and the issues that arise from the continuation of colonization in contemporary societies, the rejection of Indigenous sovereignty and attempts by settlers to address the harm done by colonization. Stirling holds a MEd from Te Uru Māraurau, Massey University, New Zealand (2007).

Martin Storksdieck is Director of the Board on Science Education at the U.S. National Academy of Sciences where he oversees studies that address a wide range of issues related to science education. He also serves as a fellow at the Institute for Learning Innovation (ILI) where he directs ongoing research studies on science learning in immersive environments; models of involving researchers and scientists in science museums and science centers; and understanding the impact of science hobbyists, such as amateur astronomers, on the public understanding of science. He previously served as Director of Project Development and senior researcher at ILI, was a science educator with a planetarium in Germany, and worked on local environmental management systems for the International Council for Local Environmental Initiatives. He holds a Masters in Biology from the Albert-Ludwigs University (Freiburg, Germany), a Masters in Public Administration from Harvard University, and a Ph.D. in education from Leuphana University (Lüneburg, Germany).

Cathlyn D. Stylinski is a tenured faculty member at the University of Maryland Center for Environmental Science with a focus on science education programs for K-12 and public audiences. She is involved in teacher education, curriculum development, media production, and education research and evaluation. Her research interests include media impacts on public audiences; teacher professional development and changes in classroom practices; geospatial visualization and analysis tools to support learning; the relationship between children and nature; and public participation in science research. She holds a Ph.D. in ecology, M.S. in biology, and B.S. in television and radio production and has also conducted environmental science research and worked in broadcast television.

Kelly Teamey is a lecturer in Education at the University of Bath. Her research interests include organisational learning and change, literacy in developing country and contexts and the policy, methodological and pedagogical issues associated with these. Her recent research was in the ESRC-funded project on Non-Governmental Public Action that focused on partnership dynamics of NGOs and governments working together to provide education, sanitation and health services in India, Bangladesh and Pakistan. Kelly finished her Ph.D. at King's College London in the School of Education in 2006.

Nora Timmerman is a PhD student in the Faculty of Education, University of British Columbia studying the concept and practice of ecological justice and how it can be employed through holistic pedagogy within higher educational settings. Having most recently taken on one of life's most educational endeavors, mother-hood, Nora thoroughly enjoys the challenge and wonder of coming to know the world anew alongside her child.

Arjen E.J. Wals is a Professor of Social Learning and Sustainable Development. He is also a UNESCO Chair in the same field. He works within the Education & Competence Studies Group of the Department of Social Sciences of the Wageningen University in The Netherlands. His PhD - obtained in 1991 from the University of Michigan in Ann Arbor, U.S.A. - explored the crossroads between environmental education and environmental psychology. He has (co)published and (co) edited over 150 articles, chapters, books and professional publications on topics such as: action research and community problem-solving, whole school approaches to sustainability, biodiversity education, sustainability in higher education, and, more recently, social and societal learning in the context of sustainability.

INDEX

245

Breinigsville, PA USA
26 August 2010
244192BV00003B/10/P

9 789460 911590